Viscountess Strangford

Original Letters and Papers of the late Viscount Strangford

Viscountess Strangford

Original Letters and Papers of the late Viscount Strangford

ISBN/EAN: 9783337109752

Printed in Europe, USA, Canada, Australia, Japan

Cover: Foto ©ninafisch / pixelio.de

More available books at **www.hansebooks.com**

ORIGINAL
LETTERS AND PAPERS

OF THE LATE

VISCOUNT STRANGFORD

UPON

PHILOLOGICAL AND KINDRED SUBJECTS.

EDITED BY

VISCOUNTESS STRANGFORD.

LONDON:

TRÜBNER & CO., LUDGATE HILL.

1878.

PREFACE BY THE EDITOR.

In a notice upon the death of Lord Strangford that appeared in one of the newspapers of the day,[1] the remark was made, "We feel sure that no correspondent of Lord Strangford ever burned a letter of his. His letters ran over alike with wit and with information; there was some happy allusion, some apt sarcasm in every line. Nor was this all. No one was ever more ready and generous in communicating knowledge. A question on any of his favourite subjects would be rewarded by a letter which was in fact a philological or political treatise composed in his own terse and amusing style. No one had a keener sense of humour; if there was a grotesque side to a thing, Lord Strangford was sure to find it out. And, like all really accurate men, like all men who really live in their work, he had the keenest appreciation of a blunder. It was curious indeed to listen to the half-provoked, half-amused way in which he would speak of the grotesque mistakes with regard to his favourite studies which he was constantly coming across. In short, a letter of Lord Strangford's, written in one of his happiest veins, was a mixture of wit and learning which it was really a privilege to receive."

[1] Saturday Review, January 16, 1869.

The conviction of this writer was unhappily far from being justified by fact. In this age we live so fast that few of us take time to appreciate our own possessions, so that even treasures become encumbrances; the few long letters that are still written are as often as not tossed aside and forgotten under the mass of daily dust that crowds out all, good and bad alike. The publication of the letters in this volume has been, I am well aware, too long delayed; I plead the excuse not only of long illness after the publication of the two volumes[1] of Lord Strangford's writings which I edited immediately after his death, but also the fact that I shared the conviction of the writer I have quoted, and for some years searched near and far to find more of the many letters my husband wrote with a lavish hand. For some long ones—almost essays—that I remembered, I willingly waited, and journeyed many miles to obtain them; but I searched and waited in vain; no more than these have been found for me. What I publish now may not appeal to a very general public, but they will, I feel sure, be gladly welcomed by a few. I have ventured to reprint also a very few of the essays and fugitive pieces written by Lord Strangford on various kindred topics; of these I would gladly have reprinted more had space allowed me, for many that were thrown off on the spur of the moment—trifles apparently à propos only of a passing event or publication—contain some golden grain of erudite knowledge, some keen bit of criticism, or some thought so suggestive and informing, that it seemed a pity not to collect them into a form that might be pleasing to the scholar or useful to the student. There

[1] Selections from the Writings of Viscount Strangford, 2 vols., Bentley, 1869.

is food in this volume for those who study other subjects than purely scientific philology and ethnology. The
same writer quoted above adds:

" The linguistic and philological attainments of Lord
Strangford were simply amazing. It was wonderful to
talk to a man to whom all the languages of Europe and
civilised Asia seemed equally familiar. It was wonderful to hear a man who could discuss the peculiarities
of Basque, and Lithuanian, and the Romance of Dacia,
and who could address a native of Sogdiana in the
peculiar forms of Turkish and Persian spoken in his
native province. But this was not all. The power of
speaking a vast number of languages and dialects has
often existed in company with very little real philological
knowledge, and with very little real intellectual capacity
of any kind. It was not so with Lord Strangford. He
was a scientific and historical philologer of a high order.
There are few men who more emphatically know whence
words come and whither they are going. He not only
knew a vast number of languages, but he knew all
about the languages which he knew. He knew their
history, their several stages of growth, their exact
relations to one another; and he knew all this in the
most intelligent and philosophical way. He had too,
beyond most men, his knowledge, as the phrase is, at his
finger's ends. And he was one who thoroughly realised
the way in which cognate though not identical studies
must be brought to bear upon one another. This is,
we need hardly say, especially needful in the case of
comparative philology and of history strictly so called.
The comparative philologist will be sure to go astray
without a pretty considerable knowledge of the political
history of the nations with whose tongues he is dealing;

b

and the political historian is equally sure to go astray unless he clearly grasps the relations between the languages of the different nations whose history he writes. Now Lord Strangford could perhaps hardly be called an historian in the strictest sense of the word, one with whom political history was in itself an object of primary study; but on the one hand he had always studied philology in its proper relations to history, and on the other hand he had mastered, as few men have, the political history and condition of those particular nations with which the events of his own life brought him into special contact. Lord Strangford was, in short, an ethnologist in the highest sense of the word. And he brought ethnological knowledge to bear on times and countries alike with the past and the present. He was at the same moment an authority on the present state of Eastern Europe, who might rank side by side with Mr. Finlay, and an authority on the earliest state of England, who might rank side by side with Dr. Guest. He was equally ready to discuss the relations of the Turk, the Greek, and the Bulgarian at the present moment, and to discuss the exact relations of the Briton, the Scot, and the Englishman in the days of Ceawlin. It seemed wonderful to have to go to one man for the details of the ecclesiastical movement now going on between the Danube and Mount Hæmus, and also for the details by which the Welsh tongue retreated before the English, from the Axe to the Parret, and from the Parret to the Tamar."

And though the criticism in these letters is sharp and the humour keen, not the most tetchy of authors can detect the faintest breath of ill-nature: he was indeed utterly

incapable of it. He used to call himself the "Literary
Detective," and the "Chronicler of Current Error;" and
when he thought he detected wilful imposture, he was
certainly unsparing in his denunciations; but not the
faintest shadow of a personally unkind feeling ever
darkened his mind.

As it happens, the long delay in publishing these letters
has brought them to an opportune moment, for scarcely
a page of the volume can be read without the feeling
that here was a mind which had mastered what is vulgarly
called the "Eastern Question:" one who knew both the
upper and the nether springs of all that caused and concerned that question: one who had read deeply in the
history of all that led up to the complications of to-day:
one who had watched and touched the hidden intrigues
that traded on the various characteristics of the races
engaged in it: "one who knew the peoples as he knew
their languages:" one who, looking back, could also look
forward with the eye of a true prophet: one who had
thought for himself, and formed his own judgment upon
that thorough knowledge which comes of personal experience and understanding. And many a one may now deplore
his loss, besides those sorrowing friends who loved him.

I have ventured to add two letters which explain
themselves. Prince L. Lucien Bonaparte kindly permits
me to publish the affectionate *éloge* for the scholar and
the friend whose loss he still mourns; the letter of Professor Arminius Vambéry is the honest outpouring of a
grateful and appreciative heart written on hearing of the
intended publication of this book. My warm thanks are
due to both for the permission kindly granted to me to
share these two letters with the world.

Permission to reprint articles already published has been kindly accorded to me by the proprietor of the " Pall Mall Gazette," by Admiral Spratt, and by Mr. Matthew Arnold; and I here most gratefully acknowledge their kindness.

E. STRANGFORD.

August 3, 1877.

FROM H.I.H. PRINCE L. LUCIEN BONAPARTE.

LONDRES, *le* 19 *Juin* 1877.

MADAME,

C'EST avec beaucoup de plaisir que j'apprends par les journaux votre retour à Londres. J'espère que vous me permettrez de rappeler à votre bon souvenir les liens d'estime profonde et d'amitié sincère qui m'attachaient à votre mari. Lord Strangford était un de ces hommes rares dont la perte ne saurait être assez regrettée par quiconque s'intéresse à la vraie science philologique.

Ce linguiste très distingué unissait, en effet, à la connaissance la plus approfondie des langues orientales, telles que le persan, l'arabe, &c., celle non moins étendue des langues slaves, des langues celtiques, et surtout du grec moderne. Que de doutes ayant trait à la comparaison de cette dernière langue avec l'ancienne hellénique n'a-t-il pas résolus, sur ma demande, d'une manière aussi complètement satisfaisante, que celle de plusieurs hellénistes que j'avais consultés avant lui l'était peu! Je me souviendrai toujours des heures qu'il venait passer dans ma bibliothèque et du plaisir qu'il prenait à examiner quelques volumes de la plus grande rareté, soit Valaques, soit Albanais, soit Bulgares. J'étais heureux de posséder ces trésors linguistiques, puisqu'ils servaient à rendre heureux cet homme excellent, aussi modeste que savant, et dont l'aristocratie anglaise doit être fière.

On m'assure que vous comptez publier des notices biographiques et littéraires sur Lord Strangford. C'est assez vous dire, Madame, que j'attends avec la plus vive impatience l'apparition de cet ouvrage, qui, j'en suis certain, surtout venant de vous, sera rempli du plus grand intérêt scientifique et littéraire.

Veuillez agréer, Madame, les hommages respectueux de votre très-dévoué

L. L. BONAPARTE.

TO THE

MEMORY OF LORD STRANGFORD.

———————

THE writer of these lines passed many years searching for and studying East-Turkish manuscripts in the libraries of Constantinople; he haunted the mosques and Tekyehs to obtain information from Mid-Asian pilgrims arriving on the shores of the Bosphorus; and, later on, in order to complete these studies, he took a journey to the Oxus and Zarafshan, which was then a difficult and dangerous undertaking. Enthusiastically devoted to these studies, he may well be excused for the boundless surprise and admiration which filled him, when, on his return from the East, he met, in the British metropolis, a man who was better acquainted with the collected works of Newa'i than many a thick-turbaned Hodja in the high schools of Bokhara, Samarkand, and Herat; and who was as familiar with the writings of Fuzuli, Bidil, and Meshreb[1] as are only the best of their *Bakshis.*[2]

This man was Viscount Strangford, a bright star in the firmament of philological science; but one who studiously hid his light from public view. And therefore I congratulate myself as all the more fortunate that I was one among the privileged few who were permitted to

---

[1] The popular poets of Central Asia.   [2] Oriental troubadours.

draw near to that light which shone for as brief a moment
as a meteor, and to profit by its genial warmth. Alas!
for those happy and never-to-be-forgotten hours that I
passed in the company of one who was as witty and
learned as he was unassuming and modest! and why
should I conceal the truth that it is to these same hours
I trace the germ of my more recent as well as of my
future labours?

It needed but the slightest allusion to the dialectic use
of this or that sound, to elicit Lord Strangford's views
upon Anatolian or Azerbaijanian dialects, whence he would
break into the most minute discussion of the Mohakemet
ul Lugateïn (a philological dissertation of Newa'ï's); for
his Lordship was not only a brilliant linguist, speaking
and writing Turkish, Persian, and Arabic with thorough
fluency, but he was yet much more a scholarly philologist,
carrying, not on his book-shelves, but in his head and
heart, the colossal materials of Comparative Philology;
he could not only trace every termination or affix in the
various linguistic groups on the Volga, the Oxus, and the
Jaxartes, but he could follow them across the Sajan mountain ranges to the Jenissei and the Lena.

Never shall I forget the eager glance with which the
learned Lord seized upon some of the private correspondence of several of my fellow-pilgrims from Kashgar, written
in pure Eastern-Turkish. At that time Jetishehr[1] was a
sealed book; we still fed upon the meagre and unsatisfactory literary fragments which Klaproth is said to have
received orally from a native of Komul,[2] and the most dar-
ing optimist would not have ventured to hope that within
ten years' time we should be possessed of such a grammar

---

[1] The collective name of the seven cities of Turkistan.
[2] A native of Komul, one of these seven cities. *Notes by the Editor.*

of Eastern-Turkish as Shaw's meritorious work. The scientific Turkologue of that day indulged in quaint dreams about the dialects in the south-western dependencies of the Tien-Shan mountains; while, misled by the hypothesis of Quatremère and Remusat, it was believed that uncorrupted remains of the Uigurian language (which even in the Middle Ages was richly endowed) might yet be traced there. It was in such a conversation with Lord Strangford that he first drew my attention to the deciphering of the Kudatku Bilek in these words: "If you could master and edit that manuscript in the Vienna Imperial Library, you would do a greater service than even your Dervish performance in Central Asia." I was aware that many others had unsuccessfully attempted to unravel this most difficult writing; but a word from my noble patron sufficed, so to say, to imprison me for four years with this manuscript. And when, after incredible efforts, I had succeeded in contributing to some extent to a comprehension of this, the earliest linguistic monument in Turkish, I felt that the first rank in the merit of this service should be assigned to Lord Strangford, now removed from us by a premature death. My noble friend lived to learn from me that the characters of the once official languages of Jengis Khan had been cast in metal types at Innspruch; but the end was already drawing near, and when my "Uigurische Sprach-monumente" appeared, that true English heart, ever inspired with the love of science and of liberty, had ceased to beat.

Lord Strangford was not only a thorough—nay, *the* most thoroughly grounded scholar in the Turkish language and literature, but he was, besides that, intimately acquainted with all the other dialects of the Moslem populations of Asia. In addition to the perfect know-

ledge of Turkish, Persian, and Arabic that I have already
named, he read, spoke, and wrote Afghan and Hindustani;
and what is yet more remarkable, he combined with all
this immense knowledge of living and dead Oriental
languages a scholarly knowledge of the ancient and
modern languages of Europe. His own countrymen know
how deeply versed he was in Celtic lore, but what most
astonished the writer of these pages was his intimate and
thorough knowledge of the Slavonian tongues, nearly all
of which he had mastered in their most minute details.
He could repeat by heart innumerable poems from the
Gusle of Vuk Karačić; he knew the entire collection of
national songs of the Kačič which live in the mouths of
Bosnians and Herzegovinians; and if by chance the conversation turned upon the Bulgarian, his favourite child in
the family of Eastern Christians, his habitually downcast
eyes were raised and lightened up as in eloquent words
he discoursed upon the value of this nation of herdsmen
and agriculturists.

"Love for all, hatred for none," was the principle of
his life. He wished to see all the peoples of the Bal-
kan-countries enjoying prosperity, without detriment to
the just rights of the Turks. He had most thoroughly
studied the lights and shades of Moslem national life, in
the defence of which he was ever ready to break a lance,
though no man was more alive to the misrule and the
Byzantinism of the Stamboul Effendi class, which he
frequently lashed with due severity.

As in his individuality, so in his views Lord Strangford differed widely from the statesmen of England, and
from their knowledge of Eastern affairs. In the present
time, members of Parliament or ex-ministers of State
take a trip to the East in order to study the land and

the people while the steamer is coaling, and on their
return home loudly proclaim their superficial experiences,
making often an astounding display of distorted facts
and absurd views. Five-and-twenty years ago, Englishmen had still the good sense to abstain from expressing
their opinions on the virtues or defects of a foreign
country and race, until the local experience of years and
a sound knowledge of the languages, habits, religion and
history, had given them the right to pronounce judgment
upon that country and people. What would the noble
Viscount have said and felt had he heard a well-known
member of the late Liberal Government last winter
inform his constituents that "the Turks possessed no
literature, and never had any poets,"—the Turks,
observe, to whom old Hammer-Purgstall assigns no less
than two thousand poets !

It may be thought by some an exaggeration on my
part, but it is nevertheless an indisputable fact that
England's perplexity in the East, her disquietude whenever the " Eastern Question " comes practically to the
front, is mainly due to her want of true, sound knowledge of the Moslem Asiatic countries and peoples.   It
is from this cause and not on account of a superior
number of troops, that she is overreached by the Colossus
of the North. What some few had done in Eastern
Asia, some English diplomatists succeeded also in ac-
complishing in Western Asia, where they made the name
of " Ingiliz ". shine with a brilliancy which even the
blunders of their successors have been unable altogether
to obscure.

We need not hesitate to acknowledge that the soundest
of all the diplomatists of the period was the Lord Strangford whom death struck down in the flower of his age,

and whose great capacities were as little recognised by contemporary statesmen as his rare learning and marvellous intellectual powers were during his life appreciated by the English nation.

To-day, when a man of his stamp might render the most eminent services, we look in vain for his equal. There is no one like him. Nothing meets the eye but a dismal void, and the dark shadow of an extinct meteor.

A. VAMBÉRY.

BUDA-PESTH, *June* 10, 1877.

TABLE OF CONTENTS.

CONTENTS.

LETTERS AND PAPERS

OF THE LATE

LORD STRANGFORD.

A

LETTERS AND PAPERS

OF THE LATE

LORD STRANGFORD.

———

OBSERVATIONS ON THE TURKISH LANGUAGE.[1]

It has been thought useful to supply the traveller with a brief sketch of the mechanism of the Turkish language, such as may assist him in understanding what he hears, and in applying any words which he may pick up; although in the limited space at our disposal it is impossible adequately to explain the remarkable structure, both grammatical and syntactical, of this beautiful language, which is justly admired by philologists.

The Turkish is, like the English, a mixed language. With a Turkish construction it works up Arabic and Persian words. Common Turkish is almost pure Turkish, but the old literary language introduces Persian copiously. The leading literary school now reduce the foreign elements, and use more Turkish. It is expressive, soft, and musical, not difficult to speak, but not easily written. The Turkish characters are, with some slight difference, the same as the Arabic and Persian. They are written from the right to the left, in an oblique direction. The chief

---

[1] Written for the "Handbook of Travellers in Turkey," and published by the kind permission of John Murray, Esq., Albemarle Street.

books of the Turks are those on poetry, law, and theology. Printing was introduced at Constantinople in the sixteenth century; but the copies of the Koran are still chiefly multiplied in manuscript.

The Turks have several styles of writing, each used for different purposes; such are the *nessik,* which is the foundation of all the others, and in which are transcribed copies of the **Koran** and other sacred books; the *diwani,* for firmans and official documents; the *rik'a,* for ordinary correspondence; and several others.

All consonants are to be pronounced as in English, *g* always hard, and *ch* always soft, as in *girl* and *church;* *k* and *g* before the soft vowel, *e, i, k, eu,* are *mouillés,* that is, they have a slight sound of *y* after them; thus, pretty is *gyuzal.*

When *p, t, k,* and *g* occur at the end of syllables or words, and, in the process of inflection or conjugation, any addition is made, they become, for euphony's sake, *b, d, y,* and *gh* respectively, as *git,* go; *gider,* he goes; *kalpak,* a cap; *kalpaghi,* his cap; *gelejek,* one who is coming (venturus); *gelejeyim,* I am coming. We have observed that one of the chief causes of an Englishman's unintelligibility in speaking a foreign language is his inattention to the proper pronunciation of the letter *r.* This one character in English represents two distinct sounds, one initial, as in *ring,* when it is a consonant; another, medial or final, as in *horn, cur,* when it is a semi-vowel. This semi-vocalic sound does not exist in foreign languages (except in Sanskrit and Illyrian, where it is recognised as a distinct vowel), and accordingly the consonantal sound should be carefully pronounced: thus, *firman,* an order, should not be made to rhyme with our word *sermon,* if meant to be understood by a Turk, but with "*there, man,*" as an Irishman would pronounce it. Difficulties in foreign languages may often be usefully illustrated and explained by our own provincial peculiarities. An Irishman will observe this rule instinctively. In addition to our vowels, there are the French *u*

and *eu*, and a peculiar thick sound of *i* or *u*, found in the
Slavonic dialects, and existing in English, but not distinguished.

Turkish belongs to what has been called the **Altaian or**
Turanian family of languages, but more properly to the
Ibero-Turkish, which includes the Iberian (Basque), Majyar
or Hungarian, Fin, Lap, and numerous others. It has dis-
tant affinities with all, but nearer with Majyar. The
relatives of its own branch are the Turkish languages and
dialects of **Andalusia,** Turkestan, and Siberia. The Turkish
language is so widely distributed and understood, that a
traveller may make his way by its use from Algiers to the
great wall of China, and from Egypt and Arabia into
Siberia. Beyond its own proper area it is extensively
used as a foreign and cultivated language in Persia, Cir-
cassia, and the courts of Turkestan. It has left its traces
in India.

Ethnologically, the **Turk is neither a Kaukasian**—an
absurd denomination—nor a **Mongol;** he belongs to a high
race, which, like the Indo-European or **Semitic, has a**
wide range, ranging from the high-bred Osmanli, equal to
any Indo-European or Arab, down to races having the
sloping **eyes and rounded** cheekbones **of the** Mongol.
There is a roundishness of skull, and, in the **lower** members of the race, a tenderness of skin. As the Semitic
race has tendencies towards the negro, so has **the Turkish**
towards the Mongol.

Vulgarly, **in philological works, Turkish is classed with**
the agglutinative languages,—a fanciful and unscientific
appellation.

There are **no** peculiarities **to an Englishman in the**
Turkish consonants, but in the Anatolian and Turkoman
dialects some of them become harsh gutturals. For centuries the tendency of the Osmanlis has been towards
softening, dismissing the gutturals and nasals.

There is, practically speaking, no definite article in
Turkish, though *o* is sometimes used, and inflection will

often supply its place. The indefinite *a* or *an* is expressed, as in some other languages, by *bir* (one).

The various relations of nouns expressed in other languages by prepositions or by cases are, in Turkish, represented by a set of affixes, which differ from cases in the fact that they are simply attached to without being incorporated with their noun, as in home, home*ward*. These affixes are as follows, with the old names of cases for convenience' sake:—

Genitive (of), *een, yn, ün, oon*—after a vowel, *neen, nyn, nün, noon.*

Dative (to, for), *ah, eh,* . . . . *yah, yeh.*

Accusative, *ee, y, ü, eoo,* . . . . *yee, yü, yoo.*

Ablative (from), ***dan, den.***

Locative (at, in), *da, de.*

Associative or instrumental (with), *lah, **leh**.*

It will be observed that each affix is written with different vowels; this arises from a peculiarity of the Turkish system of sounds which is common to the Altaian languages, and which is recognised in Basque, Majyar, and Fin, called the "harmony of vowels," which is as follows:—The vowels are divided into two classes, which may respectively be called soft and hard, there being four of each, and every soft vowel having its corresponding hard one. They are *ah, y, o, u,* hard; and *ay, ee, eu, ü,* soft. Very few words contain two vowels of opposite classes, and the use of all affixes is regulated by the character of the vowels of the root. This most important rule should always be borne in mind, as applying to all increases of the root, whether in nouns, pronouns, or verbs. Such a word as *goldsmith* is impossible to the mouth of a Turk, who would pronounce it *goldsmŏŏth*. Thus ***adam*** makes *adamyn*, the *a* in the root being hard; *e* being soft, *sherbet* makes *sherbetin*; *geuz, geuzün;* and *top, topun.*

The plural is formed by adding *lar* or *ler* to the root. The affixes are joined to this for the plural cases; thus, *adamlar, adamlaryn.*

Adjectives are indeclinable, as in English, and, as in English, always precede the qualified substantive, as *güzel kary*, a pretty woman, and *güzel karynyn*, of a pretty woman.

The numerals, cardinal and ordinal, do not make the noun plural, as *yüz adam*, not *yüz adamlar*.

The personal pronouns, *ben, sen, o*, take special affixes to make them possessive; thus, *benim, senim, onun*. These, again, when declension is necessary, take the affixes of cases above given; thus, *ev*, a house; *evim*, my house; *evimden*, from my house. After a vowel, the possessive *i* or *u* of the third person becomes *si, sy, sü*, or *su*, according to the character of the preceding vowel; thus, *kapu*, a gate; *kapusu*, his gate; and *kapusuna*, to his gate; *na* and *ni* being used for *a* and *i* in the dative and accusative of the second person possessive.

There is no relative pronoun in Turkish, its absence being supplied by a most complicated construction, with a verbal gerund taking the possessive affixes.

In Turkish, when the idea of possession has to be expressed, the object possessed always takes the third personal possessive affix, the possessor taking the genitive termination; thus, *pashanyn evi*, the pasha's house, not *pashanyn ev; karynyn geuzü*, the woman's eye, not *karynyn geuz*: literally translated these words mean — the pasha his house, the woman her eye; reminding us of our own "for Christ his sake," or the Latin "suo sibi gladio hunc jugulo."

The observing of this rule forms one of the chief difficulties in Turkish. The genitive affix is only added when we in English would use the definite article, whose want is thus supplied by inflection; *pasha evi* and *kary geuzu*, without the genitive, mean a pasha's house, as distinct from any other kind of house; a woman's eye, as distinct from a man's; where *pasha* and *kary* may be considered as adjectives, qualifying and describing the object rather than as implying possession.

The verb has its infinitive in *mek* or *mak*, declinable like a noun. The Turkish verb, like the English, makes a distinction between "come" and "am coming," "came" and "was coming," and so throughout, including the passive. What is called in English the participial form is in Turkish represented by *yor*—*gelyorim*, I am coming, *gelyordim*, I was coming, &c. Its root, or simplest form, is the imperative. The tenses are mostly formed by adding person-endings to participles, which latter are capable of being used separately. An example is given:—*gel*, come thou; *gelir* (a separable present indefinite participle), one who comes; *geleer-eem, geleer-sen, geleer, geleer-eez, geleer-seeniz, geleer-ler,* I, thou, he, we, you, they, come; *geliyur* (a separable present definite participle), one actually coming; *geliyür-eem, geliyür-sen,* &c., I am coming, &c.; *gel-ejek* (a separable definite future participle), one about to come; *gel-ejeyim, gel-ejeksen, gel-ejek, gel-ejeyiz, gel-ejeksiniz, gel-ejekler,* I, thou, he, &c., will come. The past definite is *gel, -deem, -deen, -dee, deek, -deeniz, -deeler,* I, thou, he, &c., came; this is not a separable participle. The past indefinite, *gelmish,* one who has come, is a separable participle; *gelmish-eem, -sen, gelmish, -eez, -seeniz, -ler,* I, thou, he, &c., have come. The optative, present and past, *geleyeem* and *geley-ideem,* I may and I might come; the person-endings are respectively as in *gelirim* and *geldeem.* The conditional is *gel-sem, -sen, -seh, -sek, -seniz, seler,* if I, thou, he, &c., come. The imperative is *gel, gel-seen, gel-elim, geleen, gel-seenler,* come thou, let him come, let us come, come ye, let them come.

For a verb whose root has a hard vowel, of course the endings must also be used with hard vowels, as *bak,* look; *bak-arym,* I look; *door,* stop; *doorooroom,* I stop.

The negative verb, which has a separate conjugation, is formed by the insertion of an *m,* under euphonic rules, before its person-endings. We merely give one or two examples, as being irregular and in most common use: *gelmez,* he comes not; *gelmeh,* do not come. For verbs with hard vowels the syllable is naturally *mah* and not *meh.*

An *e* or an *a*, according to the vowels of the root, placed before the *me* or *ma*, changes the negative verb to one expressing impossibility; thus *gelmem*, I come not; *gelemem*, I cannot come. This admirable mechanism of the verb is followed throughout with the most perfect regularity ; and there are reflective, causative, reciprocal, and the derived conjugations, which are formed in a similar manner by introducing different monosyllables.

An interrogative verb is made by the addition of *mi*, *my*, *mü*, or *mu*, after the endings, as *geldinmi*, didst thou come ? It precedes, however, instead of following the endings, as *-eem*, *-sen*, *-eez*, *-seeniz ;* as *gelejek-mee-eez*, are we coming ?

This particle can be added to nouns, or all other parts of speech, as well as to verbs, and serves to specify the question as belonging emphatically to the word to which it is joined. This is a great convenience, which is unknown to other languages, except the Russian, Illyrian, and partially the Latin. The working of the principle is beautiful; thus, *sen mi Istambolah gitdin-mi*, did you go to Stambul ? *sen mi Istambolah gitdin*, was it you who went to Stambul ? *sen Istambolah-mi gitdin*, was it to Stambul you went?

A simple verb may, therefore, have six forms—an affirmative, negative, impossible, and an interrogative of each. But the difficulty is more apparent than real, as the person-endings are simple and never vary, the tenses few, and the root itself is never changed or disguised.

The working of this system has a great likeness to that of the English verb, as it exists in fact, not as represented commonly in grammars.

The Turkish idiom, in many cases, has extraordinary resemblances to English, and particularly to the Cockney dialect.

The construction of sentences follows the inverted order, as in Latin, the verb always closing the phrase.

In speaking Anatolian, the guttural *kh* must be used,

and the language made rougher; but in Stambul every-thing is softened, as in English.

The traveller who wishes to obtain any further insight into the language on the spot is especially recommended to learn what he can as colloquially as possible, rather than by taking lessons from a professional master, who will prove completely wedded to a defective routine system of teaching. Let him avoid encumbering and embarrassing his brain by any attempt at formally studying the literary Turkish, which will only create inextricable confusion, and, even if learnt, would be quite useless for conversational purposes, a great proportion of the words used in the written language being quite unknown to the middle and lower classes. There are several Turkish grammars. Mr. Redhouse is the author of the best grammar of the language, but it is unfortunately in French; and he is also the author of a very remarkable English and Turkish dictionary, besides other works.[1] A fine sketch of the language will be found in Professor Max Müller's "Lectures on Language," though mixed up with the conventional High Dutch nomenclature.

[1] Since this was written, Mr. Redhouse has issued a useful pocket volume, under the title of "The Turkish Vade-Mecum;" containing a copious Ottoman Grammar; a carefully selected Vocabulary, alphabetically arranged in two parts—English and Turkish, and Turkish and English; also a few familiar dialogues and naval and military terms—the whole in English characters, the pronunciation being fully indicated. How well the book answers to its title is thus noticed in the "Saturday Review" of 14th July 1877:—"Mr. Redhouse has packed into a very compact little volume, readily carried in the pocket or knapsack, a guide to Ottoman colloquial language, which seems to be of a very practical and useful kind. He dispenses with Arabic characters, which, he thinks, only mystify and confuse those who desire rapid and rudimentary instruction, and gives the words in English letters; together with a carefully prepared vocabulary, and a short appendix of military and naval terms."—*Publishers' Note.*

19 MANSFIELD STREET, W., *April* 1, 1861.

MY DEAR SIR,—I must beg you to excuse me for not having sooner sent you Lascarato's book, according to promise. I have only just succeeded in recovering it from a friend to whom I had lent it. To my mind, the book is so curious and interesting, both for its contents and its language, that I am anxious you should not be without some help towards understanding it, and I therefore venture to give you a hint or two, which I hope may not be unacceptable. I recommend you to begin at once with the political or third section. The language there is, at first, much easier and less idiomatic, and the matter just at present has immediate interest. He is bitter and fierce beyond anything, but is perfectly impartial, showing up alike the "Come-stà" or toady party, the clamorous annexationists who usurp the name of the people, and the Ἄγγλους ἀδιαφόρους. The other sections, which are on domestic economy and the priesthood, are to an English reader mere truisms and platitudes couched in quaint vigorous language, though to a Greek they are audacious and shocking to the last degree.

I have been cudgelling my brains, but I fear without much result, to find out for you a royal road or clue to the labyrinth of modern Greek phonetics. Lascarato is as defiant in form as in spirit, and he spells anyhow, with most perfect wantonness, not because he knows no better, but because he does not think the matter worth caring about, and uses any vowel that comes uppermost to his pen. Of course you are prepared for all the letters representing the *i* sound being used indifferently; ϵ and $\alpha\iota$ are used with equal indifference; $\alpha\iota$ is the *exact* equivalent of ϵ, and softens γ and χ in the same way into y and that peculiar soft χ which can only be expressed on paper by *hy* [*we* have the sound only before *u*; thus *Hume, Hughes,* are *exactly* rendered by $X\iota o\hat{\nu}\mu$, $X\iota o\hat{\nu}\zeta$, in Greek transliteration]. Lascarato would be quite capable of writing $\alpha i\tau i\alpha$ as $\acute{\epsilon}\tau o\iota\alpha$. When you are at a loss for the meaning of a word—of course barring such vulgarisms as are impossible for you to know—your best plan will be to repeat it to yourself as it were with your eyes shut, and to try at the meaning by applying every possible variant in place of such letters as happen to have equivalents. Final ν is hardly ever pronounced except before vowels and π, τ, or κ, which coalesce with it and take their respective medial sounds. In these cases it is constantly put on where not wanted, especially by Albanians and Western Greeks; thus Lascarato writes $\nu\alpha\nu$ for $\nu\alpha$ constantly; but a Greek has no conception of a medial consonant pure and unaffected by a nasal: this is from Albanian influence. He not only writes "madama" as $\mu\alpha\nu\tau\acute{\alpha}\mu\alpha$, but he also pronounces it "mandama," and tells you it is all the same. I have even heard old R——, who has been thirty years in England, say "to ndeserve it," instead of "to deserve." Another way of avoiding ν as a termination is to put on an extra vowel, as $\alpha\dot{\nu}\tau\acute{o}\nu\epsilon$, $\dot{\epsilon}\kappa\epsilon\acute{\iota}\nu o\nu\epsilon$, $\tau\hat{\omega}\nu$ $\dot{\epsilon}\chi\theta\rho\hat{\omega}\nu\epsilon$. Lascarato is very fond of this. In the aorist plurals it comes as a matter of course, being favoured by the wish to obtain uniformity in accentuation—thus you have $\dot{\epsilon}\kappa\acute{\alpha}\mu\alpha\mu\epsilon$, $\dot{\epsilon}\kappa\acute{\alpha}\mu\alpha\tau\epsilon$, $\dot{\epsilon}\kappa\acute{\alpha}\mu\alpha\nu\epsilon$, for $\acute{\epsilon}\kappa\alpha\mu\alpha\nu$; sometimes even $\dot{\epsilon}\kappa\acute{\alpha}\mu\alpha$, but this is rare. Here is an instance in Lascarato. $\varDelta\acute{\nu}o$ $\gamma\alpha\ddot{\imath}$-$\delta o\acute{\nu}\rho\iota\alpha$ $\pi o\hat{\nu}$ '$\mu\alpha\lambda\acute{\omega}\nu\alpha$ (two donkeys who were quarrelling—for $\dot{\epsilon}\mu\acute{\alpha}\lambda\lambda\omega\nu\alpha\nu$). You must therefore be prepared for $\delta\epsilon\nu$ appearing before consonants as $\delta\grave{\epsilon}$, and not allow your eye to mislead you into mistaking it for $\delta\grave{\epsilon}$ of the old Hellenic firm of μὲν and δὲ, now bankrupt, Athenians and their Philhellenic dupes to the contrary notwithstanding. Be prepared for the omission of otiose gammas, as λέει, φυλάει, for λέγει, φυλάγει (φυλάττει), as also for the insertion of γ, when it has the sound of *y*, before the *i*-sounding letters, as γιατρός, γυιός. This is done to quicken the pronunciation, making these words sound *yatròs*, *yòs*, instead of *i-atros*, *ios*. There are several new abnormal presents formed by the phonetic influence of the aorists. Aorists in -ησα, -ισα, -υσα, are practically the same, though etymologically different; and an aorist in -ισα, for instance, though arising from a present in -ίζω, reacts upon the latter, and changes it arbitrarily into one in -ῶ, from -εω or -αω. So in the third page we have μεινάει. It would not be easy to recognise μηνύει. The first error is mere wantonness; of course -άει arises out of ἐμήνυσα becoming treated as though it were ἐμήνησα, like ἐμίλησα or ἠγάπησα, and thereby forming a present μηνάω, -άεις, -άει, like ἀγαπάω or -ῶ, ἀγαπάεις, ἀγαπάει. So ἔκοψα from κόπτω has got a new present κόβω, or with an otiose gamma, κόβγω; so κάβω or κάβγω for καίω, from ἔκαψα = ἔκαυσα.

At this rate I shall be writing a grammar instead of a letter, so I will not now trouble you with more than a few miscellaneous hints. Εἰς may become σὲ and ὥς, the latter not being the old Atticism retained, but a contraction of ἕως——ἕως τὸ σπῆτι being = εἰς τὸ σπῆτι (when εἰς means *to*, not *in*). Πουλιὸ (*pŭlyō*) is πλέον, constantly pronounced più, piò, pliò. Puliò is an Ionism or Cephalonism; I never heard it or noticed it. Δικῶ for φθάνω (to suffice), ξεδονω and derivatives for ξεφαντόνω or διασκεδάζω (to divert or amuse), and the aorist passive employment of εἴπω, as εἰπόθηκα (or ’πόθηκα), να ’ποθῆ, &c., *e.g.*, ’μπορεῖ να ’ποθῆ, "it can be said," are Ionian peculiarities, at least I never heard the last one. Feminines in -ις are, as you probably know, colloquially equivalent to those in -η or -a; thus, τάξις, πόλις, are pronounced by all,[1] and written by

---

[1] *Exceptis excipiendis*, the educated and conscious.

Lascarato, as τάξη, πόλη, and in the plural τάξες or τάξαις, &c. Before concluding I will give you a short lift over a passage neither easy nor hard—page 2, beginning Μία ἄλλη.

Παντρέβει for ὑπανδρεύει. In the combinations νδρ, μβρ, δ and β retain[1] what was their old sound, *i.e.*, our *d* and *b;* and to denote this the Greeks change the writing, and spell as above, or as γαμπρός, πρικιό (προικιον), portion. Τῆς δινει gives her. Genitives' were rapidly going when the spoken language recovered its consciousness : they are constantly used for the dative and objective case in pronouns. Γιά, *ya,* for διά, regularly so pronounced. Δαύτονε for ἐδαύτον = αὐτὸν, arising from ἐδώ + αυτον, *i.e.,* "just him." Φχαριστηέται for εὐχαριστεῖται, regular colloquialism. For ἀγαπῶμαι, -ᾶσαι, -ᾶται, it is usual to say ἀγαπιοῦμαι, -πιέσαι, -πιέται, -πιούμαστε, &c. (pĭume, pĭese, &c., as two, not three syllables). Translate the last bit, "As he turns back from his father-in-law's house, the money which he carries with him is his market purchase, and the wife is the makeweight." Ψῶνι or ψούνι, a purchase of meat or provisions; τσόντα, *ts'onda,* the makeweight, such as fat, bone, &c., such as you must take in with the good part when you buy meat. Ποῦ is the regular relative; it is also used for ὅτι, and, through Oriental influence, like Mrs. Gamp's *which,* as ὁ ἄνθρωπος ποῦ τὸν εἶδα, the man which I saw him = whom I saw.

Ἀξένω, in next page, is for αὐξαίνω : the combination *fx* being clumsy to pronounce. If there are any difficulties which you may find in the course of reading, pray do not hesitate to consult me, as I am an idle man, and shall be most happy to satisfy you as far as I can; at the same time, I must confess that here and there I am puzzled from want of special Cephalonian experience.—I remain, my dear sir, very faithfully yours,

STRANGFORD.

---

[1] In practice, not in theory.

19 MANSFIELD STREET, W., *March* 12, 1862.

MY DEAR SIR,—I have a great deal to answer for, both to you and to my own conscience, in having suffered a correspondence so auspiciously begun, and to me so profitable, as ours to fall into neglect. Travel and matrimony are my only grounds of excuse for this. As I am now settled and at rest, I lose no time in resuming our correspondence, being more especially moved thereunto by a passage in your last letter to W——, read to me by him, from which I gather that my opinion on your Ἄγγελος article, or on some of its details, would not be unacceptable. Before going into this, however, I should like to say a word or two about Maltese. I think I am not wrong in attributing to you an article on Sallack's "Malta," which appeared some time last autumn, and expressed a wish to know the real state of the case about Phœnician and Arabic elements in Maltese. That pleasant jargon, for which I have a weakness quite out of proportion to its merits, is wholly and exclusively Arabic. Not only this, but Barbary Arabic, and distinctively that of East Barbary, or Tunis and Tripoli. It must have been fixed pretty early, and affords valuable testimony in proof of the early origin of modern Barbaresque colloquialisms, which do not exist in Syria or Arabia. The use of *shi* = thing, in negative sentences, like the French *pas*, as an extra negative, this is unknown in classical Arabic and in the East, but begins in Egypt. It has also lost two hard gutturals, and makes no distinction between the emphatic and the ordinary dentals. On this last point, I have observed all Barbary men that I have talked with to be very shaky. Of Phœnician there is absolutely and positively not a trace in Maltese. The one word which exists in Maltese and Phœnician (*i.e.*, Hebrew), and does not exist in classical or Eastern Arabic, is *f'tit*, a little, *un peu*. But I have heard it also from the mouth of a genuine Tunisian Mussulman; and it must be a *Punism*, therefore, of Barbary

and Malta, not of Malta distinctively. *Yāser*, very
much, is another Punism from Barbary, which, however,
is *not* found in Maltese. There is no such thing in existence as a vocabulary of Tunisian provincialisms, and such
a one would be of great value if well done, or decently
well. The Maltese vocabulary is overloaded with Italian ;
yet not more so than the town Greek of Corfu, Zante,
or Smyrna used to be in the pre-Koraï days, or, for the
matter of that, even now among Levantine Franks. An
unusual proportion of decent Arabic verbs have become
deflected into indecent meanings in Maltese, causing end-
less amusement and mutual misunderstandings between
the two parties. *Defá*, Arabic to pay, let go, set free, in
Maltese means πέρδεσθαι : *hasha*, Arabic, to stuff or fill in ;
Maltese, coire : '*ush* (*sh* doubled), Arabic, a bird's nest; Maltese, pudendum muliebre. As to the Maltese blood, there
is no doubt that it is mainly Phœnician, and that this
latter language would have yielded easily, and as a matter
of course, within a generation or two to the Arabic, being
intimately allied, when the blood would have been little
affected. Moreover, Mohammedan conquest never seriously
affects the blood of the conquered, whereas the conquerors
are always affected by the latter. They are ever apt to
commit ethnological suicide, and obliterate their original
selves, indeed, by overmuch intercourse with the native
race; as the Turks, or so-called Moguls, have done in
India.

You will say that I have ridden my Maltese hobby to
death, and that it is time to mount the Byzantine "unreasonable." I know nothing myself about the ″Αγγελος, but
suspect it to be one of the numerous abortive efforts made
to attract public attention by one Pitsipiòs, who calls himself a prince, who left the Greek Church for Rome after
writing a very violent and amusing " Roving-Englishman"-
like attack on the abuses of orthodox prelacy, and who is
now in the pay of the Propaganda at Rome for the purpose of writing up Latin and Greek union. He is a poor

weak creature, and his ideas vague, shadowy, and baseless; but it is easy for a Greek to produce the impression of superior ability through the wonderful rhetorical power and copiousness of the language which has come down to him.

Your article is perfectly correct in matters of fact, with two slight exceptions, which are over- or under- statements rather than errors. I have looked carefully at the Albanian language, and believe, with the best Germans, that it is not only Indo-European, but that it stands in special and intimate connection with the very oldest Greek. I cannot here go into the evidence of this in detail. Its vocabulary is ruined and overwhelmed with Latin borrowings of eighteen hundred years, from Augustan Latin—evidenced by the retention of the hard sound of *c* before *e* and *i*—to the modern Romanic of their South Wallah neighbours, to say nothing of Adriatic Italian. Its forms and synthesis are much broken down; but, such as they are, are all Indo-European, and one has no more right to separate them on this account from that class than to separate modern French and call it allophylic, if it were now to be first discovered, and if Latin had been completely obliterated. Latham, who puts them in the same unclassed category as the Basques, is utterly untrustworthy and no *scholar*, though his destructive criticism is often of great value, and unjustly ignored or run down by the Germans. It is not this old connection which helps their assimilation to the Greeks proper. It is the total uncultivation of their language, and absence of writing and of all literary or home-grown religious traditions among them, which does this. An orthodox Albanian becomes a Greek at once the moment he comes under the civilising influence of the Greek language as an instrument of education and literature, and where they exist in small bodies they lose their own language in a generation or two. In large bodies, as in Hydra and Attica, they keep it up, but for all practical purposes are Greek. Ethnologically, of course, they are a

B

far more important factor than the Slavonians in the
modern Greek race. The Greeks have equally incorporated, and are incorporating, the Romanic population of
Northern Greece, because these have, most unfortunately,
left their language uncultivated, have no traditions separate from the Greeks; for with them *un Romanu* is an
exact equivalent to ἕνας Ρωμαῖος, and does not imply a
sense of Roman descent, but of citizenship of the later
Roman or Byzantine Empire, and the language of their
religion and education is wholly Greek. But the Bulgarian cannot be incorporated, because he has a cultivated language for his liturgy, and hitherto, when he
wrote at all, for his secular literature, and all his sentiments and traditions are bound up with that language,
which he is trying hard to use for the improvement of his
vernacular, and as a standard and source of literary correctness, as the Greek does with Hellenic. The Greeks do
not mete out to the Bulgarians the measure which they
claim for themselves, and have succeeded, among races
subject or quasi-subject to them who have any independent
feeling, in making themselves thoroughly hated by their
attempts to crush vernacular education. And when they
now tell the world that these people were all the same
two or three thousand years ago, it will be thought pleasant and clever at Athens and in Finsbury Square, but at
Sophia and Bucharest people will wonder whether the
Franks think them fools enough to be caught by such very
poor chaff as that, and deluded into lending themselves to
any scheme of Neo-Byzantine supremacy. You now see,
no doubt, why the word *Rouman (lege, Romăn* or *Romŭn*
—РОМЬН, with a special Slavonic vowel—in South
Wallachian *Rŏmanu*, as in Italian) is ἄδοξον καὶ εὐτελές τι.

It embodies the consciousness of the North Wallachian's
descent from the great people, and is the very source and
key of his rising self-respect and his future political rege-
neration. This will always be a stumbling-block to the
Greek's aim of supremacy; and he would fain replace it

by some other more profitable tradition of the Wallachian's identity with himself. But the Greek's eager
vanity overlooks the fact that neither Boyar nor peasant
are likely to thank him for substituting a theory of connection with the race of Mavroyeni for one of descent
from that of Trajan. As for Dr. Beron and his Thracians,
and all these shadowy and meaningless theories, the writers
no more believe them than the readers, if there are any ;
and they are really not worth powder and shot, and neither deserve nor obtain serious consideration out of the
Hellenic Buncombe for which they are manufactured, just
as Dublin manufactures analogous stuff for the Celtic
Buncombe.

The word Γραικός is not only common, but fixed and
universal. It is the regular modern substitute for the
Ρωμαιὸς (accent always so in speaking) of thirty years ago.
Of course, it arose from the necessity of finding a correct
and comprehensive term to include all Greeks which
did not suggest any political meaning, like the word
Ἕλλην.

This last word is in practice purely political, and only
applied to the whole race as a figure of rhetoric and in the
high style ; as, for instance, when we call ourselves Anglo-
Saxons. Ξέρετε γραικικὰ is the regular current expression for "Do you know Greek ?" It is now as much a
point of honour to sink ρωμαιϊκα as to sink ἀφέντης ; but
plain country folk and sailors will long continue to use
both—at least I hope so ; for I honour and respect a Greek
who sticks by and is not ashamed of his honest Byzantine
tongue and traditions.

I don't quite agree with you about Queenstown, &c., but
there is no space for more, and I may have bored you
enough as it is. I must say, however, that your Γιλβερ-
τόπουλος would infallibly be taken by plain Vasilaki or
Dimitraki, who knows no tongue but his own, and who
reads his regular newspaper gossip, for Major Yelverton.

W—— tells me you will be in town before long. I

hope to have the pleasure of seeing you when you come.
—I remain, very sincerely yours,

STRANGFORD.

———

CORFU, *May* 25, 1863.

MY DEAR FREEMAN,— .... I suspect that the person you met in Switzerland who said *Ne parla Almane*,
was no genuine Rhætian, but more probably an Italian
speaking dog-French, his only available means of communication with a Western stranger. You hear very little
Romansch even at Coire, and it has gone down very low
in all the Rhenish valleys, though in the Engadine it has
much more vitality.

I am writing with much shortness of temper and bitterness of spirit, having been much provoked by the hotel
waiter, who has called this island Kérkyra instead of its
real name. I blew him up strongly for so doing, but I
don't think he followed or appreciated my arguments. If
he had said Korkyra, I should have forgiven him; but to
go and dig up a dead old bone of a word which never was
vernacular anywhere out of Attica at any time, and to be
ashamed of the good, picturesque, descriptive word of his
grandfathers before him, is a thing which rouses my wrath,
and impels me to lift up my voice and testify against this
race of pedants. Well, perhaps we may live to see a
younger generation of Anglo-Saxons ashamed of Derby
and Whitby, and reviving Northweorthig and Stuóneshalh.

There is no political talk, ferment, or agitation here, but
much silent anxiety as to the time and the manner of ac-
complishing the union. They seem to me to wish that they
had had a longer notice, and to have been universally
taken aback and unprepared at the sudden change of prospect. As far as I can see, even the lowest and howl-
ingest town-rowdy is not wholly glad to be annexed; nor,
on the other hand, are the great landowners wholly without consolation. What they fear more than anything else

is an armed rising of the peasants when we withdraw. With the peasants, as you probably know, ἕνωσις means ownership of the soil, as far as it has any real definite meaning at all. I am very much afraid that we are making the Greeks a present of seven islands, and that the Greeks, who have always been extremely lukewarm about these islands, are fully aware of the fact, and apprehensive of its dangers; having only encouraged the cry for annexation because it rested on the same principle as that which would put them in possession of Thessaly and Crete, which they do want. The people here are coolly and openly arranging and discussing schemes of future Corfiote supremacy in Greece, and devising wonderful factious combinations of votes and parties, which are to put and keep all power in their hands. But I think now, and have always thought, that the most hopeless thing about the Greeks— and what makes me almost despair of them, putting aside the sailor and farmer classes—is their universal cleverness. Fancy a nation entirely composed of multiples of Disraeli —none cleverer, none duller, and all striving for the same objects.

There is nothing for it but to sluice them well with Albanian and Bulgarian blood, and produce a new ethnological combination or race.

I am going on to Constantinople very shortly.—Ever yours truly,   STRANGFORD.

CONSTANTINOPLE, *June 24,* 1863.

MY DEAR FREEMAN,—I am glad you got our letters, though they were of no avail. I quite agree with you in thinking that you could have done what you had to do in Switzerland perfectly well without them, though something of the kind would be quite indispensable at Vienna or St. Petersburg. Here anything of the kind would be quite useless as regards the Embassy people; and the diffi-

culty for a historical inquirer would be, first of all, to find
anybody unconnected with money or politics in their most
sordid form, and, secondly, to get speech of him. It is very
odd how people here run on in old grooves; nobody cares
in the least about philological and ethnological questions
here, even when they bear upon politics—I mean, English
people don't care—and accept any fact as such put into
their hands with perfect acquiescence, especially when it
tends to support their policy, or chimes in with their pre-
judices. I can find out next to nothing about the Bulgarians, what they are feeling and doing. It is only by
means of a bookseller's shop-window that I have seen that
an Anglo-Bulgarian dictionary has last year been published, and this is an American, and not an English doing.
The old stagers are quite content to go on looking on them
just as Turks do, as so many Greeks belonging to the
Rum milleti or Greek "nation," and the more advanced
ethnologists have discovered them to be Slavonians. Meanwhile, as far as I can see, their anti-Greek feeling is being
made use of by an active Russian and Servian propaganda
(the former more literary, the latter more political) to turn
their sham Slavonism into a real one; in other words, to
make them think of themselves as Slavonians and brothers,
&c., representing them meanwhile in Western Europe as
true identical Slavonians already. If this propaganda
were genuine and national, I should respect it, and cherish
its natural growth till it choked out and killed the Turks,
which is the best thing that could happen perhaps. But,
in truth, and for all its mask of Christian sympathy and
cry of civilisation, it is mere Government machinery,
worked by the triple agency of despotism in its worst
form—the Czarism, old and, so to speak, respectable of
St. Petersburg, the Czarism you know of at Paris, and
the *Othonism* of Belgrade. Prince Michel's master-spirit
on the spot is Garashanin, who has his own ambitious
views; but the Prince is acting as a regular indigenous
double of Otho. He has raised the cursed spirit of Pali-

karism, and imposed military rule, martial law, and arbitrary taxation; and has given them whatever may be the Slavonic for ἡ μεγάλη ἰδέα, instead of the "benefits of civilisation" with which the House of Commons give him credit. He wants to rule Othonically and by Othonic means over Bosnia, &c., and Bulgaria, which, as you know, is not as yet to Servia what Thessaly is to Athens, however much it may pass as such in England. The Turks are strong on their military legs just now, and there may be no immediate row. If there is a row, and the Turks go to the wall, Garashanin will be Minister and practical ruler of a great kingdom. If the Turks win, down goes the Prince, and Garashanin is believed to look to his place instead. I don't much like rural policemen living at free quarters in Bulgarian villages (though I cannot get into a divine wrath about it, more especially when I see the mechanism of the details with which it is exaggerated); but I dislike much more, and find it come much more home to me, that we should have people of station in England, M.P.'s, "Timeses," &c., absolutely without power of criticism of any alleged fact on one side or the other with regard to this country. L——'s cool offhand optimism with regard to the general condition of the Turkey question in the home provinces has nothing to make us fly in the face of our Government when they endeavour to bring to his bearings, in the interest of his own subjects, a prince dependent on Turkey, who is ambitious, unruly, and faithless towards that country. But L—— is very riling, I admit. The best proof of the merits, speaking generally and broadly, of our imperial policy here, putting aside the recognition of it by men like Eugène Forcade in the "Revue des Deux Mondes," lies in the fact of its adoption by the Greeks and by the Montenegrins. The latter have not, of course, lost their old ancestral hatred of the Turks, nor is it right they should; but they are on good terms with them, and they are disposed to keep faith with them in spite of all temptation, having learnt the inutility, as I hope they learn the immorality, of breaking faith at the instigation of foreign despots, who leave them in the lurch after all. The Greeks here, at all events the industrious and mercantile Greeks, I am assured, talk with much sobriety and patriotism. They are hotter than ever at the prospect of a Byzantine Empire, and at what they call the reversal of English policy, at the same time that they seem, and in their present mind are really, in earnest about working for it and not filibustering for it. This is, in other words, a reversal of their own, or their late king's own policy, and an adoption of ours. I can say sincerely that I wish them success, and I honestly admire their good management in Greece of late. But I can hardly, from past experience of their want of ballast and of the power and policy of the despotisms which are working for chaos in these countries, believe in their ulti- mate success. Our fault of policy in these parts seems to me to have always lain in our acting from hand to mouth, and taking for granted the perpetuity of Turkish domi- nion. This last has no bottom to it. The exclusive con- scription and other causes (principally connected with taxation) must cut the ground from under the Turks at a period which of itself would not come so soon as people idly talk, but which for all that has to come. If this is granted, a Government really representing English ideas should take an active course, and not be content to drift. It should be in more active communication with the lead- ing men of one race to succeed the Turks, such as one would fain and fondly see the Greeks, or of all races, with a view to your federation; to teach them what to eat, drink, and avoid when growing up out of barbarism or political childhood, and to prevent, above all, their being demoralised by our own or other people's political partisanship—our own, which spoils a child; that of France and Russia, which makes a thief of him. Light and more light is what we want; no jobbing little wretched consuls made out of bank- rupts; but no expense spared in covering the land with men of the Leake type to lighten our darkness, which can

be felt, and to tell us at home who is a true man, and who
is the dupe or tool of the Frenchman, who wants a row
for a row's sake, or the Russian, who wants a row to get
at his neighbour's property. Then we should not have the
discredit of Baillie Cochrane talking of there being six
millions of Greeks (!), or Mr. Maguire boasting that there
were only ten thousand Turks in Samos (!!) (a semi-detached
and perfectly quiet dependency, where there are *none*);
nor, what I regret to have seen, a Professor of History at
Oxford losing his head and temper because he read a letter
in his "Times" one morning from its correspondent at
Scutari in Albania, where that excellent man made the
Turks horribly massacre and mutilate the Albanian pri-
soners, who were on their own side (!!!). Goldwin Smith,
I think, is not bound to know that the Miridite country is
a loyal Montenegro, the inhabitants of which are Catholic
Bashi-Bazuks, with a loose sort of independence, who have
always fought with the Turks, and neither could nor did
side with the Montenegrins; but he might have his sus-
picions aroused, by seeing a trace of foreign idiom here and
there, that Civis Romanus was no Romanus after all. A
. . . . may be found a useful correspondent at the Palais
Royal, where much Tuileries dirty work is done, as
well as in Printing House Square, and that in the ratio
of his ascertained influence and private friendship at headquarters. This is allusion, but it is knowledge as well.
I suppose it not unreasonable to think, even *à priori*, that
means of influencing English opinion on the Eastern question is not unacceptable to the Emperor. I do not think
that —— —— is directly paid by the French; but I should
not think he went unrewarded. As to his mistake, he of
course made it on purpose, aware of our ignorance, and
eager to excite our hatred against the Turks on the eve of
Garibaldi's supposed invasion of Albania, as planned for
him, from which it was part of the greatness of Garibaldi
to hold aloof.

I must have bored you to death with this long story of views on matters regarding which it is a public misfortune that all have views and none have knowledge. However, I cannot help a little animation on the subject after having just read the wonderful debate of the 29th May. I ought to have written more about Rhætia, but that I must adjourn indefinitely, as I shall leave this in a week. Very probably I shall next be in Rhætia itself during August, where it will be a pleasure to fall in with you. My wife has gone with one or two ladies and military people from Corfu to Joannina, of which she writes in very high praise. Your view of Londres and Albertville I devoutly hope may prove true. I had rather turn Turk and live here than that Londres should come first; and Londres will come first if we go shutting our eyes and ears to all but loyalty with a strong conventional element.—Ever yours truly,   STRANGFORD.

---

58 GREAT CUMBERLAND STREET, W.,
November 7, 1863.

MY DEAR FREEMAN,—When I was at Constantinople in June, I had the satisfaction of reading and profiting by your article on the Landesgemeinde of Uri—which, by the way, I observe the Swiss write shortly and colloquially Land*s*gemeinde. When at Lugano in September I saw the same article turned into French in the "Journal de Genève," a paper which I like, and consider above the Continental average.

I took notes of the numbers, and on my way through Geneva the other day I got them to send to you, under the impression that you may not have received them from any of your Swiss friends, who, probably, would not recognise you in print at first sight.

I cannot congratulate you on your appearance in French clothes, which ought properly to have been mountain German clothes; but, anyhow, you make a better show than Kinglake in the *feuilleton* of the Κλειώ of Trieste, where it is melancholy to see all his vigour frittered away under the treatment of high Athenian penny-a-lining and Gradus Greek.

After leaving Constantinople I went round by the Danube and joined my wife in Lombardy, bound from Scutari, Montenegro, and the Dalmatian towns. She was delighted with the Montenegrins, whose ways are much more primitive and genuinely Homeric than I had any idea of. To be sure, they were seen at the right moment, in full summer and perfect peace. After which we dwelt among ex-Rayahs for two months in Tessino and Vaud, with a visit or two in Rhætian Switzerland. My chief philological inquiries had reference to the dialects of Western or Burgundian Switzerland, and they have been quite fruitless. I tried the chief booksellers of Lausanne, Vevey, and Geneva, and could get nothing worth having—nothing but school-books for teaching French to the little Vaudois boys; and about the side valleys of the Valais, such as the Val d'Anniviers or Einfisch Thal, I could neither get nor hear of anything. So I have nothing to go by but local names, glosses, and guide-book statements, such as "On parle un patois mêlé de Roman et de Français." You will be glad to hear how Berlepsch, a Swabian citizen of Zurich, the reigning guide-book man, talks of *les armées françaises* having crossed the Lukmanier with Charlemagne. This is in a French edition, made to sell in France. I have not seen the German original.

I made at once for Miss Yonge's book on returning, and am deep in it. It is, I must say, wonderfully well done; but there is something to be corrected in every page. The best parts by far are when the materials are her own and the criticism too; the worst, when she follows blind or bad guides. It is dreadful to see pages wasted on those wretched Triads and sham Welsh myths; yet I find it easier to bear the burden of Triadism, Hu Gadarn, Helio Arkites, and all, than the cool arrogance of the "sound common sense" people, such as we have it in the "Edinburgh" article which is supposed to have smashed up and extirpated the Druids.

Now just look at this. The common-sense man chatters and grins like a monkey over the absurdity of Ogham inscriptions, and treating accidental or meaningless scratches as actual alphabets. Well, Dr. Graves claims to interpret these scratches by means of the old Irish language, existing in remains fairly well known and investigated. Meanwhile an Ogham and Latin bilingual is found at St. Dogmael's in Merionethshire. It can hardly, therefore, be accidental. The Latin is *Sacrani Fili Cunotami.* But the application of Grave's method gives the same with *magi* for *fili.* So you get at once the proof of Graves's system and an older stage of a Celtic genitive, identical with the Latin and that of the old Gaulish inscriptions. When will people read Zeuss, and when will Whitley Stokes reprint his Celtic articles in the "Saturday"?

I suppose I have something to say upon all your articles except the purely historical ones. But I must confine myself to the current "Saturday," in which I have two points to treat of. Both you and Miss Yonge (and indeed everybody else) write Iona. But Whitley Stokes says this is a mistake arising out of Iona being spelt Ioua, *i.e.,* Iova — a Latinisation out of (I forget the exact literal spelling of the Celtic original) *I-columb-cille,* "the island of the dove's cell" (or of Columba of the cell), to which one may add a conjecture that the mistake may have been fostered by literary monks under some sense of the Hebrew Jonah, "the dove." Some of the German people who don't make enough allowance for direct derivation want to make St. Columba an original dove, not a Latin one; but I don't believe this. Whitley Stokes compares the mistake with "Hebrides," arising out of a misreading of "Hebredes."

Another matter is Liudprand and his Greek. I was aware of his mission, and had some faint knowledge of his history, but I had no idea of his glosses. I would give anything to see them, or a selection of them. You are not verbally accurate in saying that he represents exactly the modern pronunciation. If he did so throughout, it would be a phenomenon in a spoken language to last so long unchanged. *En ti echmalosia autû* deviates in two places from modern pronunciation—one small, the other interesting. *En ti* would now be *en di*. All Greeks agree, and never vary in this point, as ἐν τῇ, ἐν πολέμῳ, ἐν Κρήτῃ, pronouncing the initial *tenuis* as a medial, and reacting on the nasal so as to make it suit its class : *-nd, -mb, -ng*. I suspect this is not very old, though, as I have observed, it is the one point of Greek phonetics that a Western most often fails to catch or to practise. Liudprand may have failed to notice it. *Autû* for *aftû* is very curious. It is the shibboleth of the Trebizond Greek, where it survives in company with ποιῶ and the κ of οὐκ before a vowel, written in plays, &c., where that dialect is represented ἀουτὸς. *Διληάσεται* is pure Lascaratoism, except that Liudprand does it on purpose. But I am very curious to know the way *o* and *ω* are treated—*υ*, in fact, has retained its sound in many words and many places, *e.g.*, *tumbanon* for a drum, which, of course, the spelling is modified to suit, τούμπανον.

I want to go to war together with France, in order that France may get the Rhine ! It would probably only be held for a time, and I see nothing but a surgical operation like that which would unite Germany and sweep away all the little kings and frontiers. Besides, I want to be able to look a Pole in the face, which is impossible now.—Ever yours truly, STRANGFORD.

58 Cumberland Street,
November 25, 1863.

My Dear Freeman,—Many thanks for Liudprand. His Greek is very curious and interesting. The very first thing that I lighted upon when I opened the book anyhow was the explanation of the heathenish modern name of Scaramangà, which has always puzzled me—"Σκαραμάγγιον hoc est pænula," with σκαραμαγγᾶς for its tailor or confectioner of course. But the manner of his Greek is queerer than the matter, and puts me strongly in mind of the bits of Latin for Latin's sake which Walter Scott so loves to put into the mouths of his monks, dominies, and antiquaries, without the least regard to its appropriateness or importance. As for *autu*, I think it may very likely be as you say, and, at most, inconclusive one way or the other. I believe with firmness that the German and Italian sound of *au* represented the classical and Alexandrian, and probably the Roman and *early* Byzantine sound of *aυ*—as such combinations of sound as -φτ-, φσ-, and the like, are quite contrary to ancient phonetics, and become changed into ππ, or φθ, or ψ, when they occur. But it is exactly the other way in modern phonetics. I am sorry to see by Liudprand that a German of the tenth century could not pronounce ἀλήθεια, but called it *alitia* : only I am not sure whether a Lombard of that time would not be entirely Italian—in fact, on reflection, I am pretty sure he would be so.

My charity to Miss Yonge is much less than it was, now that I have read about Christian names among the Tscherkessen, which is the last hair that breaks the camel's back. As for the people whom she calls by that pretty name, I know my place a deal too well to think or talk or write about them in the present state of English opinions. They are a pack of savage, irreclaimable slave-dealers, only fit to ride down and slaughter the Polen, just as Polen are notoriously incapable of governing themselves, and are only good for bayoneting Tscherkessen under the orders

of Russen, who get on by setting honest men to exterminate
honest men, just as Angelsachsen set a thief to catch a
thief. They are like unto Savoy, which we know to be
only a few barren mountain slopes not worth making a
row about, having read as much in the "Times." Upon
my life, out of the two unready nations among whom I
have spent my days, I sometimes prefer Osman the Unready to Athelstan the Unready, for he has no conscience,
which is better than too much of a one, and he doesn't
bother his own or other people's heads with excuses for
inaction or shirking duty, nor does he abuse or belittle or
abandon friends whom he does not care or fears to help—
at least, not out loud. As for the Tscherkessen, they put
me in mind of my old friend George Olympiern, of whom
I had read in a copy of her book which Miss Bremer presented to my wife (I could not have sent to a library for
such stuff) before you denounced the absurdity in the
" Review."

I always leave out the principal point of what I want
to say or write. When at the Hotel Byron I came upon
a copy of Sir Charles Lyell's last book on stone periods
and the like. In one part he leaves geology to talk about
language and the "Aryan controversy," which is very
absurd and irritating, and as though one should say the
Copernican controversy because Mahometans hold that
the sun goes round the earth. However, that is not what
I was going to say. In treating of the corruption of
Pennsylvanian German by the admixture of English, which
he does from his own experience, he gives instances, and
more particularly mentions the *Anglo-Saxon* words *fencen*,
to fence, and *flaur*, flour. Is it not curious, the force of
penny-a-line slang on even a man of science ? How would
he translate "La plus fine fleur de la farine de la race
humaine" into *Anglo-Saxon?* I had this in my head to
write to you, but forgot it. As for Schleswig, it drives me
wild. Dr. Latham and you are the only people who write
it as Englishmen should write it, and used to write it.

But I have a deadly hatred of *sch* generally for a clumsy and newfangled corruption—it is either the older *sc-*, or it is the High Dutch way of pronouncing *s* followed by a consonant, whether written as in *schlangen*, or written as in *stein;* and it is a pity that the literary language has kept the writing in so many words. The Nether Dutch of Germany hasn't got it at all except as the representative of *sc-*, and that of Holland has kept the old pronunciation of *sk*, even though written *sch*, except as a termination, when I believe it is pronounced *s*.

But what has become of all the old school geography books of my youth which used to tell us about Sleswick? What makes me hate *sch* is chiefly the memory of Reshid Pasha, who used, of course, to be Reschid in Germany, and then became Redschid in the "Times." They always wrote him so, and were deaf to their correspondents' complaints, they being above the laws of spelling, and writing it as they chose, just as they do *diocess* and *escocheon*.

On the whole, I am for having Denmark to the Eyder, and am ready to accept the doctrine with all its consequences. The lesser interest and lesser sentiment must give way to the greater and stronger; and if the Germans, or rather Nether Dutchmen, of Sleswick have to become Danes in the long run, and to learn Danish at school, I think the world will manage to get over it. What I know about the matter of nationality and language I get from Latham, who seems to me to be very good indeed, as he always is when he is master of his elementary facts. Many of his paradoxes are mere excrescences, and many arise from simple ignorance; but some seem to me to be unanswerable, at all events unanswered. Of these, the last, the chiefest, seems to me his theory that no German became or appeared as a Goth till he occupied the ground of Lithuanians. But the Lathamic style and manner is a fearful thing.—Very truly yours,   STRANGFORD.

SATURDAY MORNING, . . . 1864.

My Dear Freeman,—Good heavens! what *have* you done? You have been mutilating and slashing an especial favourite of the old "Saturday" period, one who was declared in '58 to have the "true trumpet-ring in his ballad notes," more especially in the "noble 'Forging of the Anchor,'" which, therefore, you will have seen cheek-by-jowl with your own revilings. This was Whitley Stokes's doing; and I very much fear that he was led into that dreadful sentence about the trumpet-ring by a mixture of college friendship, clique influence, and a little bad taste, not to say by the sight of the green flag of Erin. I have long been filled with sorrow and sickness at seeing the flagrant puffery of that "noble" ballad which has been going on, and it does me good to read you on the subject.

One word, though, about *Maer* or *Medhbh*. They have just excavated a place traditionally known as her treasury in Co. Roscommon, and found her tomb with an Ogham inscription containing her name, the only hitch of which is, that she appears in the genitive with what has been hitherto considered in Gaulish and Ogham-Irish as a masculine termination only, as in Latin—*Medbi*, as in *Sagramni*, &c. This is not inexplicable or unparalleled, however. But the two points which come out clearly from Oghams are, first, the verification of the hypothetical system of declension raised, in one case-ending at least, by Ebel, out of the oldest MS. Irish; and, second, the verification of Dr. Graves's system of reading them, partly suggested by hints in MS., and by means of bilingual inscriptions.

Mr. Ferguson has, furthermore, missed the Irish stories which have a distinct element of fun or absurdity in them, such as "Conn of the Hundred Fights," "Milesius, or the Fenians." Welsh absurdity, on the contrary, is deadly dull all through; in proof whereof, I send you the most absurd book, on the whole, ever written.—Ever yours truly,

STRANGFORD.

C

MY DEAR FREEMAN,—There is no difference of opinion between you and Whitley Stokes as regards the new poems of Ferguson, for he has not spoken yet: it was the "Forging of the Anchor" only that the —————— overpraised, alluding to it in the course of a very amusing review of the sham Irish ballads of the Lover and "Rory o' More" school. The "Cow-Foray," and such like, are dull and worthless. Ferguson, I now remember, is a New York Irishman, and once wrote a book called "Hibernian Nights' Entertainments." He will end, I suppose, as a Fenian Tyrtæus or Yankee Ossian. Is it not fair, by the way, to compare the word "Fenian" with the word "Achaian," each denoting its respective nation under its early heroic and rhapsodic aspect, with Fin MacCumhal for Achilles, and the Ossianic for the Homeric poems, and Argyleshire for Asia Minor?

I am glad you don't see any difficulty about *ánthrōpos* with simultaneous tone and quantity; but I am sure other people, dons and dilletante students of modern Greek, will. Old Norris says he can quite understand a short syllable being accented, but he cannot understand a long syllable being unaccented, and sacrificed to the short one in a dis-syllable. For reply to that I had to Lithuanise, and to appeal to some of our own dissyllables, rare, and generally compounds, such as headache (ŭ-). He understood it at last. Your difficulty in σοφία I quite understand, but I do not allow it to become a difficulty to me. I have not, without taking of much thought, and whipping up my moral consciousness, as it were, sufficient firmness of ear to distinguish *ĭa* from *ĭa* in hearing and speech without hiatus, which won't do. I think, too, that it was in these words that accent first began to kill quantity. Perhaps this may be even shown historically; but I should be un-willing to judge of the fineness of an old Greek's ear by my own. Neither the don's nor the Klepht's theory make head or tail out of the accentuation of πράγμάτι, for instance. I can only realise it by taking thought; but still I can realise it by so doing.

No; I don't think your theory about quantity being only kept for verse and solemn occasions will quite do for pre-Christian Greek. I have seen this view somewhere, but not worked out. I hold by the entire, absolute, simultaneous use of the two, with a minimum of encroachment on either side, as illustrated by dead Vedic Sanskrit and living Lithuanian. I am content to accept accent as an ultimate fact, without seeing how it arose, until Bopp, Müller, & Co. shall have fairly settled the matter. As it stands, it is an accident of the language, not necessary to its grammar,[1] and dependent on quantity. Quantity, on the other hand, is absolutely essential to the grammar, and to the accent, which it regulates and limits. The two cannot be taught together in England; and if one must go, it had better be the accent. But I would like to draw a line somewhere, and the best would be, I think, at the New Testament. It would be very good, I think, to teach this accentually, and with modern pronunciation, except for the diphthongs, and so to pronounce all Christian Greek, and all late Greek except such authors as Lucian, Longinus, the later epigrammatists and poets, and the like avowed imitators of classical models. I dare say Nonnus and Homer would have been mutually unintelligible in common talk, while Nonnus and I would probably get on very well; but I am pretty sure that up to his time and later they kept up quantity, dead in the common speech, by scholastic pronunciation recording it; in fact, by doing as you say. Your view to me is good for post-classical, but not for classical Greek. To my mind Etacism is by no means an unpardonable sin, though of course utterly wrong; for it is a common process in the transition of other Aryan languages. So is the change of the medials *b, g, d,* to their respective smooth

---

[1] **Surely the** compounds like θεοτόκος are the only important point?

and continuous sounds, especially when preceded or flanked by long vowels. Brag and self-righteous *à priorism* apart, the unpardonable sin to me is the way the Greeks stultify the known phonetic and accentual systems of their ancestors, even under their own theory. What is the use of grammarians telling you that no word can end in any consonant except *ν, ρ, ς*, and two in *κ*, when they insist in the same breath that *Ζεῦ βασιλεῦ* must have been always, and *ab initio, Ζὲυ vasilèv?* The Romans wrote foreign words phonetically. When they heard of a city called *Triá*, why did they go and write it *Trōja, i.e., Troyya?* Those sort of details can be multiplied to any extent.

I don't believe in *être* from *essere*. I don't know the age of *essere*, to begin with; and it may be Italian only, and not Romanic. The Spanish *ser* seems to support the latter, but Diez says that it is from *sedere*. This seems over-refinement; but really in old Spanish documents the word seems to have been always *sezer*. *Être* comes particularly well from the older form *stăre (stăti)*, and is better than *stâre* or *cstăr* in Italian and Spanish.[1] I don't in the least believe in immemorial distinctions of dialect, nor yet in such a thing as a High Dutch unity of language at the historical beginning. I'm afraid the Dutch are not much better than modern Greeks as regards some points of their language, and will talk foolishly and vainly about their *w* and their *cu*, though one was actually written *uu*, and the other *yu*, in many cases at least. And they are bringing in the fashion of writing *v* for *w* in our own old language, and giving us *vringan* and *vyrean* and *treov*, which I can't stand. By the way, I had quite forgotten to beg of you not to call Lithuanian *Lettish*. The last will long outlive the first, but it is in a Romanic, or at least a Romaic stage, and only good for vocabulary here and there. I don't know much about it, anyhow. The verbs in *-mi* are more to my taste than *ale* and *bull* even. And

---

[1] No; I fear it will hardly do, as *stăre* must have become *stăre* very early.

what do you think of *platus* for broad ? Your ancient Greeks are in Switzerland; my ancient Greeks are on the Niemen.—Ever yours truly,   STRANGFORD.

I break open my letter to say that I have just now done what I should have done before writing my last paragraph. I have looked out *être* in Diez, and find that he is distinctly for *essere.* I should not have been so decidedly for *stare* if I had not forgotten my prosody, and been under an impression that it was short like *dăre.* Perhaps it was so at first, but not in classical times, I fear. *Stāre* would make *ester, éter,* not *être.* Diez's analogy is from *texere* or *tessere* becoming *tistre* and *titre.* *Étant, été,* of course, are from *stare. Soyons, soyez,* &c., seem to be from *sedere.* There can be no doubt about *sedere* for the Spanish : they actually wrote (1032) in Latinised Romanic "quod sedeamus perjurados." But it seems very hard at first sight to say that the Italian *sia* is from *sit* and the Spanish *sea* from *sedeat. Seja* in Portuguese is a strong confirmation, however.

―――――

ST. JAMES'S CLUB, ST. JAMES'S STREET,
Wednesday, J. 25, 1864.

MY DEAR FREEMAN,—E. A. Sophocles is as big and as square as a paving-stone, and I fear I can hardly manage to send him to you by book-post, as I should like to do. His dissertation is very brief, but very good. The mass of the book is the lexicon, a condensed sort of Ducange, but much too concise. He says nothing about accent and quantity, probably thinking it unnecessary to point out the fact of their co-existence in the ancient language, and impossible to indicate it upon paper to us who cannot conceive such a fact. I myself have not the least difficulty in conceiving it as regards theory ; and as regards practice, it is not difficult to see how, in the course of time, either quantity must kill accent in a language, or accent kill quantity:

Lithuanian is the only Aryan language where the two fully co-exist without mutual interference, at least to any extent. There you can see syllables short in quantity bearing a tone-accent at the expense of syllables long in quantity left untoned. *Sūnŭs*, a son, of the *u* declension, like *gradŭs*, or as the same word in Gothic and Sanskrit, has the accent on the final in the nominative singular: thus, *sunùs*. In the nominative plural the final is long in quantity, like *gradūs* (and for the same reason). But it is accented *sū́nūs*, on the first. It is hard to realise this, equally for a modern Greek and a college don, but it is a fact in a living language for all that. Again, *bŭlŭs*, a bull, in the nominative singular is accented, as above, on the last; in the nominative plural it shifts its accent to the radical vowel, *bŭlūs*, without its quantity being lengthened. In this word the old pre-scientific German spelling indicated the shortness of quantity by the same orthographical means that we use for the same purpose, and doubled the consonant thus—*bullus;* just as we double the *v* in *navvy* to express the short of *a*. The third word which I shall take is the most instructive of all. *A lus*, ale (or rather small-beer), is ˘ ˘, like *bŭlŭs*. But when the accent is shifted to the *ă* in the nominative plural, that short *a* becomes long in quantity from the very fact of the accent falling on it; and this is the case with the vowels *a* and *e*, but not *i* and *u;* so *geras*, good, is ˘ ˘ in the nominative singular, but *gerai* (˘ ¯) in the nominative plural. Does not this illustrate the first step of the process by which accent killed quantity in modern Greek, and usurped all its authority? Take a last case, which the curiosity of the words themselves being so well preserved makes it a pleasure to quote—*esmì, esì, ésti*, for the verb substantive; *cimì, cisì, cíti*, "I go;" and *edmì* (second person lost), *ésti* or *est*, "I eat." The final *i*, accented or unaccented, is exactly the same in all these words in point of quantity. But in our own language, and all others we are accustomed to, *csmî* would infallibly be pronounced *esmēē*.

Servian is the only other living language which retains longs and shorts together with betoned and unbetoned; but it is not so good for illustration, as its sound-system is comparatively modern. I have, moreover, Lithuanised you to death. But Diefenbach was right in saying that the discovery of Lithuanian was hardly of less importance than that of Sanskrit itself—a pardonable over-statement. . . . .

Your "middle" on comparative philology being taught for practical purposes is uncommonly after my own heart, being, in fact, entirely and of old my own view; so that on reading it I said to you, "Pereas tu, qui ante me meum dixisti." I always thought of it with special reference to Haileybury Persian as taught to grown boys, having to learn as much as they could in a short time; saving labour, so to say, by telling them that the *ṁ* of Rustam was the *m* of *optimus*. I cannot trust myself to go into this in a letter. . . . .—Ever yours truly,

STRANGFORD.

MY DEAR FREEMAN,—No; I don't think *chasse* is from *hetzen*. A Dutch *h* is always, so far as I know, retained in Dutch words passing into Romaic. *Cucciare* in Italian, *cazar* in Spanish, are surely from a vulgar Latin *captiare*, the *ch* being the regular letter change, as in *cheval*, when the word became Gallo-Welsh, pronounced, I have not the least doubt, with the English, Spanish, and queer-Welsh sounds of *ch*. *Captare*, without the *i*, has become the regular word for searching or finding in queer-Welsh, or rather Inn-Welsh and East-Rum-Welsh; and these last people have alone kept the Latin *venari* for hunting.

I should like to write my heart out on the subject of

the word *Aryan*, a word I do not quite like in Max Müller's comprehensive sense, nor do the Germans themselves.
It is very short and handy, and so far good. But I hold
that its conventional meaning should be restricted, and
kept within the same limits as its intrinsic meaning, which
denotes the Indian *plus* the Iranian families. These, one
way with another, form about the best-defined group of the
whole set of languages, and it would be a pity to make the
word mean two things, or to merge the real meaning in the
arbitrary extension. The Germans are apt to call the
Eastern group *Arisch*, and the Pan-Aryan set *Arisch-
europäisch*, which is definite, but clumsy. Whitley Stokes's
Pataric for the whole set is absurd. Perhaps it is best to
keep *Aryan* as at present, and call the Easterns *Aric*. But
then the special marked character of the latter must be
brought forward as prominently as possible, and as often as
possible; for people are very apt to forget the importance
of old Persian, and its peculiar affinity with Sanskrit.

The man who wrote about no Gothic plurals in *s* deserves to have his nose cut off. Except neuter plurals in
a, like Latin, there are no Gothic plurals, in nouns at least,
which do *not* end in *s*. But it is very curious how they
seem to have dropped the *s* from the very first in old High
Dutch—forming its shibboleth, in fact—but keeping the
length of the vowel, *wulfós, wolfā*. This process is precisely identical with that of the masculine plural of the
Sanskrit declension corresponding — -*ās* appearing in old
Persian as -*ā*.—Ever yours truly,

STRANGFORD.

19 MANSFIELD STREET, *August* 9, 1862.

MY DEAR MÜLLER,—I have not answered your letter hitherto, as I have been away from town for some days. The words you mention are all true Persian—*ward* unquestionably so; but whether the old Persian presumed form *ward* be the origin or the issue of the Greek ῥόδον, it is difficult to say, and perhaps is more for the botanist to settle than the philologist. *Gul* means flowers generally in *modern* Persian, *gul i surkh* being a rose. *Sārī*, another word for rose, seems related to *surkh*, *çukhra*, *thukra*. *Satranj* may possibly be from the Indian direct. In *Shah māt*, the *māt* is the Arabic verb, *i.e.*, "the king is dead." This verb has naturalised itself in colloquial Persian as a metaphor derived from chess in the common phrase *māt shudam* or *māt māndam*, "I am at my wits' end," or "done for." From this it has got into Pushtu, where *mātēdal* means to be broken, *mātāwal* to break, words one would hardly like to call other than native without very sufficient cause. *Bābūsh* should be *bābūj* in Arabic, and it comes through a Turkish channel, the Turks pronouncing the Persian word as *pāpūch* (or rather *pāpūch*, as they are averse to real long vowels). I add one or two more which come into my head.

Arabic *zībak*, Persian *žīva*, "*quick*-silver." This is well known, I suppose; but it is interesting as showing the Persian pronunciation of *v* to have been our *v*, as it is now in Persia, and not *w*, as taught in our grammars after the Indian tradition or school of Persian.

Arabic *tāj*, Persian *tāj*, a crown, or arched skull-cap.

This is certainly the *taka* of the *Yaunà takabará*, which also, I think, gave rise to the Arabic *ṭāk*, an arch or vault; from this last is derived in the ordinary Semitic way *ṭāḳiyya*, a skull-cap, in Arabic and modern Turkish. This last is the word which Klaproth recklessly compared with the old Chinese gloss *thu-kiu* for a helmet, which would have been well enough if Semitic terminations could have been found in the Altai before Islam.

Arabic *serāb*, the mirage of the desert—found in the Koran. It is not likely to be connected with *sharaba* (the root, "he drank") in any way, and surely must be *caput aquæ*. *Ser* means everything in Persian idiom, almost; and here would be the appearance or burst on the sight of water.

Arabic *zamkerīr*, the bitter cold of winter (in the Koran), I think I mentioned to you.

Arabic *'āj* (with *'ain*), ivory. I suspect a connection with an assumed old Persian word, lost in modern Persian, but represented by *gāz*, a tooth, in the dialect of Ghilān, *ghāsh* in Pushtu.

I have no Arabic dictionary at hand, but shall look when I go to the Asiatic Society to see whether the Persian *birinj, burinj*, bronze, has passed into Arabic, as it has into Turkish. I have a strong impression that it has done so, and would therefore be a more natural origin for the Italian and Spanish forms *bronzo, bronce*, than Muratori and Diez's *bruno, brunizzare*, &c., or Pictet's *brass* with a nasal in it. There is, I believe, a Zend original form, *běrězya*, Arabic *jauhar*, Persian *gauhar*, jewel, originally the core or essence of a thing.

Māl, wealth, property; Persian ditto, but best in Kurdish, where it means a house. Rawlinson says he finds it in this last sense in his old pre-Assyrian Hamitic, about which I know nothing.

Arabic *ustuwanat*, a pillar; Persian *sŭtūn*.

I have a suspicion of there even being roots or verbs in Arabic of Persian origin. *Shād*, glad, is certainly a true Persian word, with well-known and widespread Aryan affinities. *Sa'ada*, he was prosperous or happy, **sa'īd**, prosperous (just as *bakhīt* in modern colloquial **Arabic**, from the Persian *bakht*, through the Turkish), *sa'ḍān*, a monkey (blessed or prosperous animal, like the Persian *shādī* or *shādū*: compare Arabic **may mūn**, blessed and monkey, a curious euphemism), seem to me to be not so much accidental coincidence as real borrowing. The word does not exist with this meaning in the other Semitic languages, but occurs with that of supporting or propping; and with this is connected Arabic *sā'id*, the wrist or forearm (as the fulcrum), *musā'ada*, the giving help or support, and thence affording a man what he wants, conceding. On the other hand, *Sa'ad* occurs very early as a proper name, and **Sa'ūd** is a Wahābi and Bedouin name of the remote interior. What I have said is mere conjecture, but at all events I think "Arabic roots" require looking into, and are not to be taken on trust. Take, again, **zayn**, good; *zayyana* (secondary conjugation), he ornamented; *zīnat*, ornament; *zayy*, dress, appearance; with the Persian *zī*, costume, dress; *zībā*, beautiful; *zivar*, ornament; *zīb*, ornamenting (as in *Aurang-zib*), the participle used in composition of an obsolete strong verb, *ziftan*, to be inferred from it. You will be able to settle this last case at once with the help of **Sanskrit**, for want of which I am brought up suddenly half-way in all philological speculations.

There are plenty of Arabic names of plants, drugs, objects of art, or articles of civilisation, borrowed from the Persian; but they have to be gone through systematically with a big dictionary. What I have given above are meant to be a few of the less obvious ones, most of which, after all, must be known to you. But I do not think that any words representing abstract ideas of religion, politics, or literature will be found, and have no doubt that your informants overstated the evidence of Persian words in Arabic, however correct they may have been in maintaining the fact that Persian civilisation influenced that of the Arabians. I believe that the Persian words in the Koran are to be accounted for by the Sassanian occupation of, and political connection with, Yemen and the neighbouring coasts of Africa, of which the Persian geographical term *Zang-bār* is a record, and by the circulation of their romances among the Arabian educated classes, alluded to and announced in a passage of the Koran, as Mecca was the literary centre of Arabia in the times immediately preceding Islam, and not the country bordering on Mesopotamia and the Aramean dominions of Persia.

If I remember rightly, there is a passage in your Lectures in which you mention the Persian words in Turkish as coming through an Arabic channel. It is the converse: the Arabic words in Turkish come through a Persian channel, and are used with a Persian construction and idiom. The Persian words in Turkish are very numerous indeed, and out of all proportion above those in Arabic. They are also curious in one respect, which I have not seen noted anywhere: I mean, that many of the religious and ceremonial terms of Islam in Turkish are Persian, and not Arabic.

Oruj, a fast, Persian *rūza*. The *Bairam*, of Persian origin, though the modern Persians use the Arabic word *'id*. *Nāmāz*, prayers, *ikindi namazi*, Turkish the afternoon prayer, Persian *sālāt i digar—ikindi* being a derivative of *iki*, two, as *digar* is the old ordinal of *du*, preserved in the sense of *second* in Parsi and in Firdausi, but meaning *another* only in modern and classical Persian. *Giaour, i.e., Gawr*, with the Turkish *mouillé* sound of the soft *k* and *g*, is the Persian *gabr*, a fire-worshipping infidel; which last is no corruption of *Kāfir*, but the Aramean *gabra*, a man, pronounced *gaura* by modern Chaldeans and Nestorians, and probably preserved in the name of the Kurdish serf or subject tribe of *Gurān*. *Abdest*, religious ablution. *Dīn*, faith, *yaumu'd dīn*, the day of judgment, had already got into the older Semitic languages, and, through them, into Arabic, under which head I forgot to put it. I suppose it must be the

Zend *daēna.* *Khudā,* in Turkish, is bookwork rather than true vernacular, but it seems to have become the latter among the Turks of Siberia, to judge by vocabularies. *Bihisht* and *duzaleh,* in Turkish, are also more often written than spoken.

I hope you will not think it too great a liberty if I ask you to allow me to send you a note or two upon one or two little points of detail in your Lectures about which I have had opportunities of obtaining firsthand information. One is the "*langue boukhare,*" which is in a fair way of taking its place unchallenged as a separate substantial Persian dialect in modern works on philology, instead of being actually and identically Persian, which it really is. But I have taken up too much of your time already, and must remain, very truly yours,   STRANGFORD.

P.S.—Have you ever looked, or do you know where to tell me to look, for a monograph, if such exist, upon Persian words north of the Caspian in the Ugrian languages? Of course, I don't mean words that have come in since the great centralising Tartar conquests, but those of the pre-Islamic, or early post-Islamic period. Diefenbach, *sub voce* Guth, in half countenancing the old God and Khodā theory, alludes to the Hungarian *Isten* as being probably also Persian, and I am curious to know where he got the idea from, if not his own. The Persian *Yezdān,* no doubt, is his word; but many others occur to me, though I know next to nothing of these languages. *Ezer,* a thousand, must be *hazār; khubavi, -va, -vo,* in Bulgarian, "good," is un-Slavonic, and must be *khūb (which has never got into Turkish),* and a relic of the old times before the Bulgarians got Slavonised.

19 MANSFIELD STREET, *August* 23, 1862.

MY DEAR MÜLLER,—I only returned yesterday from a ten days' tour among the Channel Islands, and found your letter on my arrival here. *Serāb* is the true Persian as well as Arabic form of the word. I once thought it might be a corruption of *sahrā-āb*, "the desert water," but it is not at all likely. Anyhow, I am pretty sure it contains the element *āb*, and it is as old as the Koran. I don't think it has anything to do with *shīr;* a word, by the way, which I can't help thinking the legitimate representative of *tigris* (*tigrā*, arrow, and probably also tiger, the origin of our Latin and Greek word). The names of felines are quite loose and interchangeable in Turkish and Persian. Such words as *kaplan* and *palang* really mean any large feline animal rather than a positive tiger or leopard. *Shīr* is probably *shēr, i.e.,* with the so-called Majhūl or *ē* sound, lost in modern Persian, but preserved in the Indian-school Persian, which always represents either a diphthong *ai* or a consonant (generally a dental, as *pēsh* for *patish*) in the old language; to speak with more philological accuracy, an original *ai*, or one arising out of a lost consonant.

The Arabic words in Turkish have all decidedly come through a Persian channel. I can hardly think of an exception, except in quite late days, when Arabic words have been used in Turkish in a different sense from that borne by them in Persian; and this, after all, is deviation of idiom rather than separate borrowing. Nothing is more obscure than the history of the early distinctive formation of the Ottoman Turkish, and its separation from the Eastern dialects. I believe myself that it took place under the Seljukian emperors, whose dominions coincided pretty accurately with Persia for a long time, and that it was then that Turkish received its first literary impress and germs of cultivation from the already Arabised Persian. The latter was the exclusive language of literature among Turks for a long period; and when these latter began to write in their own language, they naturally used all the abstract terms of religion, politics, science, &c., borrowed by the Persians, the earliest cultivated nation of Mohammetan converts from Arabia; and in adapting them to

their own language, they cast them in the mould of Persian
idiom and construction, which they have continued to do
ever since they have studied Arabic books and literature
at first hand.   I ought to have said Western rather than
Ottoman Turkish, as the latter conveys too modern and
limited an idea.   The Turkish of North-Western Persia is
in reality far more Western than Eastern (though it does
not appear so from the Ottoman point of view), and I look
on it as the best and most archaic representative of the old
proto-Seljukian Turkish.   The Anatolian Turkish I take
to be an offset from this formed under the Seljukian Empire of Rūm or Iconium, which subsequently became
polished up and developed into the current Osmanli.   It
is difficult to treat of this subject without going into details for which the limits of a letter would be too narrow.
The chief *literary* difference between the true Eastern
Turkish and the Western dialects, in which I include Per-
sian-Turkish, as far as it is written at all, is the absence
of the future in -*jak*, -*jek*, from the *former*, and the much
greater *Aryanisation* of the way of expressing the relative.
Mir Ali Shir, for instance, uses *kim* as a regular relative
pronoun, after the analogy of Persian.   Even the Otto-
mans use it as a conjunction like the Persian *ki*.   The
gerund or verbal noun in -*dik*, so conspicuous in Osmanli,
used to express the relative by pronominal suffixes (*aldy-
ghym* **para**, "the money which I took"), is not found
among the Eastern Turks, who properly use -*ghan* (the
Ottoman participle -*an*) in the same way as a relatival
gerund, but, in their books at least, are inclined to make
to themselves a true relative pronoun.

About the common root for "a hundred" in Aryan and
Turanian I am very doubtful indeed.   Uncivilised tribes
are very apt to borrow high numerals from their civilised
neighbours; and I strongly suspect that the Ostiakian
sāt and the Hungarian *szāz* are borrowed from the same
source whence the Goths of the Crimea got their *sada* and
nazer.   Moreover, I don't think the word occurs in any

Turanian language far removed from Persians or Persian-speaking Turks. As for Turkish *yüz*, Yakut *sus*, I am not quite sure whether the archaism of Yakut has not been overstated, and would like to be cautious in admitting its forms to be always the oldest. *Yakut* itself, for instance, I believe is a Tungusian plural, equal to the native plural *Sakhalar;* but is it not the same word in the original native form as brought by the Yakutians into the north-east, subsequently changed by them into *Sakha?* If it were not so, then the Tungusians must have the change of *s* into *y*, and it is necessary to prove this to be the case in Tungusian previous to admitting the *s* to be older than the *y*. *Sätä* for seven in Yakut offers a tempting analogy for this, but on comparing the Turkish forms *al-ty* and *ye-di* the dental looks as if it belonged to a termination, not to the root. Some dialects, it is true, pronounce the *d* double, *yeddi, jitti.* I suspect that this Yakut *s*, so far as it answers to the Turkish *y*, has in reality arisen out of the North Turkish or Siberian pronunciation of the latter like our *j*, which is the shibboleth of the Siberian Russian and Kirghiz Turks, as distinguished from the true Jaghataians, or whatever they may be called, of Independent and Chinese Turkistan. In the extreme east of the latter, as known by a higher vocabulary from Turfan given by Klaproth (*valeat quantum*), *y* in the middle of a word is represented by *d*, as *adakhi* for *ayak*, foot. I would give a good deal to have a good rummage in the libraries of Yarkand and Kashgar.

I have not read Schott, as we have not got him, unfortunately, at the Society. Boehtlingk accuses him of comparing the Turkish terminations *-lik, -li*, with our Teutonic *-ly* and *-lich* in *freundlich*, friendly; the Russian *polk* with the Turkish *beulük;* and the Persian *murden* (*-den*) with the German *morden* (*-en*), and thereupon calls him many hard names. Boehtlingk, though not amiable, is right enough in this, which must go some way to make one cautious in accepting Schott's views and facts unchallenged.

Pray do not put yourself out of your way to answer my letters. Time is valuable with you, while I am an absolutely idle man, with nothing to do but to rove about in body and mind. I am almost ashamed of the desultoriness I should show if I wrote to you upon any other philological subject or hobby besides Iran and Turan, yet I shall not be able to resist the impulse which I have of disburthening myself of a few notes upon the Southern dialect of Wallachia, in which I have been dabbling a good deal of late, and which has been kept far too much in the background by Diez: though he says a good deal more about its verbs in the new edition of his second volume this year than in his prior edition. The only two books treating the subject at all fully are out of print, and I am afraid of the language dying out before we have a third, more especially as it is likely to fare but ill in the forthcoming millennium of "liberated" nationalities on the Danube and Adriatic.—Very truly yours,

STRANGFORD.

Part I.[1]

In 1839 the British Government committed itself to an
undertaking which practically amounted to the conquest,
military occupation, and civil administration of a remote
mountain land, inhabited by a savage and warlike race,
animated by the strongest feelings of nationality. Yet
it was all but wholly unprovided with the means of
acquiring or imparting a knowledge of the difficult and
peculiar language in which that nationality found its
strongest expression and support. Such knowledge, indeed, was not absolutely indispensable for the purposes
of official or social intercourse and correspondence. The
requirements of current business were sufficiently met by
the employment of Persian, generally known among the
educated class of Afghans, and strictly vernacular with
that large population of Afghanistan which is Persian in
its origin and Shiah by religion. But the inner life and
distinctive character of the Afghans remained a sealed
book for want of a knowledge of Pushtu. A vocabulary
inserted at the end of Mountstuart Elphinstone's travels, a
translation of the New Testament into Pushtu, and a brief
grammatical sketch and vocabulary by Major Leach, con-
stituted at that time the whole of the materials accessible
to the English or Anglo-Indian student desirous of making
himself acquainted with this language. These were scanty
in amount, of little use for practical purposes, and of not
much intrinsic value. The translation of the Testament
was executed with haste and carelessness, and though
every allowance must be made for the zeal of the

translators, and the difficulties of a little known, and, to
them, uncultivated language, with the literature of which
they were evidently unacquainted, such an error as the
often quoted rendering of "Judge not, that ye be not
judged," by words meaning "Do not practise equity, lest
equity be practised towards you," was more than mere in-
accuracy in Pushtu, as it indicates fundamental ignorance
of the real meaning of *insāf*, a word universal, and of quite
common and vernacular use in every language spoken by
Mahometans. Leach's grammatical sketch goes a very
little way in facilitating the student's progress, being
slight, imperfect, and not always accurate or consistent in
rendering Afghan sounds into Roman letters; but his
dialogues are original, animated, and apparently idiomatic.
An ode of Rahman, subjoined to his sketch, is so dis-
figured with bad misprints that it is of no use to any one
who is not proficient enough to restore the text by means
of the translation at the side; in other words, it is useless
to a learner. As this work bears the official countersign
of Mr. Torrens, certifying it to be a "true copy," the
responsibility of these misprints must be borne at least
as much by the censor as by the author. The late Dr.
Leyden appears at one time to have turned his attention
to Pushtu, and to have succeeded in adding some knowledge of that language to his other great and varied
accomplishments. A memoir by him on the Roshenian
section in the eleventh volume of the Asiatic Researches,
contains some extracts from the "Makhzan i Pushtu," the
earliest extant work in the language,[1] and the main
authority for his subject. This, however, was not
philology, and he added nothing to our knowledge of the
language. A gallant and distinguished officer, Lieutenant
Loveday, whose barbarous murder, at the instigation of

---

[1] Captain Raverty, however, in a letter contained in "The News of the Churches," of February 1st, 1861, mentions the existence of at least two older works, of one of which, the "History of the Yusufzai Tribe," he was able to obtain a copy.

the dispossessed Khan of Khelat, caused a deep and painful sensation in England at the time, is understood to have contemplated a systematic study of Pushtu, with a view to publishing the result; a project which was abruptly stopped by his untimely death.

It must not be supposed that the same neglect or disregard of the Pushtu language, which so markedly characterised the period at which our political relations with the Afghan states acquired a sudden and prominent importance, had always prevailed among the authorities in India. Early in the century the East India Company, always the ready and munificent patron of Oriental studies, authorised a learned native gentleman, Mohabbet Khan, son of the famous Rohilla chief, Hafiz Rahmat Khan, to draw up a grammatical sketch of Pushtu, together with a vocabulary, the whole being written and explained in Persian. No current practical use appears to have been made of this work in India; but two copies were found by Professor Dorn of St. Petersburg in the East India Company's Library in London, and the learned Professor was thereby supplied with the groundwork of his subsequent valuable labours in the field of Pushtu grammar, a study which he was the first to establish on anything like an accurate and scientific basis.

From the commencement of the century, Continental philologists had begun to include the Pushtu among the objects of their research. Owing to the scantiness of the material upon which they had to work, their labours were mostly imperfect and untrustworthy, and are described by subsequent investigators as abounding in errors. The researches of this period are represented by the Afghan portion of Klaproth's "Asia Polyglotta," and by the treatises of Eversmann and Wilken. A marked improvement on these was a brief notice by Ewald, in which the great Semitic scholar pronounced decisively upon the un-Semitic character of the language, which, indeed, no philologist, with any genuine materials before him, could fail in perceiving at a glance. But Professor Dorn was the first to publish *in extenso* a real grammar and vocabulary of the language, and to determine its true philological character and affinities with accuracy in detail. Not having lived in the country, however, and having had few or no opportunities of acquiring the language in a living form by 'oral and vernacular intercourse with the natives, his works are described by Captain Raverty as not being wholly free from error, at least in their lexicographical portion, where the meanings of several Afghan words are stated to be merely "guessed at." Considering the comparative want of resources at the Professor's command, it is more to be wondered at that so much precision and accuracy should have been attained, and that Captain Raverty, a ready censurer of the errors and shortcomings of his precursors, should have found so little cause of complaint.

Our associate, Captain Richard Burton, the celebrated traveller, contributed an interesting article upon Professor Dorn's work to the Proceedings of the Bombay Asiatic Society for 1849, in which, from his having acquired both a literary and vernacular knowledge of Pushtu during his service in Upper Sindh, he was able to supply many valuable additions and corrections to the work in question.

The first Pushtu grammar written in English, and containing more than a mere outline of the rules of the language, is the useful and unpretending little work of Colonel Vaughan, published at Calcutta in 1854, and followed in 1855 by a second volume, containing an English-Pushtu vocabulary. This work is entirely practical, and does not meddle with philology or grammatical theory; its use, therefore, is less for the comparative philologist or the ambitious student of Afghan literature than for the soldier or the man of business desirous of obtaining a knowledge of the elementary rules and common words of the language by a simple and easy method. Its accuracy, though not unimpeachable, is quite sufficient for the ordinary purposes of business, or the rough and ready wants of the officer; and it only requires more idiomatic phrases and dialogues, to be pronounced by far the most practically useful, if not the most theoretically perfect, of existing Afghan grammars. Colonel Vaughan's grammar was immediately followed by Captain Raverty's more complete work. It is to the latter gentleman that the credit undoubtedly belongs of being the first student to combine a mastery of vernacular Pushtu acquired upon Afghan ground with a thorough knowledge of its literature—a literature far more extensive in its records, and of greater intrinsic merit, than is generally supposed even among Orientalists. He has communicated to the public the results of many years' labours in a series of works apparently intended to comprise the whole subject of the Pushtu language and literature in all its branches. These works consist of a full grammar of the language, which has reached a second edition; of a dictionary, Pushtu and English, having a transcription of the Pushtu words in Roman letters; of a chrestomathy, or a series of selections from the prose and poetical writings of the best authors; and of a literal English version of the poetical portion of the last-mentioned work, preceded by a popular introduction to the subject. Whatever may be the merits or demerits of the system upon which Captain Raverty has deemed it advisable to construct his grammar and explain its rules, it is probably beyond doubt that his works contain a complete and trustworthy record of all its actual facts; and it is in this point that the real value of these works lies. The accumulation of materials by the linguist is a matter of primary necessity to the philologist, without which the latter is unable to pursue his science with any prospect of success; and in the present case his gratitude is fairly due to Captain Raverty for the ample store of such material which he has placed at the disposal of the learned public at home and abroad.

When the linguist who is no philologist, but has mastered a language by rule of thumb or routine study, contents himself with a plain statement of the grammatical facts of that language, respects the limits of his own and his fellow-workman's art, and refrains from dogmatising on those problems in philology and ethnology which lie beyond those limits, he acquires the good-will of his readers, and the voice of censure or criticism passes over his occasional slips or mistakes in silence. It is quite allowable in a writer upon language at Peshawar who has lived most of his life cut off from Europe, to treat M. Klaproth, who died some thirty years ago, as a living author, or to be manifestly ignorant of the processes and chief results of the science of Comparative Philology. But if he lends the weight of a name and authority fairly earned by the successful cultivation of one branch of study to the reiteration of baseless, untenable, and exploded theories in ethnology, the utter futility of which a proper view of his own special study should have led him to perceive, and to the support and propagation of such theories by arguments of his own, wholly unworthy of serious consideration, he incurs a heavy responsibility, and he has no right to complain if he becomes the object of severe comment. These remarks are unavoidable in the presence of Captain Raverty's various prefaces to his works, especially that to his grammar, and of a very able paper by Dr. Löwenthal, a missionary at Peshawar, which appeared in the Journal of the Bengal Asiatic Society for 1860 (No. IV.), under the title of "Is the Pushtu a Semitic Language?" animadverting in detail upon the arguments contained in the above prefaces, where Captain Raverty makes himself the advocate of that curious delusion, the Semitic character of the Afghan language, and the Jewish origin of the Afghans. Incidentally, the doctor has brought forward many new and most valuable illustrations of the Pushtu phonetic system and vocabulary, as also, in a less degree, of its forms; and it is therefore all the more to be regretted that he should have been thus forced to treat this really necessary and important branch of inquiry as an object secondary to the refutation of an absurd theory, in which no one capable of appreciating his arguments now believes, and the believers in which seem to be proof against his or any other man's demonstration.

"Error is immortal," says Dr. Löwenthal, with perfect truth, and it would therefore be sheer waste of time to try and kill the Semitic theory or to gainsay a writer like the Rev. Mr. Forster, when he tells us that *āsmān* is a Pushtu word, derived from the Hebrew *samim* (*sic*), with the article, *hesamim* (*sic*); that *ōr* is Pushtu for "light" (which it is not) as in Hebrew; that the Hebrew *nahar*, "a rider," is contained, in that sense, in a Pushtu compound (not a word of which is true), and that therefore the Pushtu is a Semitic language. It is more to the purpose to inquire how Sir William Jones came to countenance this theory, as he unquestionably may be said to have countenanced it, when he stated the Pushtu to be an actual dialect of Chaldee. It is probable that his opinion, in the first place, was uttered more or less at random, and was hastily conceived, without more than a mere cursory examination of the language. In the second place, one or two remarkable, though superficial and accidental, coincidences do really exist. The genitive is formed in Chaldee by a prefixed *di* or *d'*, in Pushtu by *da*. They are wholly unconnected in origin, as the Chaldee word is simply the Aramaic relative pronoun, while the Pushtu word is probably part of the demonstrative pronoun *dagha*.[1] Dr. Löwenthal compares it with the Latin *de* and the Polish *od;* referring both—the former, after Bopp, conjecturally—

---

[1] Dr. Trumpp compares it with the Punjabi postfix *da*, which he shows to be originally an ablative derived from the Prakrit *do*, itself a corruption of the Sanskrit *-tas*. It is more convenient, however, to assign Pushtu forms to a native and Iranian origin, as long as it is possible to do so without violent assumptions. *Hagha* is also found in Assyrian in exactly the same form, but in the sense of the near, not, as in Pushtu, the remote demonstrative. *Ha* is, without doubt, the Zend *ĥa*, Sanskrit *sa*, old Persian *ha-uva* (Sanskrit *sa-sva*), whence the Persian *ō*, in modern pronunciation *û*.

the latter, with certainty, to the Sanskrit *adhas*. The demonstrative pronouns, moreover, are not unlike in the two languages at first sight. The Chaldee *dēk, dēn, hādēn, dāk, dā*, masculine and feminine, "this," resemble the Pushtu pronouns *hagha, dagha*, on the surface, but are of quite different origin.

Rawlinson compares *hagha* with a presumed Zend form, *hakha*, corresponding to the Sanskrit *sasva;* but as the Pushtu *gh* rarely, if ever, answers elsewhere to the Zend *q* or *kh, gha* is more probably a mere phonetic or inorganic increment, while the *da-* and *ha-* are no doubt respectively cognate with the Zend demonstrative *ha*, Sanskrit *sa*, and the Zend and old Persian base *da*, found in the enclitic pronouns *-dim, -dis*, in the inscriptions *-dish*. Whether these dental bases, which are found both in the Semitic and the Aryan languages, be real instances of primeval connection or mere accidental coincidences, is a question to be determined only by Semitic and Aryan philologists of the highest authority and experience respectively, such as Ewald and Müller. It is, at all events, quite certain they are no evidence whatever of special and distinctive affinity between the Semitic languages and Pushtu. The word *or*, "fire," probably reminded Sir William of the well-known Semitic word for light, and it is possible, though not probable, that he may have remarked a curious resemblance to the ordinary process of formation or derivation of words in Arabic in such instances as the Pushtu *tōr*, black, *tiāra*, blackness; a change not easily explained, from our not possessing the Pushtu language in any other than a quite modern form, and our having, therefore, but limited means of comparison. The above examples, it may be said, constitute the amount of those "treacherous indications," to use the words of Dr. Dorn, which misled the great linguist and man of letters into the hasty utterance of an opinion which has been employed to shelter idle theories that its gifted author would have been the first to disavow and refute, had he lived long enough to become acquainted with the modern science of Comparative Philology, of which he himself unconsciously helped to lay the foundations.

It may be worth while here to call attention to the undue stress which has been laid upon the so-called native tradition of the Afghans, connecting them with King Saul, son of Kish, and upon the name of Beni Israil, which they are said to give themselves, at the same time that they reject the title of Yahudi.. This affiliation of themselves upon a historical personage of the Old Testament is in their case looked upon as an exceptional and unique phenomenon, instead of being, as it really is, the rule in all analogous cases. Wherever a rude and un-cultivated people have been brought within the pale of Islam, they have never failed to connect themselves with the traditionary quasi-Biblical ethnology of their con-querors or spiritual instructors through some patriarch or hero of Scripture, the knowledge of whom was derived by the early Mussulmans from corrupt Jewish sources. Thus the old Turkish traditions of Central Asia make an eponymus for that race after the usual process, out of its own national title, and connect them with Japhet under the name of *Yafet oghlan Turk*, Turk, son of Japhet; and the Berbers or Amazigh of North Africa make eponymi out of their native and their Arabic names, and affiliate themselves upon Ber, son of Mazigh, nephew of Canaan, grandson of Ham. The Persian civilisation and native religions and heroic traditions were far too strong and deep-seated to yield to this process, and in Persia, accord-ingly, there are no traces of it to be met with. As for Beni Israil, it is obviously, and on the face of it, a mere Mollas' Arabic phrase, derived from books, and therefore those who represent it as a national title prior to, and independent of, Mahometan influence, do what is equivalent to putting Latin words with a Latin con-struction into the mouths of the Highland clans of Scotland previous to the Christian era.

The most complete analogy to this so-called Pushtu tradition is furnished by that of the Gipsies, which affords, perhaps, the most perfect and typical example of a spurious and insitive tradition, as opposed to a genuine home-grown one, having been instantly and universally adopted by a race from its neighbours, and by it passed off in turn upon the latter as being really its own. In every country of Western Europe, where the Gipsies made their first appearance during the course of the fifteenth century, their invariable reply to all questions as to their race and origin was the legend that they were the descendants of Egyptians who had inhospitably driven the Virgin Mary from their doors. On the faith of this, their Egyptian origin was always recognised in Europe as a matter of orthodox belief, until Grellman published his researches based upon an investigation of their language; and this delusive belief stands recorded in three extreme points of Europe, by the English, Spanish, and modern Greek names of this race, *Gipsy, Gitano,* Γύφτος. The legend is not found among any Asiatic Gipsies, and was manifestly forced into the mouths of the European wanderers by the leading questions of their Christian interrogators. It vanished into air at once before the first examination of the Gipsy language, from which we are now enabled to know not only whence they came, but from what particular part of India they came, and through what countries of Western Asia and Eastern Europe they passed on their way to the west. The strong elements of Persian, Byzantine Greek, and Wallachian, which their language contains, suffice to show their route as clearly as a written itinerary. The acquired and spurious tradition of the Jewish origin of the Afghans appears to have its exact parallel in the above fable of the Egyptian origin of the Gipsies. It would be an interesting inquiry to ascertain how far the former is really current among the Afghans, and whether it is to be met with at all among the clansmen and primitive classes living comparatively out of the reach of the influence of Mollas.

It is impossible to conclude this brief notice of the Jewish or Semitic theory without expressing great regret that Captain Raverty should have thought it answered any practical or scientific end to support his paradoxes with regard to the language by arguments derived from the fact that numerous Arabic words are contained in the Afghan vocabulary, and from the use of the technical terms of Arabic grammar in the treatment of their own language by Afghan grammarians. If Pushtu be Semitic for the former of these reasons, so is every language spoken by populations professing Mahometanism; if for the latter reason, so is every language that has ever been grammatically taught and cultivated by Mahometans, and we therefore must fain look on Persian and Turkish, Malay and Mandingo language, French and modern Greek, as comprised one and all in the category of uniform Semiticism on the strength of their being expounded by Turkish, Arab, or native teachers, through the technical apparatus of *ism* and *fi'l*, and *māzi* and *muzāri'*.

The real fact is, that the language of the Afghans corresponds, with great and exceptional exactness, to the position in which we should be inclined to place it upon *à priori* grounds, from a mere consideration of the geographical conditions and political history of the country in which it is spoken. We should expect to meet with a language descended from either the ancient speech of India or that of Persia. We should be more inclined, upon geographical grounds, to favour the Persian alternative, as the highlands of Afghanistan, even now called Khorasan by the inhabitants of the plains of the Indus below the passes, and thus, by them, identified with Persia, belong physically to that country rather than to India. At the same time, we should look for the evidences of the language of the Afghans having been

powerfully influenced in its formation by the neighbouring dialects of India, as well as by the vernacular form of
its more ancient and cultivated language; and we should
expect the vocabulary of a mountain tribe, that never
worked out its own civilisation, but has always adopted
that of its settled and powerful neighbours so far as it is
civilised at all, to be fully loaded with importations from
those languages in all their different stages. The result
which, upon inquiry, we do find, precisely corresponds
with all these expectations. There is no reason for
doubting that the forms Πάκτυες and Πακτυική χώρα,
met with in Herodotus, express the modern national
name of Pushtu in the pronunciation of the Eastern
Afghans, with whose geographical position they completely coincide. They are of sufficient importance for
the contingent supplied by them to the host of Xerxes
to be noticed by the Greek historian, at the same time
that they do not constitute a special satrapy, nor is any
such satrapy mentioned either by Herodotus or in the
Behistun or Naksh i Rustam inscriptions. It is probable that
they were at this time a mountain tribe of limited extent
and importance, situated in the most easterly parts of their
present area, upon whom the Achæmenian yoke sat lightly,
but dependent upon some one or more of the great adjoining
satrapies of Gandára, Thatagush, Haraiva, Hara'uvátish,
or Hindush; settled countries with a population, then, as
now, with the exception of the last, almost entirely pure
Iranian, and speaking a form of Persian of which, if it
were not actual Zend, at all events Zend is the nearest
representative that has come down in documents to our
time. The distinction between the Pushtu as we now
have it and the Persian languages, properly so called, in
their various forms and stages, is so deeply and clearly
marked, that it is reasonable to conclude that, even at
this early period, a considerable difference already existed
between the Zend or old Aryan of the plains and the
contemporary form of Aryan then spoken by the ancestors

of the Afghans, from which the present Pushtu is descended. This separation must have been widened and rendered permanent by the absence of Persian, and great preponderance of Indian influence, to which Eastern Afghanistan was subject during the whole period between the downfall of Achæmenian power and the rise of Islam. The traces of Græco-Bactrian and Indo-Scythian dominion and influence to be met with in the Pushtu language are imperceptible, but the constant intercourse with India, and the direct Indian rule, which prevailed during most of this period, have left a strong and indelible stamp on Pushtu, not only in its vocabulary, but even in its forms, idiom, and general character. So strong and pervading is this effect, that it is not easy to determine, without minute investigation, whether the Pushtu is to be ranged among the Indian or Iranian dialects. The nature of the words which it has borrowed from the Indian dialects is sufficiently remarkable, as indicating the source whence the Afghans obtained many of the rudiments of civilisation and the means of expressing them. "To write," for instance, is called by the Indian root *likh*, not the Persian *pish*. Even to the present day many insulated tribes in the Hindu Kush, such as the Dir, Tirhai, Laghmani, and Pashai, specimens of whose languages are given by Major Leach, speak dialects of distinct Indian rather than Iranian origin, and therefore ethnologically represent either an actual population of Indian ancestral settlers, or else of a thoroughly Indianised native race. Far more important than all these are the Siāh-pūsh Kafirs of Kafristan, whose language, as exhibited and illustrated by Dr. Trumpp in a late number of this journal, is a genuine Indian dialect, and whose physical character, at all events in the instance of the men seen by the doctor, is no less Indian than their language. The safest general conclusion about the Pushtu would seem to be that it is the descendant of a language belonging to the western rather than the eastern branch of the true Aryan people,

and therefore allied more intimately with Zend than with
Sanskrit; but that during the period of the disintegration
of the old Persian languages, and the gradual formation of
the modern Persian, it was from political causes far more
exposed to Indian than to Persian influences; this period
being that in which the spoken Sanskrit language was
ceasing to be vernacular in its purest form, and was
gradually becoming corrupted into the colloquial Prakrit
forms, which are now generally acknowledged to have
immediately preceded, and truly and directly given birth
to, the modern vernaculars of Northern India. The Neo-
Indian dialects, while thus undergoing the process of
formation, powerfully affected the Pushtu while itself in
the same presumed transitional state, and the Persian
does not seem to have recovered its lost influence until
it had substantially acquired its modern form under the
late Sassanians and in the post-Islamic period. Since
then it has modified the whole nature and character
of the Pushtu, which in its modern, and especially its
literary form, appears entirely recast in a Persian mould.
Yet it is quite possible to determine in a majority of
instances, not only whether Pushtu words, of which the
affinity with Persian is evident at first sight, have been
directly adopted from the latter language, or belong
strictly and originally to Pushtu; but even, in the former
of these cases, to ascertain within some sort of limits at
what period and from what stage of the Persian they have
been adopted.

In order to assign to the Pushtu its proper position
among the Iranian languages, it is necessary to enumerate
briefly, yet with sufficient detail, the different dialects of
which that important group consists, according to the most
natural classification and arrangement of which they admit.
For this purpose it is convenient to assume the Persian
language proper as the central unit or standard of comparison, by which to test the nearness and remoteness of
the affinity of the rest. This arrangement is natural as

well as conventional, for the Persian language covers more
time in its records and more space in its distribution
than any of the others, and occupies a position central
to, conterminous with, and directly influencing all, or
nearly all, of them. By the Persian language proper is
understood, firstly, the old language of the Achæmenian
inscriptions, the direct parent of modern Persian, to which
may be added the two dialects, whether they be contemporary dialects or successive stages of the Zend,
most intimately allied with old Persian; the transitional
dialects spoken during the Sassanian period, comprising
the lapidary, numismatic, and literary Pehlevi, in so far
as it is Aryan and stripped of its Semitic element, and
the language formerly called Pazend, but now generally
known as Parsi, differing very slightly, if at all, from
the former, and being the penultimate stage of modern
Persian; the classical modern Persian of literature during
the Mahometan period, from Firdausi and his immediate
predecessors and contemporaries downwards; and, finally,
that which has furnished philologists with fewer materials
than any, the true living language of modern Iran. It
must not be forgotten that Persian is spoken as a native
and vernacular language much beyond the limits of the
Persian empire, in the settled parts of Turkistan and
Afghanistan, far into the heart of the Chinese Empire, by a
population whose Persian origin and agricultural habits are
variously indicated in these countries respectively by the
names Tājik, Sārt, Dihkān, and Pārsīvān. Besides these,
the pastoral and nomadic tribes of mountaineers dwelling
in the ranges which traverse and enclose the plains of
Eastern Persia and Western Afghanistan, of whom the
Eimāk [1] and Hazāra are the principal, are known to speak

---

[1] Generally so pronounced, but
written Uimāk, اوىماق. The word
is Turkish, meaning a clan or tribe;
چهار اوىماق. "the four tribes,"
is the usual Persian name for this
race. The word is lost in Osmanli,
but survives among some Turkoman
tribes of the interior of Asia Minor,
by whom the main tribe is called
'ashira, and the next minor sub-
division oymak. I am indebted for
this information to Mr. Edmund Cal-

Persian as their own language. Their native traditions, whatever they may be worth, point to a Turanian rather than an Iranian origin, and one of the four clans of the Eimāk is actually called Moghul, and speaks a corrupt dialect of Mongol; but the other Eimāks, the Hazāra and the settled Tājiks of the plains, all speak the Persian language in an archaic form, which may be generally described as being the Persian of Firdausi. But of the provincialisms, archaisms, and special differences of this Tājik or extra-Iranian Persian, there does not exist any notice whatever in detail; and it would be well worth the while of linguists and scholars in Persia, or the neighbouring countries, to endeavour to form a collection of the kind. One or two vocabularies of the Persian of Bokhara have been compiled and published, but as they were drawn up, not with the object of contrasting Tājik-Persian with Iranian-Persian, but of showing that the language of Bokhara was Persian rather than something else, they have done more harm than good, as they have served to induce comparative philologists to accept and admit the "langue boukhare" into their essays and vocabularies as an independent dialect, having its own ordinal value, and standing towards Persian in the same relationship, more or less, as Kurdish or Ossetish. The "Fārsi" of Bokhara in reality differs from that of Teheran in the same manner and degree as the "Français" of Canada or the Mauritius differs from that of Paris, or the English of Boston from that of London. Each, in the rates of its consciousness, accepts the metropolitan standard of literature and conversation; each considers itself, and really is, of the same

vert, for a long time resident among the Turkomans of the neighbourhood of Kaisariya. A vocabulary of the dialect of the Moghul Eimāks, drawn up by Major Leach, has somehow given rise to the impression that the whole body of the four Eimāks speak Mongol and are of Mongol descent; and they accordingly figure as Mongols in all modern works on language and ethnology. This is quite incorrect, and there is nothing whatever in Leach's words to warrant or give rise to such a supposition. Whatever their descent may be, their language, with the one exception of the Moghul Eimāks, is exclusively Tajik Persian.

E

name, form, and virtual identity with the main branch
from which it sprung; and though each may contain many
curious provincialisms and archaic expressions, that circumstance of itself does not elevate them to the rank of
separate substantial languages, or even dialects.

The dialects standing nearest to Persian, being its
genuine sisters, and not modern offsets or corruptions of
it, are the Mazanderāni, Ghilek, and Talish, spoken in the
wooded and mountainous country south of the Caspian.
They are closely allied to each other, and form a natural
family which may be conveniently called the Caspian.
They are known through some brief specimens of popular
poetry published, with notes, by M. Chodzko; the Talish,
moreover, through a grammar and vocabulary published
at St. Petersburg, the province in which it is spoken being
partly Russian. More remote from Persian than the
Caspian group, and respectively about equidistant from
it, stand the languages of the north-west and south-east
frontiers, the Beluchi and the numerous Kurdish dialects.
The former, well illustrated in Germany from materials
supplied by Major Leach's vocabulary, is unfortunately
only known to us as spoken by the Rind Beluchis, the
conquerors of Sindh, and it bears many traces of Indian
influence accordingly. The dialect of the Nhārūi, or
western Beluchis, bordering on Kirman and Sistan, has
not yet, to the writer's knowledge, been noticed. Regarding the various Kurdish dialects, it would be more
convenient to call them by a less limited and more
comprehensive term, such as Kurdo-Lurish or Lĕkī, as
they are not only spoken in Kurdistan proper, including
the area of Kurdish migration and settlement in Asia
Minor and Northern Syria, and among the extensive
settlements of true Kurds in Northern Khorasan, but by
the Lurs and Bakhtyaris of Luristan, and by the whole
of those Ililyāt, or wandering tribes of Persia, who are
not of Turkish race. These latter are called Lek in
Persia, and of their distinctive dialect absolutely no

record exists. The same may be said of the Luri, for though everybody who has been in the East, and inquired into the subject, is aware that the Lurs speak Kurdish, yet there is nothing to show in proof of the assertion save a few words in the Kurdish vocabularies in Mr. Rich's work on Kurdistan.

A very peculiar and insulated dialect must be classed in this stage or degree of proximity to Persian. This is the Baraki, spoken by a small hill tribe in a secluded district of Afghanistan. Their tradition, pointing to a recent Arabian origin, and to a language invented for purposes of secrecy by themselves, though accepted by its chronicler, Major Leach, is worthless in presence of the language itself, which is an interesting, and in many points truly archaic, Iranian dialect. *Kshār*, for instance, Persian *shahr*, old Persian *khshatram*, *ksha*, the number six, Zend *ksvas*, Persian *shash, shish*, which could not, of course, have been invented out of nothing, could not, any more, have been adopted from the local Tājik Persian of the plains, from which the old initial compound sound must have disappeared long prior to Islam. Leach only gives a vocabulary and dialogue, without any outline of the grammar, but the construction of sentences, as shown in the dialogue, is far less Iranian and more Turanian than would be expected from the wholly Iranian forms and words of this language.

Next come the two well-known Ossetian dialects, which have now for some time attracted the attention of European scholars, owing to their outlying and insulated position in the Caucasus, and to their unexpected philological affinities. They have been fully illustrated by the labours of Rosen and Sjögren. The numerous Indian characteristics, and the strongly marked sound system of the Pushtu, and the special and peculiar nature of much of its vocabulary, serve to remove it further from Persian than any of the dialects previously mentioned. Yet it does not close the list, and, upon the whole, after due consideration, the

extreme position among the Iranian dialects should probably be reserved for the Armenian, the affinities of which
to Persian, nevertheless, are numerous, clear, and undoubted.

The above enumeration, it is believed, will be found to
have comprised the whole circle of Iranian dialects that
have come down to us, and that are at present known to
exist. They are all of them closely connected with one
another, and each one of them is capable of supplying great
and effectual aid in throwing light upon the difficulties and
explaining the peculiarities of any or all of the others.
Pushtu, obviously, and as a matter of course, has to be
illustrated by Persian, but the dialects are also capable of
rendering it equally efficient services. Dr. Dorn has thus
drawn useful comparisons from the Caspian dialects in
two or three instances, and would have done so more fully
had it been his object in that place to explain, rather than
to state, the rules of Pushtu grammar. The principal end
with which the Persian dialects have been examined in
the preceding survey, has been to show how very scanty,
after all, are the materials which lie at the disposal of the
philologist for their due investigation, and to stimulate
the linguist who may read these pages, and who may have
opportunities for such researches, to dig and quarry in a
valuable mine, which, so far from having been exhausted,
is as yet in many places unworked and undisturbed.

A TOO PERSONAL PRONOUN.[1]

To the *Editor of " The Realm."*

[THIS curious letter, the address of which a huge blot has partially
obliterated, must have reached us by mistake, the reviews referred to
having never appeared in our columns, and the critic being unknown
to us. It is dated on the evening of the Ascot Cup Day. We shall
be glad to hear further from the writer, whoever he is, when he is
quite sober. He shows traces of a talent for critical omniscience
even while he kicks over them.]

SIR,—You are not fair upon me. You are my taskmaster
and the lord of my benefit; I am your servant and your
workman—your hireling reviewer. In this capacity I have
no reason to doubt that I have given you entire satisfaction, nor do I believe that you can point out any contemporary instance of omniscience and effrontery superior to
that which I love to bestow upon you among my brother
workmen in the employ of other masters. Omniscience,
indeed! Why, before I have done with you, I shall just
take the liberty of pointing out to you what I have done,
and thus leaving you and your readers to judge for your-
selves. But of this more further on. For the present, I
have only to remind you that even the omniscience of a
weekly review writer has its limits; that his endurance or
his impudence are not proof against all wear; and that his
conscience is occasionally seen to put forth the germs of a
feeble uneasy vitality. Why this noise and grumbling?
say you. Because, say I, you have called on me at a
moment's notice — and it would have been much the

---

[1] These amusing letters appeared in a short-lived newspaper called the
" Realm," June 15 and 22, 1864.

same thing if it had been a year's notice—to pronounce from the judgment-seat of your columns an authoritative and skilled opinion on a book about law, archæology, and philology, all these three strands being most cunningly twined together into one rope and tied into one knot, which I have no power to untwine, no knowledge wherewith to untie, and not enough impudence to cut. And, as if law in itself were not bad enough, you vex my soul with the law of Anglo-Saxons and Romans, and the like old-world people. "A Neglected Fact in English History. By H. C. Coote, F.S.A. London: Bell & Daldy." Such is the smooth unpretending outside or husk of the very hard nut which you have called on me to crack, in order that your readers may delight in the kernel. Now, I vow and declare that I know absolutely nothing about these occult sciences of law, philology, archæology, and Anglo-Saxon, and I care as little as I know. No more, between you and me, do our readers, in practice at least, whatever they may do in theory. But it is not fair upon a reviewer to expect him to make his bricks without the straw of knowledge, nor is it quite fair to newspaper readers or skimmers to expect them to lean with full confidence on the support of columns constructed with plinths such as I make without straw. Nor, while talking of straws, can you expect that you will be allowed to place the last straw on the camel's back, and thereby to break down your beast of burden, without his treating you to a spice of the angry camel's mettle? He will creak and groan at you; he will sway his great neck round at your legs, and make grass of your flesh with his herbivorous grinders; he will chuckle and bubble at you, with great pink globes of angry foam—half wrath, half rumination—bursting from his injured querulous mouth. No, sir; I have long proved myself in your service to be no angel, fearing to tread on unknown and sacred ground; but rather to be one of the other sort, who will rush in at anything from trigonometry to the Vedas. But I must draw the line somewhere, and I choose to draw it at Roman and Anglo-Saxon law, at the Domas of Æthel-red and Siculus Flaccus de Conditionibus Agrorum.

Bethink yourself, sir, for one moment, I pray you, of the nature and amount of work done by an active literary reviewer, going well in single harness, let us say, between the shafts of a moderately light weekly newspaper. Give yourself the trouble of reading the books which he professes to review for you, just in order to see whether he has read them at all, let alone the question of his possessing, or having acquired or crammed, the collateral information which will enable him to confirm or to refute. He cannot do it, or, at all events, he hardly ever does do it. The pace is too good; the necessity of saying something is too urgent; the amount of new patients waiting, as it were, in the dentist's anteroom is too great; the competition with other, and perhaps rival, contemporaries is too strong. So I and my brethren, who have nothing to do, please remark, with the scientific labour of skilled and trained critics, such as those whom you will find shining in such constellations of wit and special knowledge in the earlier numbers of the "Edinburgh" or the "Saturday Review" —I and my brethren, having neither time nor knowledge, waste the former by simulating the latter; for the bricks must go to the kiln, straw or no straw. The results of such manufacture are appalling to the individual reviewer to behold, if his moral stomach be at all squeamish and his conscience qualmish. But here is seen the great advantage of anonymous writing, namely, the protection it affords to the reviewer's conscience; otherwise how could any human conscience withstand the remorse, let us say, of having assumed and arrogantly put forward knowledge about the Binomial Theorem when the writer is ignorant of simple equations.

But let us turn from general propositions to particular instances. I will just pass briefly in review the work which I have contributed to your columns since the beginning of the year. First and foremost, of course, comes

my famous review of the book of the season. Sir Emerson
Tennent's "Story of the Guns," in the very clever author
of which it is my delight to recognise an omniscience, a
pugnacity, and a two-thousand-competition-wallah power
of cra—of assimilation, on which I would fain model my
own, and up to which I gaze in admiration as at a star on
high. Of course I shot the steel-headed bolt of my criticism
through and through the iron plates; but if you think I
had anything to do with the forging of the bolt, you are
very much in error. Then came Dr. Percy's "Metallurgy;"
then came Mr. Freeman and the Achæan League; then
came "A Handbook of Uterine Therapeutics;" then came a
"Handy-book to Modern Corruptions; or, Clippings from
the Queen's English;" then Mr. Gorst's book on New Zealand, with my remarks on the whole land question as between
the settlers and the Ngatimaniapoto and the Ngaruawahia
tribes—and I beg of you, sir, be mindful of the spelling of
these words, because Maori orthography is my strongest
point but seven. Then the books on that weary old
Ottoman Empire, dear and precious among empires as it
is to reviewers for its inexhaustible fertility in book-crops;
then that Asian mystery, the Eastern Question—and I
hope, sir, that neither you nor your friends will ever be
called upon to answer the inquiry, 'What is the Eastern
Question?' Then came Shakespeare and the parasiti-
cal literature thereunto pertaining; then Dr. Schiefner's
"Tschetschenzische Studien," a nice light work for summer wear; then the "Zeitschrift der Abendländischen Por-
nologischen Gesellschaft;" then Dr. Sandwith's "Hekim
Bashi," in which I find three false concords in his Turkish,
and so bruise the Kars hero's heel, as he is about damaging
his own knuckles by knocking the Grand Turk's numskull
lying sick on his couch—a chronic invalid, who won't
die, won't get well, and won't take his physic. The last
thing I did was the drawing-room edition of Halayudha's
"Abhidhanaratnamâlâ" (having previously glanced at the
bell-tent edition for the use of subalterns), just published

at Ahmednuggur for the festivities held there by so many millions of our dusky fellow-subjects in honour of the ter-millenary of that sweet swan of Nerbuddha. I daresay I missed many of the best points, in humour and pathos, of the mighty Sanskrit tragedian. Dr. Max Müller would soon settle my hash, and perhaps even the titular Sanskrit Professor himself might have *beau jeu* with me; but at least I put my horse at the fence boldly, and without swerving, craning, or, I think, falling; and I think I was graphic in describing the ceremonies—the public fountains playing *ghee* or clarified butter, the gratuitous distribution of sacred cow-dung to the poor, the nautches, and the widow burnings. Do not, then, bother me about Roman law and the *Trinoda Necessitas*, about *burhbot, briegbot,* and *fyrd,* after that, for I am exhausted intellectually and morally. If you want anybody to tell you whether Mr. Coote is right or wrong in his use of these cabalistic words, go elsewhere, and do not come to ME.

A NEGLECTED FACT.

To the Editor of " The Realm."

SIR,—The real fact is, that if you ask me what Mr. Coote's book is, I can tell you with no more difficulty than is inherent in making a summary of a work on a subject which is quite unfamiliar; and such difficulty is much lessened in the present case by Mr. Coote's way of breaking up his paragraphs, or rather of making his paragraph and his sentence commensurate. This is apparently imitated from M. Guizot, though, to a profane student of novels rather than of history, it looks uncommonly like the works of M. Alexandre Dumas, *père;* but it is a great help to the eye and memory. If, on the other hand, you ask me what Mr. Coote's book is worth, I can no more tell you than I can tell you what is the relative worth of the Armstrong and the Whitworth gun. Nor do I believe you will find six men in England who can; for though the work is perfectly clear, and not in the least abstruse, the subject is very abstruse, and hardly anybody is equal to it in all its bearings. Perhaps it will be handled some day in one of the Quarterlies or sober-sided periodicals. But, to be done properly, it should be done by a commission or board. Mr. Home should be at once called on to summon the ghost of Mr. J. Mitchell Kemble, and to him should be adjoined the German trio, Professors Leo, Lappenberg, and Pauli; there should be Mr. Wright, and there should be that priceless pearl of anonymous and somewhat crotchety erudition, who goes on week after week pouring out historical criticism from unexhausted stores into the "Saturday Review"—a nameless contributor,

yet with force and learning enough to make the fame of
ten men—one who alone will keep his review sweet
through ten times the current amount of dripping stuff
about Early Rising (which comes regularly once a year),
Flirts, Lords and their Lackeys, and the like. Such a
body, or, for the matter of that, any one of the Germans
singly, would be able to establish or confute Mr. Coote's
propositions decisively and once for all.

It is easy to state what the propositions themselves
are. The mass of Englishmen are not descended from the
ancient English whose name they bear. They are not
sprung from a small dominant caste of Teutonic invaders,
but from a subject race of provincials, Romanised Britons,
"Welshmen," or Lloegrians. The last were not exterminated by the English or Teutonic invaders, but they
remained under them as the great majority of the population, and impressed on their rude conquerors, almost unchanged, the laws and institutions which they had enjoyed
under the dominion of Imperial Rome. The population
in Anglo-Saxon times is divided into *gesithas*, subsequently
called *thegnas*, and *ceorlas*. These respectively represent
the Roman *possessores* and the *coloni*. The borough with
its territory constitutes the shire, which exactly represents
the Roman *civitas*, or city with its territory. The hundred
represents the Roman *pagus*, but bears a name applied
from the ancient Teutonic itinerant assessors, one hundred
in number, moving from township to township. The so-
called sixhyndman, intermediate in some measure between
the thegn and the ceorl, is an actual Roman, at least in the
earlier times, and belongs to the old Roman population of
the towns. The termination in -*tun* belongs to one-tenth
of the local names in England, and it denotes the old
Roman enclosures of land as found and retained by the
English invader, with his own name prefixed; such a
termination and such enclosures not being found, or
having been swamped, on the Continent. More than this,
the very hedgerows of England are genuine Roman

demarcations, preserved in Britain alone. All these points are supported by copious reference to Roman jurists and Anglo-Saxon documents, through the vast mass of which latter, contained in Kemble's "Codex Diplomaticus," it is evident that the author has worked his way; and though I can tell you nothing about his correctness, I can readily bear witness to his industry.

Philology is the author's weak point. Not content with institutions, he maintains that our very language came to us from the Romanised Britons, whose language was the classical written Anglo-Saxon, the earliest stage of modern English. So that both in blood and speech we English bear the name of English merely as the Italians of North Italy bear that of Lombards, or the provincials of Gaul that of French from their Frank conquerors. The Jute, Saxon, and Angle invaders, speaking Scandinavian or Teutonic dialects only remotely allied to our own, forsake their own forms of speech and adopt that of the Romanised Britons, themselves no Celts, but an antecedent Teutonic population descended from the Belgæ. This philological part of Mr. Coote's theory will not hold water in the least; and some of his statements are such bouncing blunders that it is astonishing how they got to Mr. Coote's pages. Certain abstract terms of religion, distinguished from ceremonial terms of alleged later origin, are found in Anglo-Saxon, such as *husel*, a sacrifice. These indicate a pure and primitive form of Christianity existing in the island previous to the Teutonic or Saxon invasion, and were borrowed by the Saxons from the Britons. Now, here is how and where Mr. Coote breaks down. The oldest Teutonic form of *husel* is the Gothic *hunsl*, found in Ulphilas, and it is absurd to suppose a bishop on the Lower Danube to have borrowed it from the Britons. But Mr. Coote knows nothing about Ulphilas and the older Teutonic dialects of the Continent, otherwise he would never have said anything so shocking as

"It (the Teutonic of Anglo-Saxon England) has two letters and sounds unknown to the Continent of Germany, viz., the *theta* and the *w*. It has an inflection which no German dialect has ever had, viz., the formation of a plural of nouns in *as* and *es*."

Go to your Grimm, Mr. Coote, to your Massmann, your Gabelentz, and your Diefenbach; learn their ways, and the ways of *a*-stems in the *Ur-Deutsch;* avoid paradox when you do not know all your subject, and be thankful you hear no more on this from   ME.

DOG-PERSIAN "IN EXCELSIS."[1]

Vient d'être nommé Chevalier Grand Cordon de la Légion d'Honneur I Am Your Faithful Obedient Servant Russell Knight of Thegarter. Let us suppose this delectable piece of nonsense to have appeared some fine evening in the official portion of the Paris "Moniteur," great with the dignity of leaded type and authoritative heading; and let us further conceive it to have been duly copied, circulated, and commented upon in the unofficial ordinary newspapers of France. What commentary should we suppose the French papers likely to make upon the English system of nomenclature? What would they say about the godfathers and godmothers who "assist" at the baptism of infant "Anglo-Saxons"? The first ejaculation would probably be the same as that which was provoked by the representation of "Othello" in English on a Parisian stage some fifteen or more years ago. "*Iago, Iago—ces noms Anglais—tiens, c'est comme le miaulement d'un chat!*" Think of the outburst of jokes both coarse and keen, of the inextinguishable laughter among the happy gods of the European Paradise. Think how the ignorant majority, and the evil-minded majority, and the clever majority, would all go their ways exulting in one more proof of that perverse insularity which begins even at the baptismal font. M. Assolant and all the tribe of *feuilletonistes* would put forth the most brilliant little leaves of writing, all of a glitter with glass-dust not to be distinguished from real diamond-dust. The voices of De Porquet, or Fleming and Tibbins, or whoever may be the recognised interpreters of English words and ways for the benefit of the French, would be dull and silent amid the chaff and gay clamour. But a

[1] From the "Saturday Review," December 24, 1864.

small minority would assuredly be found, versed in the method of our language, and ever irritated at signs of international misconception, who would not spare their denunciations of the utter carelessness and slovenliness in a public office which lets an insane jumble of titles and names and formulas go and do duty for an unprotected foreigner's own decent Christian patronymic.

The scene and the names must now be changed, and the story must be narrated of ourselves. In one of the " London Gazettes " of last week, such as we are accustomed to read in the top corners of our daily paper the morning after publication, the following pretty piece of reading was served up at our breakfast-tables :—" The Queen has been graciously pleased to nominate and appoint His Highness Furzund Dilbund Rasekhul Itgad Dowlut - i - Englishia Rajah Rajegan, Rajah Rundeer Singh Bahadoor of Kuppoorthulla, to be a Knight of the most Exalted Order of the Star of India." This must have created bewilderment, disquietude, and annoyance among nine-tenths of newspaper readers—among all ladies, and professional people, and douce parochial-minded people—very much as though a Hindoo crossing-sweeper had intruded himself in person upon their morning privacy, or a fluttering white-robed Lascar thrust his bundle of tracts between the ratepayer and his teacup. Asia is very well in its way, but Asia must consume its own smoke, and not come into the way of its European neighbours, as it has got into the habit of doing too frequently of late. Yet there are gleams of hope through the darkness. Englishia—which seems to differ from English as Alicia from Alice—might make a pretty ladies' name, such as Andalusia, Venetia, and other provinces have done before now : and it has a friendly look, like a green oasis in the midst of this weary Asiatic desert. Rajegan is evidently the family name of his Highness, according to the punctuation of the phrase, sentence, word-drift, or whatever it is to be called ; and we sincerely congratulate the Rajah on its pleasant sound, its adapta-

bility to European organs, and its apparent resemblance to
the proper names of the exalted Irish—a race fond of claim-
ing an Eastern origin, which may perhaps be admitted
when we find names in the East made so much after the
fashion of Hogan, Flanagan, and Mulligan. Those who,
like ourselves, are professionally bound over as critics to
be mistrustful of everything, may hazard a suspicion that
some of it may be no name at all, but a mass of title, or a
bit of a sentence in a native language that has been smuggled
into the "Gazette" by enthusiastic advocates of the Roman
character, under guise of a name. Such cavil as this,
however, can be met by a ready answer. If Furzund
Dilbund, &c., be a title, why is "His Highness" written in
English, and not in Kuppoorthullese? We must take it as
we find it given to us. It is given to us as a name, and it
has been taken as such, and made merry over as such, and
had good stories told over it as such—especially the inevit-
able old one of the Spanish landlord and the hidalgo with
his string of names, a story as impossible to miss as it
seems to be to write three consecutive Spanish names
correctly—and moralised over as such, and very likely had
thanks said over it as such that we are not like those
Asiatics; and all the cheap Quintilians of Cockayne have
stared, and gasped, and told us "how much harder 'twas
than Gordon, Colkitto, or Macdonald, or Galasp." Of
course, a name like this is one more proof of Asiaticism,
Indianity, niggerhood, or by whatever name we may call
the aggregate of the perverse uncomfortable ways of our
fellow-subjects and cousins Indo-german. It seems to
afford a dim shadow of an explanation, or at least an analogy, to their other objectional points of difference from
ourselves—their dislike of beefsteaks and turn for meta-
physical brooding and clarified butter, their tendency to
be blue at the extremities in cold weather, their aggravating cerebral accent, their singular proclivity to the selling
of Christian tracts in London, combined with marked
repugnance towards the religious doctrines therein incul-

cated, and all the other details which make up the
character of the wolf we have got by the ears and are not
flinching from the duty of taming.

Perhaps Miss Yonge, at least, will thank us if we take
this name—let us say Sir Furzund Rajegan's name—to
pieces, and see of what material it is made up; in doing
which it will not be easy to avoid the discovery, at the
same time, of what materials Perso-Indian scholarship in
high places is made up. It would be more exact to say
Persian at once. The sentence is made up of Persian
words, meant to obey Persian laws. The words are either
true Persian drawn from the pure well of Aryan undefiled,
or Arabic words and an Arabic phrase incorporated in that
language, or Indian words treated and inflected as Persian.
The laws of its syntax are Persian, and it is a good or bad
sentence only when tested as Persian. *Furzund*, in its
elements and its meaning exactly corresponding to the
Latin *prognatus*, is a somewhat archaic and poetical word
for *a son*, little used vernacularly, but fully living in the
high literary style and official parlance. In the latter it is
employed—or was some years ago—by the Grand Vizier's
office at Tehran in addressing Persian ambassadors abroad,
and other dependent functionaries. All Continental Orientalists would write the word Farzand or Ferzend; and
English Orientalists who have anything approaching to
book-learning, and who see the advantage of adopting one
system of transcription, generally follow that of Sir W.
Jones, who would write Farzand. But, though the vowel
is etymologically, and elsewhere really, an *a*, Furzund does
exactly express the Indian way of pronouncing it, with our
short *u* as in *but, fun;* and it is no use quarrelling with
this part of Mr. Gilchrist's system, which is, practically,
so accurate on Indian ground. The only inconvenience
attending it is that a handful of educated people here,
familiar with Continental languages, and not realising the
nature of the transcription of sounds from one alphabet to
another, *will* say *Sootledge*, and *Poonjab*, and Sir *Yoong*

F

Bahawder, as they used to show off their Spanish in M. Du Chaillu's year by pronouncing Gorilla *Gorillia*, after the analogy of Montilla and Manzanilla, just as if the great anthropoid ape were a new kind of bitter sherry. But if the carriage people go wrong, the omnibus people go right in these Gilchristian short *u*'s.

Dil-bund, or *-band*, or *-bend*, literally "heart-binding," is by itself quite unobjectionable, beyond such objection as lies against the whole, that it is written in Persian, and not in the plain English official version thereof. The words, when taken separately, though we need hardly now say they are no more the Rajah's name than the Lord Chamberlain's name, are good sense enough, as we have seen. Yet *Fur-zund Dilbund* means just nothing at all, as it stands. The word which logically connects the two, in order to convey the desired meaning of "affectionate son," or as we should say, "devoted dependant," is wanting or omitted. It is a very little word, being simply the short letter *i*; and, in the Arabic alphabet used by all Mussulmans for writing their respective languages, it is an invisible word, not perceptible as a word at all. Yet it is none the less an integral, if not quite an organically living portion of Persian speech. The Arabic alphabet has no means of expressing a short *ĭ* as a substantive word by itself, nor can it represent the sound as here uttered at all except as a vowel point affixed to the consonant ending the foregoing word, or by a *y* when that word ends in a vowel. In this case it is called the *Izâfa* (junction or copula), more properly, the sign of Izâfa. But it is not writing, but speech, which constitutes the vital principle of a language; and if the Arabic alphabet only affords an imperfect Semitic instrument for the registration of Aryan sounds, these latter, when emancipated and recorded in a more suitable character, should be represented in full, and all the more so when grammatically significant. The Parsee does this when writing Persian with the Zend alphabet, for that has a character for each vowel, whether

long or short; the Armenian does this; and we Romans
should do this, as, indeed, all scholars generally do.   The
word is a good little word, come of good lineage, with
illustrious cousins.   It is the legitimate descendant of the
Zend *hya*, the Achæmenian *hya*, which is both a relative
and demonstrative pronoun, as well as the termination of
the genitive case arising out of that pronoun, being neither
more nor less than the Homeric article.   In Parsi, the
most archaic stage of current Persian as recorded in the
books of the Fire-worshippers, the word appears not only
in its modern employment, to form the connection between
substantives and adjectives, or to supply the loss of the
genitive case as in our *of*, but as an active relative pronoun; as in, for instance, *mart i raft*, the man who went.
In the modern Kurdish declension of personal pronouns
it is well preserved in an older form—*Az*, I; genitive, *ya
men*, of me; where Kurdish has also retained the old
nominative now lost to Persian, but common to all the
other Iranian dialects, as well as identically existing in
Old Slavonic and Lithuanian, and, with more surface-
change, in each of the other members of the Pan-Aryan
group, from *aham* and *ego* down to *I*.   The word corresponds always in meaning to the English *of* or *which;*
and, if the alphabet admit of it, should no more be
omitted in writing Persian than those words should be
in English.

Here, we again miss it after Dilbund. *Rasekhul Itgad*
is intended to represent an Arabic phrase, inserted bodily
into the sentence according to Persian syntactical rules,
but, within itself, being perfect self-contained Arabic.   As
in Turkish, Persian, or Indian politics you constantly meet
with *imperia in imperiis*, so in the languages of these
countries you meet with *linguas in linguis*.   Gilchrist
would write it *Rasikh ool I'tikad*, or *I'tigad;* Sir William
Jones would write it *Rásikhu 'l-I'tikád;* and this last
would represent the Arabic spelling with mathematical
accuracy.   The Arabic article may be left alone by itself

in the Roman character without any harm being done ; or
it may be prefixed to the *I'tikád*, as it ought to be by
rights, but when affixed to the *Rásikh* it is like coupling
shafts to a cart-horse before they have been built into
the cart. *Rasekh* is an allowable variation, but *Itgad* is
nothing at all. This word, like all Arabic words, must be
written on some one consistent system, and any random
or unsystematic writing is pure error. The word should
be *I'tikád* or *I'tiqád*, or it may be written with any other
conventional sign to convey the two sounds proper to
Arabic ; one, our inverted commas, for a sound impossible
to European adult learners, being a forcible contraction
and subsequent dilatation of the throat-valves, so to speak,
when uttered by Arabs, but in other languages into which
it has passed, a mere hiatus ; the other, a guttural *k*, or a
q, for which last *g* is a misprint, but not even a misprint
can confer sense or possibility upon this word as it stands.
The phrase altogether, and by rights, we may add, is as
though the Latin *fidei servantissimus* were embedded in an
English sentence.

Dowlut we have nothing to say against, for the Gilchristian system has one or two redeeming points about it,
though we should never dream of using or advocating it.
At this point we find our little friend the short *ĭ* had got
his syntactical rights officially acknowledged at last, perhaps owing to his next neighbour's presence ; for where
you find English, you will probably also find *i* written long,
and even unduly held in honour, it is said. But why
Englishia ? It is utterly barbarous. In Persia at all times,
and in India during the Mogul period, the name of England
was written and spoken *Ingilís* or *Ingilíz*, which, with an
Arabic feminine termination added to the Gentile adjective, would be *Ingilíziyya*. Latterly, the word *Ingréz*,
taken from the Portuguese, is the one used in India for
the most part. But *Englishia*, if it be so written purposely
with the laudable intention of getting the word in its purest
form hot and hot from headquarters, is at best a case of

clipping and tampering with the Shah's Persian, which
even the Ruler of India has no right to commit. The
idiom of this language, moreover, imperatively requires the
presence of some honorific adjective in the present instance;
the phrase should be *Dowlut,* or, as we should write, *Daulat
i 'Aliyya i Ingilîziyya,* "the high English state." It is not
a mere question of politeness, nor of grammar, but of idiomatic principle; and the adjective is as indispensable as,
in French, the prefix of Monsieur in an address like *M. le
Comte, M. votre frère,* would be. Its omission is, in an Oriental's eye, a want of due self-respect. We would gladly
enter into the whole question of the method of clothing
European forms and titles in an Oriental garb had we space
enough; we can now only say that the Russians have long
been manipulating Persian for this purpose with wonderful
tact, and their greatest success in Central Asia has been a
philological success. The Sovereign of India was long
called a mere *Malika i Mu'azzama* in Indian Persian,
which a Central Asiatic understands as an "exalted Chief-
tainess." The Emperor of Russia is in all the mouths and
opinions of Central Asia the *Imperâtûr i A'zam,* the
Greatest Emperor; and this last is not mere official form,
but good Persian vernacular. Raja Rajegan will do well
enough; it does not belong to the domain of linguistic
criticism to inquire why the worthy man is called Rajah
of Rajahs, so we willingly make our salaam to His Highness, and retire from his presence, after having expressed
our entire dissatisfaction with his fine new patchwork of
European clothing.

There is no great harm or depth of delinquency in this
affair, after all; nor is the carelessness or slovenliness
with which it is put together bad enough to hurt the
feelings of Orientalists seriously, who should be thick-
skinned and long-suffering in this respect, and have much
to bear withal. It is the intense strangeness, not to say
absurdity, of writing an English Government Gazette in
Persian, and not in English, which bewilders us and pro-
vokes our comments. When it is wanted to say "His

Highness Raja So-and-so, a devoted adherent and faithful
dependent of the English Government," it is best to say it
in English when addressing English readers, and to keep
the Persian for Indian Gazettes on Indian ground, if there
be such things. When we give the garter to King George
we shall not gazette him as " Anax Andron Tondapamei-
bomenos Georgios," much less write it "Hanacks Andron;"
but we shall call him King of Men, or whatever the proper
Athenian title may be, in decent everyday English. When
Prince de Carambolesco shall be elected by universal suf-
frage Emperor of regenerate Danubia, we shall not say to
him *Maria Ta*, but "Your Majesty," however pleasant it
may be to show off our Daco-Roman. We are already
prone to dwell with more weight upon the points of difference which separate Asiatics from ourselves than upon the
points of similarity which unite us, and it is not well to
let a plain straightforward sentence in the classical language of Sadi pass, for want of explanation or translation,
as a vile uncouth tag of names worthy only of a Feejee or
Dahoman savage. The incidental questions arising out of
this—the force and vitality of the Persian language in
India, its bearing and influence upon Hindustani, adopted
by the English as the universal language, but as yet unfixed
and adrift, as regards its future vocabulary at least—the
curious discrepancies among Mahometan Orientals, in the
employment of terms denoting their styles and titles—the
difference between the living language of Iran and the
benumbed quasi-classical Persian scholastically taught in
India—these questions, full of interest, cannot now be
examined. For the present, we can only conclude with the
Arabic proverb, "*An-nâsŭ a'dâŭn mâ jâhalū*," of which the
French "*C'est la mésintelligence qui fait la guerre*" is a
feeble shadow, and which we shall freely translate, "When
men see a strange object which they know nothing of,
they go and hate it." Even in a mere trifle like the present, it is surely no waste of time to substitute correct for
incorrect impressions, and sow the seed of sympathy rather
than antipathy.

THE interior and mountainous districts of Northern
Albania are an unknown land to English tourists, and are
almost unvisited even by real travellers and explorers.
At all events, they have hitherto found no place in any
English record of genuine travel. The only account
known to me which contains any fulness of geographical
detail is a contribution of the Austrian Count Karaczay to
the Proceedings of the Royal Geographical Society. This,
however, is based, not on personal travel, but on information supplied by the Roman Catholic clergy of the country,
many of whom, Dalmatians or Italians, are Austrian subjects. I believe I may even go the length of limiting the
number of tolerably recent English travellers among these
wild mountains to two persons—Mr. Hughes and Mr.
Dunn Gardner. The former, now Oriental Secretary at
Constantinople, and son to the late well-known traveller
in Southern Albania, has travelled on the line of the
White Drin as far as Ipek, Jacova, and the curious old
Servian monastery of Dechan. The latter, I understand,
has been everywhere, even into the fastnesses of the
almost independent Mirdites. But no account of either
of these journeys has been published. On the other hand,
an account of travels which never took place, and which
there is no occasion further to specify, does exist.

The French have been beforehand with us in this field,
and have gone a long way to supply our wants. M. Hec-
quard, formerly French Consul at Skodra, published at the

---

[1] From "The Eastern Shores of the Adriatic," by Viscountess Strangford.
Bentley, 1865.

end of 1858 a volume of great interest and importance, replete with geographical, statistical, and miscellaneous information on Upper Albania, the fruit of many years' most active political employment in that country, and of a thorough knowledge of its languages. I think that much of this work, even though very dry, would well repay translation by a competent person. It was, and has as yet been, wholly unnoticed by the English press, not having even been boiled down into stock for ordinary magazine consumption. I wish that my limited scope and space would allow me to make large extracts from his valuable work for the benefit of English readers, and introduce them to the Hotti and the Clementi, to Shalla, and Pouka, and the subjects of Prince Bib—tribes of good Catholics who are more unknown to us than the Waganda and the Wagogo of Equatorial Africa.

For general information on Albania as a whole, and particularly on its central and southern parts, I cannot do better than refer my readers to the great work published not many years ago by Von Hahn, for a long time Austrian Consul at Ioannina. This is a vast storehouse of facts of every conceivable description, with archæology and philology predominating, as is natural in the work of a German, learned or otherwise. Everything is there treated, from the earliest origin of the people in the old pre-Homeric period down to their modern nursery stories, and to the question whether there really are or are not Albanians born with tails. It is an Augean stable of disorderly erudition, which strongly needs the clear and methodic mind of some French or English Hercules to reduce it to order for the use of the general reader.

Writers on Albania usually adopt the tribal or genealogical method in defining and classifying the divisions of that country, and are generally apt to tread in one another's footsteps without much inquiry how far the extent or value of such divisions may not have been overstated. Thus, M. Cyprien Robert writes of "*Les quatre Albanies*," meaning the districts of the Gheghs, Tosks, Ljaps, and Tchams, the last two, though affiliated with the second, being considered now to stand by themselves as separate divisions. I do not think my readers will thank me or be much the wiser if I fire off into their faces a mere repetition of these uncomfortable, snappish monosyllables, that fail to convey any idea of practical value which is not much better expressed in another way. Besides, such a division leaves out a great deal: ten districts are enumerated by Colonel Leake in his earliest and now rare work ("Researches in Northern Greece and Albania") which do not belong to any of these main branches. The true and intelligible division is that of religious denomination. This has the advantage of coinciding broadly with a natural geographical demarcation, and it also serves to indicate the past history as well as the present condition and future prospects of Albanian civilisation in its three forms—Catholic, Greek, and Mussulman. The true and typical region of the Mussulmans is in the centre; that of the Latins in the northern district, of which Skodra is the chief town; and that of the Albanians in communion with the Greek Church, corresponding with fair accuracy to the limits of Epirus, is in the south, with Ioannina for its capital. In the centre, the Christian population of the towns, such as Berat, Elbassan, &c., is almost entirely of the Eastern Church, and with the Greek language actually or prospectively for its speech. In the north, on the other hand, there are no Greeks, except those so called by the ordinary misuse of the term—that is to say, Sclavonians of the Eastern Church, who are found in the border districts next Montenegro. As a whole, the Christians of the north are Roman Catholics, devotedly attached to their Church. The Mussulmans are everywhere, north, centre, and south; but it is only in the centre that they preponderate so as almost exclusively to form the population.

The germs of civilisation were implanted and nurtured in the north by Italian influence, by the Church of Rome

and the Republic of Venice; in the south, by the Patriarchate of Constantinople and the Byzantine Empire, or
its offshoot, the Despotate of Epirus. The rising tide of
Ottoman conquest either overwhelmed or buried the whole
country. It destroyed the political power of the Greek
Empire in the south, and further deadened the low vitality
of the Patriarchate by turning it into a mere instrument
of control for its own purposes. In the north Skanderbeg
was crushed; and Venice, driven one by one from the
towns she held, was forced to capitulate honourably after
the great siege of Skodra. The mass of the Catholic
population were, however, able to maintain their religion
and a certain amount of independence unmolested, and
had no oppression to complain of. But the growth of
their civilisation was checked; they were cut off from
Europe, and buried from the sight of the world. This
lasted during the palmy days of Ottoman statesmanship
and military prowess; but as weakness and want of con-
trolling power set in at the centre, persecution and oppression, and the long train of evils which always accompany
weakness in a Mahometan state, became rife at the extremities. A large portion of the Catholic population was
then fain to embrace Islam in order to avoid calamity, as
well as, doubtless, to obtain a career of advancement, or
to escape the imputation, and possibly the reality, of being
the allies and tools of hostile Christian states. From the
reports of Venetian ambassadors, we know that this conversion must have been taking place during the last half
of the seventeenth century.[1] The descendants of these

---

[1] From a work, which must be of
great curiosity, published at Palermo
in 1648, under the title of "Anato-
mia dell' Impero Ottomano," and referred to by Colonel Leake ("Researches," &c., p. 250), it appears
that the Albanians were still mainly
Christians at that time. Their insur-
rection is reckoned upon, in common
with that of the other Christians of
the empire, as a means of overthrow-
ing the Turkish rule from within, to
be supported by a European league
from without. This is a curious an-
ticipation of what is supposed to be
the great discovery of anti-Turkish
diplomacy since 1856, internal dislo-
cation substituted for external ag-
gression.

Albanians have retained a great many vestiges of Christianity, not to say of actual ceremonies. This, of course, refers to the mountaineers and country people, not to the townspeople. Thus, for instance, the Mussulmans of Retchi celebrate the feasts of Christmas, Easter, St. Nicholas, and St. George; and in illness or distress they are sure to send for a Catholic priest to pray for them. The tribe of Skreli derives its name from St. Charles—Shen Kerli—to whom it was anciently dedicated; they pay tithes to the Catholic priest, and join in the Church festivals, although professing Islamism. Things have so changed, that at this day the Christian mountaineer has infinitely the advantage over the Mussulman, as he escapes the conscription by avowing his religion.

In 1846 an attempt was made to levy the conscription on one of the true Catholic tribes under the pretext of its being avowedly Mussulman, and was carried out with great atrocity and cruelty towards the victims and their families. Sir Stratford Canning was the first to become acquainted with the circumstances; he interfered promptly and peremptorily; the offending Pashas—Salih of Salonica being the worst—were punished, and the poor Albanians settled at Philadar, a mountain village near Brusa.

At the present moment all the world is forced to hold some opinion or another, whether fairly come by or not, on the subject of nationality. It may, therefore, be instructive to examine that of Albania, and consider how far it is capable of standing by itself, and what value it may assume in any political combination. There is no doubt that the Albanians have a distinctive physical and mental character strongly marked—a character in a greater or less degree common to all. They think of themselves and magnify themselves in common as Albanians, in contrast to their neighbours; they all speak one language, or rather one group of unwritten dialects full of foreign importations, and in its extreme forms, north and south, shading off into all but mutual unintelligibility. Money, force, or dexterous intrigue can unite any or all of them against any part of themselves or any of their neighbours for the purpose of mere depredation, war for war's sake, or pulling down a government. But for want of a common language of cultivation and literature, and not having any religious denomination in common, they are without the two main elements which help to construct and hold together the fabric of a true nation. Having thus no consciousness of political unity, they have in themselves no power of political construction; and therefore, to the eye of the statesman, their nationality is but negative, however much the ethnologist may be justified in treating it as positive and strongly marked. The moment an Albanian enters a church or mosque door, or takes an alphabet in hand and begins his education, he enters upon the first process of his incorporation with the body politic of his neighbours or rulers. The south affords the most striking example of this. Whether the land be held by a Turkish or by a Greek government, the Christian Albanian of the south will ultimately become a Greek to the same extent and through the same causes that the Albanian sailor of Hydra or the Albanian peasant of Attica are and have been slowly changing into Greeks. Nor is it difficult to see how easily and quietly, under these circumstances, with the conscription and the land-tax gradually wearing away the Mussulman population, the country must, in the long process of time, drop off from Turkey and on to Greece, if this impatient generation would but allow time to do its own work. Whether the people will be better off or Greece the better governed is another question. They will at all events, under the strong and special influence of the Greek educational system, have learned to feel that foreign domination is the worst of evils, and to the first generation of freemen freedom will be the one paramount blessing which will atone for any misgovernment.

The Mussulman population of the central and northern

districts seem destined in the same way to mingle and
embody themselves in the general mass of Turkish Mahometans in Europe. Under the rebellious or half-indepen-
dent rule of their countrymen, the old feudal beys or
pashas, they were able to preserve their Albanian individuality untouched. But the entire modern history of
Turkey, from the Egyptian settlement in 1841 to the
war in 1854, lies in the reconquest of its disaffected and
rebellious Mussulman provinces, and the enforced application to them of the new central system of administration.
The Albanian, after two rebellions, was reconquered, and
reduced, like the Koord, the Bosnian, and the Laz of
north-eastern Asia Minor. His old antagonism to the Porte,
though still capable of being turned into an efficient instrument for the work of demolition, is, so far as it was
national, in a fair way of being mitigated under the influence of centralisation. Besides this, the Porte holds in its
hands as a trump card the power of uniting all the people
of Islam by an inflammatory appeal to fanaticism : and
though such statesmen as Fuad Pasha would be strongly
disinclined to play such a card, they may be forced to do
so by the constant menaces of filibusters, by the fanaticism
of Christians, or of Progressionists using Christian watch-
words, or by the persistent want of fair play from Europe
in standing by the spirit of treaties. And such a course
would at once convert him into a reckless and active ally.
At present, if the greedy and corrupt bureaucracy of Constantinople forces him to become its deadly enemy, the
cause will be the same that will also alienate every provincial Turk in the land from rulers of his own race—
namely, the heavy burdens of exclusive conscription and
mismanaged taxation.

It is unsafe to hazard a positive speculation as to the
ultimate future of Northern Catholic Albania. The for-
mative spirit and training power of its old mistress and
teacher, the great Republic of Venice, has now ceased to
act. Italy has enough to do in holding her own against

open foe and uncertain friend for her to influence the
eastern coasts of the Adriatic as yet, though the influence
of Venice in the Levant is her natural inheritance, and
assuredly will be hers some day.   It will be well indeed if
she refrains from premature propagandism for other than
Italian purposes, and from doing the dirty work of other
powers in Turkey under the impulse of blind hostility to
Austria anyhow and anywhere.   The spiritual and moral
superintendence of the Latin Albanians has passed from
Venetian to Austrian hands; and, in quiet times, is likely
to remain there, without being either used as an engine of
political annexation or developed into an organised system
of education and improvement.   Austria is among the
Latin Albanians' what France is among the Maronites;
and, for the matter of that, what she would like to be
among the Latin Albanians too.   But these powers use
their position differently, according to the difference of
their policy in Turkey.   The Turkish government, the
rulers of the land, are content to let both well and ill alone
in these matters.   The Albanians have no cultivated language by which to educate themselves, and easy-going
Austria, though an Italian power, so to speak, in the
Adriatic, cannot put her heart in the work of Italianising
these people, which is the only way of training and edu-
cating them to become a European community.   Nor,
from common interests, and a now active sense of having
to stand or fall with Turkey, to say nothing of good faith
and respect for treaties, has she any wish to annex in this
direction and assume direct rule herself.

It is the misfortune of these Northern Christians that,
unlike their Southern brethren, who are confronted by
Greek influence whichever way they turn, whether to
Greece proper, Thessaly, or the sea, they have no Italian
or Italo-Sclave frontagers of their own religion, and of a
master-language.   Between them and their co-religionists
lies Montenegro, firmly knit together, aggressive and
ardently anti-Catholic.   The idea of their annexation,

together with all Central Albania into the bargain, to the
Montenegrins, a people as wild and savage as themselves,
and, collectively, less numerous, is the opprobrium of the
political ethnology of the Palais Royal, such as we find it
on the famous and useful "Nouvelle Carte de l'Europe"
of 1860. When the Pope sent forth his edict enjoining all
Catholics of the East to make common cause with the Montenegrins against the infidel in 1862, it was at these Latin
Albanians that he was made to speak, in order to detach
them from the Turks. For many generations they had not
heard such language from Rome, and, had it been perse-
vered in, it might have gone some way to make them Pro-
testants, or even Turks, rather than allies of their bitterest
enemy. We may be sure that it was not Austrian influence that sought to convert the Pope into the schismatic's
friend on Albanian ground. These tribes are practically,
and all but nominally, independent of Turkey; as regards
her, they are simply in the position of so many loyal, well-
affected Montenegros; and they will always remain her
faithful allies, so long as those privileges are respected
which they know well how to defend with arms in their
hands. The experiment of detaching these tribes from
Turkey, undermining their allegiance, and substituting the
restless influence of another and greater Catholic power for
the inoffensive, inert supremacy of Austria, in order to
make use of them in any prospective combination, has
been tried before this, and perhaps is still trying. It is a
difficult game, and has failed as yet for want of sufficient
leverage; but who knows how soon the master-hand of the
very able consular artificer who is said to have invented
Montenegro as a diplomatic reality, may be recalled to
the work of setting up and pulling down in Northern
Albania? I hope I may be able one day to believe that
some English department is able to understand and control
these matters of detail both centrally and locally.

REVIEW OF " TRAVELS AND RESEARCHES IN CRETE." [1]

(From the " Pall Mall Gazette" of August 25, 1865.)

THERE is no branch of the public service which does, or has done, more good, in a quiet, unobtrusive way, than the Hydrographic Office at the Admiralty, or one which has greater claims upon our gratitude. Nor is there any part of the world where its services are more conspicuous than in Mediterranean, and especially in Levantine, waters. The priceless advantages therefrom accruing to our own large and increasing trade with the Black Sea, Greece, and the Ottoman Empire, as well as to that of all Europe, compelled to undergo some of the most difficult and dangerous navigation in the world, where a mistake of a mile in the position of any of the innumerable islands and rocks and jutting headlands may be fatal to the navigator, are too obvious to be overlooked, even at first sight. This, however, may be said with equal truth of the China trade and the Malay Archipelago as of the Black Sea trade and the Grecian Archipelago, so far as commerce alone is concerned—or at least might be said, if the Admiralty could be induced to undertake a similar thorough and exhaustive survey in that important quarter of the world, without flinching from the necessary expenditure, and the possible outcry against it by those who only care for immediate tangible results in one block. It is the halo of classical association thrown round every spot of land or sea, and the constant appeal to our imagination and our memories which lies in every local name, that invest the Grecian

---

[1] Review of "Travels and Researches in Crete." By Captain Spratt, Royal Navy, C.B. London: Van Voorst. 1865.

Levant with its peculiar, and, in a secondary degree, its sacred character, and that enhance the services of its scientific explorers. Such travels as those now given to the world by Captain Spratt are thus always sure of our sympathising attention, even though they may be weighted with a good deal of dry antiquarian disquisition, irrespectively of their intrinsic practical or scientific value. Captain Spratt is one of the veterans of the Levantine survey. He is not unknown to the public as an author, having taken his share in a tripartite work of travel and research in Lycia conjointly with Lieutenant Daniell, R.N., and that eminent man of science, the late Professor E. Forbes. In the course of a great many years of exclusive employment in the surveying department, he has probably acquired a greater topographical knowledge of the coasts of the Levant, and, we may add, of the Lower Danube and its mouths, than any other man; and, we may further add, if any man's opinion upon the Suez Canal would be worth having, it would be Captain Spratt's. Much of his time was specially devoted to the island of Crete, minutely explored, traversed, and traced by him in all directions, both by land and by sea. In his present book he has communicated to us some of the miscellaneous results of his Cretan excursions and investigations; putting on one side, or subordinating, of course, the technical and professional matter: those who care for this last may find it in his "Sailing Directions," published by the Admiralty. The book, however, is more antiquarian than anything else.

The hundred-citied island is fortunate in this point, that it has never had an unworthy book written about it; and it stands thereby in the strongest contrast with the mainland of Greece, which, indeed, with the exception of specially geographical, archæological, or artistic works, has never had a really worthy one, except perhaps Lieutenant-Colonel Mure's. In old times, Pococke, Tournefort, the quaint old Scotchman Lithgow, the ornithologist Belon, and numerous Venetians during the rule of the Republic

in Crete, whose various reports have been translated and
edited in the "Classical Museum" by Mr. Falconer, are
the chief narrators of travel in the island. In modern and
very recent times two good French memoranda have been
published, previously appearing in the "Revue des Deux
Mondes:" one by M. Raulin, a geologist; the other by M.
Perrot, author of a work on Asia Minor, which we prefer
to his Cretan Memoir. But the best and most classical of
the modern works is that by the late Mr. Pashley, a Fellow
of Trinity, Cambridge. This is a thoroughly erudite and
scholarly production, naturally chiefly archæological; but,
unfortunately, a selection of particular items rather than a
continuous record of travel. Curiously enough, there is
no such thing as a record of touristic journeying in Crete.
Both in Pashley and in his successor Spratt, personal
narrative is at a minimum, everything being sacrificed to
archæology or natural science. None of the crude people
who write "notions," or travel for bookmaking, nor—at
least until the other day—any adventurous ladies, have
ever been there, or are likely to go there. We should,
therefore, have liked a little more fulness of the personal
element in the present case, and know more of what the
traveller said and did, and eat and drank, and rode, and
what he saw and heard. These points are apt to bore us
considerably in ordinary tours, but then there never have
been such things as tours in Crete which are mere tourism
and nothing else; and we want to be told a little more
about the ordinary everyday life of a traveller there. We
therefore hope that Mr. Lear, the artist, who has lately
rambled all over the island, will complete the set of his
delightful gossiping travels by a work on Crete. Captain
Spratt knows this island by heart, and is familiar with
every inch of the ground, in consequence of some score or
more of journeyings, rather than of one prolonged tour.
When, therefore, he gives us personal narrative, it is generally selected after the manner of his predecessor, Pashley,
and chosen with the object of supplying the deficient parts

of that gentleman's work, and describing the localities unvisited by him. We are accordingly made to roam about, in the present book, all over the island in a perfectly desultory and unsystematic way, after we have been treated to a preliminary panoramic view of the whole country from the peak of Mount Ida in the opening chapter. The worthy Captain, we should state, has a very strong archæological partiality, in which he has taken every opportunity of indulging. When an antiquary appears on the quarter-deck, it is a matter of real thankfulness, considering the constant chances of successful research thrown in his way during his professional service, and we are not, therefore, in the least disposed to repine because Captain Spratt every now and then seems to ride his hobby a little too hard. He has, finally, spared no pains to add to the value of his book by a series of appendices, contributed by various hands, on many subjects incidental to it— on Greek inscriptions found in the island; on the modern dialect; on the geology and ornithology; on deep-sea sounding, Mediterranean currents, and more still. The book, therefore, though certainly too desultory, and, we think, too inartificially put together as a piece of literary workmanship—too unlicked, so to speak—is one of standard value, and distinctly fills a vacuum and supplies a want.

Captain Spratt would probably wish for competent criticism upon his geological chapters rather than on other portions of his work. Competent criticism on geology we cannot undertake to furnish him with, but the importance of his main discovery—the ascertained fact of a difference in level of no less than twenty-two feet in the western coast of the island having taken place within the historical period—is such as to command any reader's immediate attention. The fact by which this difference is demonstrated is the discovery of the old port of the ancient city of Phalasarna standing high and dry above and at a distance from the sea; and Captain Spratt maintains that the agency which produced this was not subsidence of the sea, but upheaval of the land. We have an impression that Sir Roderick Murchison has always supported rather than opposed this theory of upheaval. Whatever may be the ultimate verdict of geologists as to cause, it is certain that the present case is one of great importance in illustrating the value to the antiquarian explorer of a real working knowledge of physical science. Our naval captain's geology stands him in as good stead, and is as indispensable to him, as the Fellow of Trinity's working knowledge of the text of classical authors. The combination of the two acquirements occurred for once in Colonel Leake, the greatest of modern antiquarian geographers, and is hardly likely to occur again. Another good instance of the great gain resulting from current controversies falling into the hands of professional men now and then, and becoming cleared up at once by the necessary technical illustration or evidence, may be seen in Captain Spratt's brief remarks on the much-vexed voyage of St. Paul in Cretan waters. He himself was for some time in the Fair Havens, and on one occasion, when under easy steam, was caught by a real Euroclydon, against which he had the greatest difficulty in making head, even under full power, the gale having acquired a truly typhonic character by rushing down from the high land. It is to this down-rush, rather than to the direction, that, with all due deference to Captain Spratt, we would fain refer the words κατ' αὐτῆς, taking them to mean not "against the ship," but "down upon the ship." The disputed term Euroclydon Captain Spratt unhesitatingly affirms to be the ancient name, either general or local, for the north winds, which prevail during the whole summer all over the region of the Archipelago, known at that time of the year to Levantine sailors by the name of *meltem*, and blowing in the same direction as true winter gales, being from N.N.W., the general point in Crete, to N.N.E., the general point in the central Archipelago up to the Bosphorus and Black Sea. It seems difficult, certainly, to get over the fact that the Eurus was distinctly an easterly wind ; and, as Eurus is represented as a rainy wind, it may even be considered as one to the southward of east. Yet, after all, a local name, once taken up and used as a general term, may ultimately find itself under circumstances locally inapplicable to its new situation. Thus, we may add, the Italian *gregale* for a north-eastern winter gale, probably arising in Sicilian waters, is quite unsuitable to the northern and central coasts, where it is also used, Greece being south-east, not north-east of Italy as a whole. This very *gregale*, much dreaded at Malta, has there decided easting in it, and may well have blown St. Paul from Crete thither. As for Jacob Bryant's paradox, recently revived by Dr. J. M. Neale, that St. Paul's Melita was the Adriatic island, we do not think it worth a moment's regard since the masterly monograph of Mr. Smith of Jordan Hill. The one point on which stress may fairly be laid by the advocates of this last theory, the expression "up and down in Adria," loses all its force if it is borne in mind that "Adria" may well have applied then, as it distinctly does now in current sailor's language, to the entrance of the Adriatic, the Ionian Sea, or the whole wide expanse between Sicily and Greece ;—of which modern usage any reader who happens to go by a Messageries boat from Messina to Athens may be able to convince himself at once. Captain Spratt has so thoroughly realised the scene of St. Paul's gale off Crete that he has given us a beautiful and useful drawing of the actual occurrence, with the position and course of the ship as first caught by the squall. It may be added that a small ruined chapel still exists, as a place of pilgrimage and occasional worship, actually dedicated to St. Paul, on a hill-top near the Fair Havens.

Limestone formations are generally supposed unfriendly to anything like picturesque scenery, but if there be any exception to this rule it must surely be in Crete. Captain Spratt has been most generous to his readers in the mat-

ter of views, and we can see by means of these a certain
uniformity and special character predominant in Cretan
scenery. This seems to consist of a most lovely varied
succession of sweeping bays and bold chalk headlands,
broken occasionally by the deepest and most magnificent
of harbours, stretching far inland, and always backed by
one or the other group of snowy mountains in the west or
the centre, forming a whole which can hardly be rivalled
on the Italian or Grecian coasts, and alone surpassed on the
incomparable southern and south-western shores of Asia
Minor. The Sfakian or White Mountains, in the south-
west, called Madhares by the Cretans, rise abruptly from
the sea to a height of more than 8000 feet—as abruptly
as the mountains around the lakes of Wallenstadt.
Uri, or Riva; and, one would think, if that *race mouton-
nière,* the Alpine people, mostly university men with a
Greek vocabulary ready-made, with money to spend, and
three months to spend it in, cared twopence about climbing for anything beyond mere climbing's sake, they would
at once rush off to these splendid untrodden giants which
guard the eastern portal of the Ægean. It would seem,
however, that we cannot climb anything which does not
fulfil the conditions of being over 10,000 feet high, of
having a glacier on its sides, and a hotel with a tub in it
at its foot. We are not among the sneerers at climbing;
the more climbing the better; only let us now and then
climb for a purpose, and climb among the unvisited
accessible spots of the earth, which are loudly calling out
"Come climb us!"

One special Cretan feature is the upland plains or
basins, surrounded by high mountains, which have no
outlet for their streams, but are drained by means of
katavóthra, or subterraneous passages, common in the
limestone formation along the east of the Adriatic, geo-
logically continuous with Crete, and well known in the
Karst above Trieste—that most weird and uncanny of all
spots on the earth. The basin of Omaló, on the western

range, at 4000 feet, and of Lasíthi in the east, at 3000
feet, are described as being absolute valleys of paradise—
Engadines with the chill off, so to speak—with a climate
of months of the divinest sunshine and freshness. The
Cretan mountains, moreover, have one attraction which we
are astonished that our sportsmen, much more enterprising
and original as a race of pioneers than our climbers, have
not yet found out. Captain Spratt, on his one ascent of
Ida, solemnly avers that he fell in with no less than forty
ibexes, real genuine Homeric ἴξαλοι αἴγες, bounding away
in all directions, and setting at defiance his companion, a
practised Highland deerstalker, from the inaccessible crags
where they stood, "with their ponderous sabre-shaped
horns curved against the western sky." King Victor
Emmanuel, who has so much ado in preserving his handful of ibexes on the Graian Alps, would give his ears for
a day's Cretan shooting, with the game as plentiful as
this; and, indeed, it is ten thousand pities that, if King
Victor Emmanuel cannot go to Crete, Crete, only 150
years ago an Italian island, cannot go to King Victor
Emmanuel. Where the island will go to is clear enough,
we are sorry to say, after reading Captain Spratt's book.
It will go to the bad. Any honest unprejudiced Englishman must feel sickened, sorry, and ashamed, not for his
country, but for other countries, and Europe collectively,
on reading Captain Spratt's unvarnished tale, told in a
subdued tone, of unprincipled efforts made from without,
for no conceivable purpose, to convert the quiet, peace-
able Cretan population into discontented political agents,
to be used as tools in any policy that may turn up. In
this way the dormant flame of nationality was artificially
kindled up into fierce opposition against an enlightened
Turkish governor, who had actually erected a public
school for the use of all religious denominations indiscri-
minately, and whom it was considered desirable by the
consuls of two lately belligerent powers to get rid of.
Captain Spratt's allusive hints, rather than direct narra-

tive, are most valuable, both with regard to the political transactions of 1858, so discreditably set on foot by our previous enemy and the new friend whom he had then detached from our side, and to the general condition of the people. One thing is certain, that in the event of any new complication of the so-called " Eastern question," we shall hear more than we like, and a great deal more than we now know, about the race of savage mountain marauders called Sfakians, who may be defined as a petty or Brummagem Montenegro, only waiting for the breath of diplomatic existence to be breathed into its veins by the sick man's unfriendly doctors. If any prophecy is safe, our readers may rely upon it this one is.

About Cretan Greeks, as well as all other Greeks, we are not going to say one single word; but mean to keep silence on principle, in the hope, albeit we know it is a vain one, of inducing other people to keep silence too. If nobody were to talk about Greece, there would be no philhellenes, and the Greeks would then be rid of their worst incubus —the people who persist in putting them in a false position; they would acquire self-reliance and exercise self-control, and become a very different community to what they now are—an odious, sickly brat to one-half the world, a blessed, sickly pet to the other half. We neither love nor hate Greeks, but wishing them well, like other people, we, in Greek interests, look with horror on the prospective advent to increased power of Mr. Gladstone and the Idealistic platform. The only true friend of the Greek is the Realist, who seeks to take him as he finds him, to learn him from the foundation upwards, read him by daylight, correct and improve him where he is bad, and make a man of him, instead of simpering at him as a woman, and bothering about the classical world. Heaven help him if the sick man dies, or is smothered, before his own frame has hardened into national manhood, or reached national adolescence! If Heaven does not, Fr—, some other power, we mean, will, for he cannot help himself.

Captain Spratt's reduction of his own Admiralty chart, constructed with so much labour and accuracy, cannot be too much praised. We wish he had spelt his Greek names uniformly, reduced to some system, Leake's Italianising method being much the best to our taste. Ψηλορείτης and Νίδα (from τὴν Ἴδα), the modern names of Mount Ida and its highest basin, are both intelligible at sight, and pronounceable if we write Psiloriti and Nidha; but to write Pseeloreetee and Neetha is treating Greek like a South Sea jargon, or Hindostanee at best; nor in Neetha do you see which *th* is the right, whether as in *think* or in *those*. The ultra-pedantic method of the Hellenizers, Hypsêloreition, we consider to be the one thing which the Realistic school in modern Greek should seek to extirpate without quarter.

ON CRETAN AND MODERN GREEK.[1]

COLLOQUIAL modern Greek (its slight and loose-fitting Turkish and Italian elements apart) is spoken with tolerable uniformity in nearly all the districts where it is the vernacular language. It is thereby strongly contrasted with the countless dialectic variations, falling into four main types, ultimately reducible to two, which characterised the ancient Greek of the early and the classical period. This uniformity arose from the diffusion of Attic as the basis of a common dialect after the Macedonian conquests. It continued its progress during the Roman dominion, and was at length fully established under and by means of the centralisation of the Byzantine Empire.[2] A quasi-classical dialect, retaining the ancient grammar and vocabulary to the best of the speaker's ability and knowledge, was spoken in formal life at Constantinople by the Court, the Patriarchate, and the upper classes until the Turkish conquest; but the popular language of everyday life had gradually assumed a form essentially identical with the speech of the present day in grammar, and only differing

[1] Reprinted from "Travels and Researches in Crete." By Captain Spratt, R.N., C.B. 2 vols., 8vo. London, 1865.

[2] The fancy of calling modern Greek the " Æolo-Doric," which originated with the poet Christopulo, and has since been taken up by dilettante students of modern Greek among ourselves, is but a fancy. It would be easy to show two Ionisms for one Æolism or Dorism in it. Such seeming cases of either peculiarity as occur here and there, probably arise from the natural growth of phonetic change, rather than from any retention of the ancient form.

in vocabulary by the absence of Turkish, the comparative absence of Italian, and the retention of some Latin words. The forms and idiom of the modern language are at least as old as the tenth century. Its pronunciation, certainly not classical, is much older than that date; and though its various peculiarities are by no means all of the same uniform degree of antiquity, some of them probably belong to the later classical epoch.[1] The long period during which Byzantine centralisation exercised its influence was sufficient to establish this popular speech, so formed, with a minimum of variation in all parts of the empire; so that true provincial dialects, analogous in any degree to those of Italy or England, are only found in remote and outlying islands, or in districts early detached from the rest by Mahometan or Frank conquest. Provincial dialects, in fact, are only found in a form more or less marked in the ratio of the greater or less historical independence of the provinces during the Lower Empire.

Putting aside the interesting dialect of the Greek peasantry at the back of Trebizond, and the Tzakonic dialect, still spoken in a few villages on the east coast of Laconia

---

[1] We in England cannot teach scholastically a foreign and a dead language like the Hellenic with the simultaneous retention of both accent and quantity, nor can we conceive without effort how any language can have been so pronounced. Yet they did undoubtedly coexist in pronunciation for a long period, without either interfering with the other, when ancient Greek was a living language. To comparative philologists such a coexistence is not only intelligible, but seems a matter of course. Our classical scholars, being generally unacquainted with the existence or nature of other Aryan languages akin to Greek, do not bear in mind the fact that to this day the Lithuanian of East Prussia fully retains the simultaneous use of tone-accent and quantity: and the same is the case in Illyrian or Servian—to say nothing of the accentual system of Vedic Sanskrit, strongly allied to that of the Greek. Nor can the modern Greek, for his part, conceive how, for example, his ancestors' words εἰμί, πλατύς, could be pronounced by accent, yet without the accent changing the time of the vowel from short to long as in his own pronunciation. Recent Lithuanian grammars will teach him how this is done in the corresponding words esmì, platùs, of that remarkable language. Controversy on the subject of Hellenic pronunciation is simply worthless and a waste of time, unless based on the principles established by the comparative study of the Aryan tongues.

(which, indeed, is not a dialect of modern Greek at all, but the representative of the ancient speech of the Kaukones,[1] being a sub-dialect of the ancient Doric come down to us in a state of extreme corruption, yet not without traces of even pre-Hellenic antiquity), the main body of modern Greek speech may be considered as tending to diverge into two types, which it is convenient to call the continental and the insular. This, of course, has reference only to the speech of the uneducated, the sole refuge of true dialects in our time: the educated (and they are more numerous in proportion to the population in Greek countries than anywhere else in Europe, as regards the elements of education and something more) speak the same language everywhere. The most marked test of the two divisions, among many others of idiom and vocabulary and some of forms, is to be found in the third person plural of verbs, ending on the continent and in the standard speech in -ν, but in the islands in -σι. Thus λέγουσι or λέσι, εἴπασι, 'κτυπήσασι are said in the latter for λέγουν or λένε, εἴπαν or εἴπανε, 'κτυπήσανε. The speech of the islands shades off into its extremest variation in the south-eastern group, in Chios, in Rhodes, in Cyprus, and in Crete. In the last two islands it may be said most nearly to amount to true dialect; but the deviation even there is very far short of the absolute mutual unintelligibility which we see in, for instance, the "Exmoor Scolding," when contrasted with the Lancashire of "Tim Bobbin," or even in the difference between two adjacent Italian dialects, such as Turinese and Milanese, or Neapolitan and the polished Sicilian of the Abbate Meli. Cretan has even a literature of its own, formed in direct imitation of that of Italy during the Venetian domination. The "Erotókritos," a long half-heroic half-chivalrous poem by **Vincenzo Cornaro**, is the earliest

---

[1] The common derivation of Tzakonia from Laconia involves a letter-change which is quite untenable. The change of κα into τζα has several analogies, as τζακίζω, τζακόνω, &c., "I break, work mischief, quarrel," &c., from κακός. It is scarcely the softening of the k, which has happened in most languages, but which Greek has for the most part strangely escaped.

of these. It was written in the sixteenth century (at the end of the sixteenth or beginning of the seventeenth, according to Leake; but shortly before 1737, according to Mr. E. A. Sophocles); its Cretan character is well marked, and parts of it are said even now to be remembered and recited by the Cretan peasantry, much as parts of Tasso by the Venetian gondoliers. The "Voskopúla," or Shepherdess, a pastoral poem by one Nikóla of Apokórona, and the "Erophile," a tragedy, of which the story and title, as well as the method and style, were taken from the Italian, have also come down to us. The latter has many Cretan peculiarities: it also contains perhaps the earliest instance of Italian metre applied to Greek, such as has since become a favourite form of versification in the Ionian Islands, and is so delightful to read in the humorous political flings of Lascarato.

The dialect now spoken is described by Pashley as differing from that of the above books to some extent, principally by the admixture of Turkish words which have crept in since the conquest of the island by the Porte; but these, after all, are but few, and it must be borne in mind that the authors of these works, though they did not go out of their way to avoid provincialism, yet certainly did not seek to represent its peculiarities in full. A few songs taken down by Pashley, a specimen or two in M. Khurmúzi's work on Crete, a long vampire-story given by Mr. Pashley in the words of his Sfakiot guide, and the talk of the Cretan in a play by M. Khurmúzi, the author of the present vocabulary, constitute all the written specimens of modern Cretan known to me. This last production, called "Babel" (ἡ Βαβυλωνία, ἡ κατὰ τόπους διαφθορὰ τῆς Ἑλ-ληνικῆς γλώσσης), is what we should term a "screaming farce," and is exceedingly entertaining. It will remind classical scholars, and those who look at everything of modern Greek through ancient Greek magnifying-glasses, of the plays of Aristophanes; in reality it and similar modern comedies, like so much else that is modern Greek, are partly Italian, partly Turkish in their origin and character. A number of Greeks are celebrating the victory of Navarino in a wine-shop; an Albanian becomes quarrelsome in his cups and fires his pistol at a Cretan, who has taxed the Albanian with having come to Crete and eaten up all the κουράδια in the island. The Cretan uses the word as meaning " sheep;" but the Albanian takes it in the sense it bears everywhere else, that of σκατά, being in fact, the ordinary gross oriental idiom with which readers of Morier's novels are familiar under the veiled translation of " eating dirt." A row ensues, and an Ionian Dogberry comes in and marches everybody off to prison. The fun of the play, which is exceedingly rich and well kept up, lies in the attempts made by the Ionian to get at a coherent story from the different witnesses when cross-examined : he talks something which is as much Italian as Greek, and he has to do with an Asiatic Greek whose idioms are mere Turkish, with a schoolmaster who will talk ancient Greek, with a rough Moreote merchant, and so on. The confusion which arises is, of course, much exaggerated, and is impossible in real life, but it is very amusing. The Cretan, unfortunately, being wounded, has little share in the dialogue, but enough is given to show the nature of the dialect.

Differences of accent prevail among the Cretan provinces—probably slight, and as imperceptible to foreigners as those which exist between different provinces or counties in Ireland, and are to be detected by natives alone. This is generally the case in Greece; and it requires experience to enable a stranger to distinguish even an Ionian islander's accent from that of a continental; nothing at all is met with corresponding to the difference between our west-countrymen and north-countrymen. In Crete, the leading distinction is between the mountaineers, or Ἀπανωμερίταις, and lowlanders, or Κατωμερίταις. Concurrently with this, the provinces group themselves into districts—the western, the Sfakian, that of Retimo and the neighbourhood of

Mount Ida, that of Megalokastron, the Eastern, and the South Central (comprising the two provinces of Pyrghió-tissa and Kenúrion). The differences are to be defined as germs of dialect rather than actual dialect; a few special words and a local accent seem to constitute the whole amount: thus Σταμόνα (i.e., στάσου μόνος), *Hold hard, be quiet*, is peculiar to Lashíthi, and ἔρωτας, for the Cretan dittany, to Mylopótamo.

The speech of the **Sfakiots** is distinguished from that of the rest of the island by the persistent substitution of ρ for λ, by some difference in their vocabulary, and by general retention of the extreme Cretan type. Owing to their secluded position and little intercourse with the rest of the island, they have been sheltered from the influence of the modern Greek educational system, elsewhere so strong and all-pervading. But this system, bearing for its first-fruits an ardent surface-desire for national union and centralis-ation, which, so long as foreign domination endures, and until he attains his wishes, is sufficient to stifle the original municipal instinct and naturally centrifugal tendency of the true Greek in all ages, has taken firm root in the island. This must end by obliterating all but the faintest traces of a popular dialect, there as elsewhere—displacing a real form of speech which might have been made to bear the same relation to classical Greek that Italian bears to Latin, and substituting in its stead a strange language, now, per-haps, unavoidable and past remedy, in which a revived or fictitious ancient vocabulary is galvanised, rather than animated, by the idiom of modern French newspaper-writing.

It is in words rather than forms that Cretan is best distin-guished from the dialect of other islands. Many of these are classical words lost elsewhere, or are otherwise of interest to the philologist. Of the first class are κατέχω ("I know") for the common ἠξεύρω, πέμπω (θὰ πέψω) for στέλνω, θὰ θέσω for θὰ βάλω, ἄγομαι for πηγαίνω, and πορίζω for βγαίνω, derivatives of νέμω and ψέγω in ἐγγαλονόμος, ξερονόμι, ψεγάδι; ἀρίδι (ἄρις[1]), "a gimlet;" ἀροδαμός for ὀρόδαμνος[2], "a twig;" χαλέπα (from χαλεπός), "a difficult hill;" φθαρμός[7], "the evil eye," (from ὀφθαλμός; the ploughman's cries of ἄνω, ἔσω, &c.; σκλώπα for σκώπα from σκώψ, "an owl;" ἔδιωξε, "it has occurred to me," very probably[3] for ἔδοξε—an excellent preservation, δοκῶ being utterly lost,—with many others, The Italian words differ from those in use elsewhere, as βετέμα[4], "a crop," It. vendemmia; ροζονάρω, "I speak," It. ragionare; μαρτί, "a fatted sheep" (i.e., fatted for the festival of San Martino); βιτσάτο, "thin," i.e., poor or vitiated; πούρι, the It. pure, used as a mere expletive or weight-giver to the phrase, like γιαμά (from the It. giammai) in the Southern Ionian Islands, or μαθές at Smyrna; ματινάδα, "a popular song," and many others.   There are a few points indicating some special connection or intercourse with the Southern Morea. Besides the local name of Tzákonas (distinctly indicating a colony from the mainland), in Leake's vocabulary of the Tzakonic dialect we find κέφαλ' ἀρία, written in two words, interpreted τὸ κεφάλι μου πονεῖ, "my head aches."   But it is manifestly the Cretan κεφαλαρία[6], i.e., κεφαλαλγία, for the ordinary πονοκέφαλο[5], a headache, with the Cretan change of λ into ρ: νομεῖς or νομεῖαι, again, for shepherds, are only found elsewhere in the Cretan words given above. Some local names, chiefly in the western promontory of Crete, contain the patronymic termination usual among the Mainotes, but nowhere else (-άκος, as in Leotzákos, Dimitrákos, Dimitrakarákos)—Spaniákos, Priniákos, Mustákos, Trakıniákos, &c.   To these may be added the name Kalamatianà in proof of Moreote affinity.   The natural bridge is the island of Cerigo.   But half a century's routine occupation of this island, a most primitive and secluded district, has now ended without a scrap of information on its dialectic or indeed any other peculiarities having once been contributed to the public knowledge by the apathetic ruling race.   It may here be said that the local name Sklavokhóri, occurring more than once in Crete, shows that the island was not without its share of Slavonian settlements; and the name Katzivelianà (from κατσίβελος, fem. κατσιβέλα, like γύφτος or τσιγγενές, " a gypsy") must indicate a gipsy colony. Of dialect, properly speaking, contemporary with, or even prior to classical Greek, it is, perhaps, just possible to detect a trace here and there. Ἄρκαλος, " a badger," seems to be connected somehow with ἄρκτος, ἄρκος, whence the modern ἀρκοῦδι. Apokórona, the modern name of the ancient Hippokoronion, may possibly preserve, as in Cyprus, a Cretan vernacular pronunciation of the word ἵππος (ἵκϜος, originally akvas), retaining the original initial vowel as perfectly as we see it in the East-Aryan or Indo-Persian and the Lithuanian corresponding words, well known to comparative philologists (açva, aspa, aszwà), slightly modified in the Gothic and Celtic words and the Latin *equus*, further modified in the classical Greek, but wonderfully maintained to this day in Cyprus: ἄππαρος or ἄππαρον is there used for the Cretan κτῆμα and the ordinary ἄλογον. It must be remembered, with regard to this word, that in Cyprus a doubled consonant is still really a doubled consonant, pronounced as clearly as in Italian or Arabic: thus ἄλλο is not pronounced as a modern Greek pronounces it, but like the Italian *allo* —an invaluable relic of Hellenic pronunciation, which is alone enough to make the Cyprian dialect outweigh all the others in philological importance.

I subjoin a Cyprian view of the Cretan dialect, taken from the " *Vavilonia*." Οἱ Κρητιτζοὶ μιλοῦσιν τὰ λωὰ τὰ λόγια τους, καὶ τὴν ἀχελομαλοῦσα λέσιν τη νύφη, τὸ λαμπρὸν λέσιν το φωτιὰ, τὸν ἄπαρο λέσιν το χτῆμα, καὶ ταῖς κουδέλαις λέσιν ταις κουράδια.

In this it is the Cretan whose words, except the last one, are the same as the ordinary Greek, and the Cyprian that deviates. Ἀχελομαλοῦσα, " eel-ringleted one," for the common νύφη or νύμφη, " bride," is worth noting in this last dialect. Ἄπαρο is here spelt with only one π; but this must be mere carelessness: I have twice heard the

II

word pronounced with a π doubled, and by Cyprians in each instance—one a gardener, the other a professor. Before proceeding to give M. Khurmùzi's vocabulary, I cannot refrain from quoting from the body of his little work the following form of disenchantment used for the relief of eye-stricken or bewitched persons, not only as a long specimen of Cretan dialect, but also for its curiosity as a bit of " folk-lore."

Πιστεύουσι τὰς νεραΐδας, τὰ φαντάσματα, τὰ στοιχειά, τὴν βασκανιάν, τὰς μαγείας, τρέμουν τὰς κατάρας, κ. τ. λ., καὶ εἰς μὲν τὸν τόπον ὅπου ὑποπτευθῶσιν ἢ ἀκούσουν ὅτι κατοικοῦν νεραΐδες ἢ στοιχειά, παντελῶς δὲν πλησιάζουν· ἂν δὲ κατὰ δυστυχίαν περάσῃ τις ἀπ' ἐκεῖ ἢ κοιμηθῇ πλησίον, καὶ ἀσθενήσῃ, ἢ εὐθὺς ἢ μετὰ καιρόν, τότε λέγουν ὅτι ἔχει βυστιριά, τῆς ὁποίας τὸ ἀντιφάρμακον εἶναι τὸ διάβασμα. Τὴν δὲ βασκανιάν, τὴν ὁποίαν ὀνομάζουν, φθαρμόν[1], ἐξορκίζουν οὕτω τὰ γραΐδια· δένει (τὸ γραΐδιον) τρεῖς κόκκους ἅλατος εἰς τὴν ἄκραν ἑνὸς μανδηλιοῦ, καὶ ἀφ' οὗ τὸ μετρήσῃ μὲ τὸν πῆχυν του, πλησιάζει εἰς τὸν ἀσθενῆ, ἐγγίζει τὸν κόμπον (μὲ τὸ ἄλας) εἰς τὸ μέτωπόν του, ἔπειτα εἰς τὴν γὴν τρεῖς φοραῖς λέγον " εἰς τὸ ὄνομα τοῦ Πατρὸς κ. τ. λ." ἔπειτα ἀρχίζει " Ποῦ πᾶς φθαρμέ[2], ποῦ πᾶς κακέ, ποῦ πᾶς κακαποδομένε ; φύγε ἀπὸ τὰς 72 φλέβας[3] τοῦ παιδιοῦ μου (δεῖνα) καὶ ἄμε στὰ ὄρη στὰ βουνά, ποῦ πετεινὸς δὲν κράζει καὶ σκύλος δὲ γαυγίζει, νάυρης τ' ἄγριο θεριὸ νὰ πιῇς ἀπ' τὸ αἷμά του νὰ φᾶς ἀπ' τὸ κρέας του (χασμιριέται[4])· ἐλούσθηκ[5] ἡ κιουρά[6] μας ἡ Παναγία, κτενίσθηκε[7] καὶ στὸ θρονί της κάθισε[8] καὶ περάσασιν οἱ ἀγγέλοι οἱ ἀρχαγγέλοι καὶ φθαρμίσασί[9] την (χασμιριέται), καὶ πάγει ἀφέντης ὁ χριστὸς καὶ τῆς[10] λέγει· ' ἠντά 'χεις μάνα ἠντά 'χεις[11] μητέρα ;' 'ἐλούσθηκα[12] παιδί μου χτενίσθηκα[14] καὶ στὸ θρονί[13] μου κάθισα καὶ περάσασ' οἱ ἀγγέλοι οἱ ἀρχαγγέλοι καὶ φθαρμίσασί[15] με' (χασμιριέται)· ' καλὲ μάνα, καλὲ μητέρα, δὲν εὑρέθηκε χριστιανὸς ἁγιασμένος καὶ τὴν ἁγιὰ Πέφτη λουτουργηγμένος, νὰ πάρ' ἄλάτσι ἀπ' τὴν ἁλικὴ[16], ἢ τρία φύλλ' ἀπ' τὴν ἐλιά, καὶ νὰ 'πῇ μιὰ φορὰ τὸ Πάτερ ἡμῶν, δύο φοραῖς τὸ Πάτερ ἡμῶν (ἕως τὰς ἐννέα).' "
Τὸν ἐξορκισμὸν τοῦτον τὸν λέγει τρὶς χασμουριούμενον συγ-

χρόνως, ἔπειτα ξαναμετρᾷ μὲ τὸν πῆχύν του τὸ μανδῆλι,
καὶ το βγάζει κοντώτερον 6 δάκτυλα ἀπὸ τὸ πρῶτον
μέτρον.

"They believe in the Neraïdes,[1] in apparitions, ghosts,
the evil eye, and witchcraft; they dread curses, &c.; and
they never by any chance go near any place which they
suspect or hear to be haunted by the water-nymphs or
ghosts. If, by ill-luck, any one should pass by or sleep
in such a neighbourhood, and should then happen to fall ill,
either at once or after some time, they say of him that he
has the Vistirià, the proper antidote to which is reading
Scripture over him. As for the evil eye, by them called
Phtharmòs, it is exorcised by old women in this way.
The old woman ties up three grains of salt in the end of a
handkerchief, measures it along her arm, and then touches
the sick man's forehead with the knot, and afterwards
touches the ground three times with it, saying, 'In
the name of the Father,' &c. After which she begins,
'Whither goest, evil eye? whither goest, wretch? whither
goest, miserable one? Fly out of the seventy-two veins
of my son So-and so, and be off to the mountains and
hills, where no cocks crow and no dogs bark, to find the
wild beast, that you may drink his blood and eat his flesh
(she yawns). Our Lady[2] the Virgin has bathed and
combed herself, and sat on her throne, and the angels
and archangels have passed by, and have bewitched her
(yawns); and the Lord Christ goes by and says to her,

[1] These modern nymphs are called
by the name of the ancient Nereids,
but their attributes are those of the
Naiads. As the ancient word νηρός,
whence their name was derived (as
also the common modern word for
water), is not limited to salt water, it
is possible that this usage may be of
high antiquity in the vernacular.

[2] κιουρά, for κυρά, being like our
conventional English pronunciation
of υ. This is found in ancient dialects, as τὰν τιούχαν for τὴν τύχην

in a Bœotian inscription, and is a
marked characteristic of the Tzakonic dialect. Υ, probably pronounced like the French u in the
later classical, the Roman, and the
early Byzantine periods, has retained
or reverted to its earlier sound in a
very large number of words belonging to the colloquial language, now
written with ου. Similarly, words
like θεριό, ξερό, σίδερο must have
arisen out of the earlier sound of η
as a long ε.

" What is it, my mother,[1] what is the matter ? "   " I have bathed, my son, and combed myself, and sat on my throne, and the angels and archangels have passed by me and bewitched me" (yawns).   " Well, mother, no Christian has been found [query, can no Christian be found ?] made holy by the Eucharist and by church service on Holy Thursday, to take salt from the salt-cellar, or three leaves from the olive tree, and say, Our Father, &c., once, Our Father, &c., twice (up to nine times)." '   The old woman utters this exorcism three times, yawning at the same time, and then measures the handkerchief over again along her arm, bringing it out shorter than the first measurement by six fingers."

In concluding these brief remarks, I cannot do better than refer such of my readers as may be desirous of obtaining clear and correct views upon the very interesting subject of the true origin and growth of modern Greek, a subject hitherto always treated confusedly, with party spirit, and with insufficient knowledge, to the admirable summary which forms the preface of Mr. E. A. Sophocles's (of Cambridge, Mass., U.S.A.) " Dictionary of Later and Byzantine Greek."

---

[1] ἤντα is generally used for τί in Chios and the south-eastern islands. Koraës explains it as a contraction of τί εἶναι τὰ (for ἁ); as τί εἶναι τὰ λέγεις for τί λέγεις, " what is it you are saying ? " for " what are you saying ? " the intermediate τῆντα being found in the earliest modern Greek poetry of the Turkish period.

VOCABULARY OF CRETAN GREEK.

A.

Cretan Greek.	Modern Greek.	
ἀγκοῦσα[1]	. στενοχωρία	Oppression, *uneasiness.*
ἄγομαι . .	. πηγαίνω	I go.
ἀθιβολή .	. ὑπόθεσις, ὁμιλία	Business, affair.[2]
ἄθος . .	. στάκτη	Ashes.
αἰγούγια .	. ἀλοίμονον	Alas!
ἀκάτεχος .	. ἀνίδεος, ἄπρακτος	A man without experience.
ἀναβόλεμα .	. ἀνήφορος	An ascent, a hill (going or looking upwards).
ἀναγκεμένοι	. φρενοβλαβεῖς, πάσχοντες . .	Madmen, those afflicted in mind.
ἀνάδια[3] . .	. ἄντικρυ	Opposite.
ἀναλαμπή .	. φλόγα[4]	Flame.[5]
ἀναλώματα .	. ἀκαταστασίαι πολιτικαί .	Political disturbances.
ἀναντρανίζω	. βλέπω ἀσκαρδαμυκτί[6] . . .	To look fixedly.[7]
ἀναστοροῦμαι	. ἐνθυμοῦμαι	I remember.
ἄνω . . .	. λέγουν τοὺς βόας ὅταν γεωργοῦν νὰ κλίνουν πρὸς τὸ ἀγεώργητον	The word ἄνω is used to the oxen when they are tilling the ground, to direct them to the part unploughed.
ἀπαρθινά .	. ἀληθινά	True.
ἀποβολή .	. ἀντὶ τοῦ ἴχνους, διότι ζητοῦντες τι ζῶον καὶ εὑρόντες τὴν κόπρον του λέγουν· ἰδοὺ ἡ ἀποβολή του.	This term is used when they come upon the trace of a lost animal ; and when they find its manure they say, literally, "droppings."
ἀπόγι . .	. ἀγιάζι	Hoar frost, dew.
ἀπομονάροι[8]	. ἐναπολειφθέντες, ζῶντες .	Survivors.
ἀπορόχια[9] .	. βρουβοβλάσταρα	Lichen, or seaweed.
ἀποταχυάς .	. πρὶν	Before.
ἀπύρι . .	. θειάφι	Brimstone.
ἀραγός . .	. ἀσκὶ μικρόν, ἀσκόπουλο . .	A small water-skin.
ἀργατινή[10] .	. ἑσπέρα	Evening.
ἀρίδι . .	. τρυπάνι	Gimlet.
ἄρκαλος .	. ἄσβος	Badger.
ἀροδαμός[11] .	. βλαστὸς νέος τῶν ἐλαιῶν .	A young olive-shoot.
ἄρτικας . .	. ἀγριοσέλινον, μαγκοῦτα . .	Wild parsley.
ἀφόρεσι . .	. ὑποψία	Suspicion.
ἀφορμάρης[12]	. φρενήρης	Mad, hot-headed.
ἀφόρμησι[13]	. φρενοβλαβία	Madness.

Cretan Greek.	Modern Greek.	
ἀφοροῦμαι .	. ὑποπτεύομαι	. I suspect.
ἀτσέλεγος[1]	. σπορ$γί$της	. Sparrow.
ἄχνα . . .	. σιωπή, τζιμουδιά[2]	. Silence, quiet.[3]

B.

βαβούρα[4] .	. βοή.	. A shout or cry.
βαρεμένη .	. ἔγκυος	. A woman in the family-way.
βαστάγι .	. σχοινάκι	. A small rope.
βετέμα[5] .	. εὐφορία ἐλαιῶν	. Good olive-crop.
βίσαλα .	. κεράμια, τοῦβλα	. Tiles, bricks.
βιτσάτο* .	. λιγνόν	. Lean.
βλάβος[6] .	. ἔχει βλάβος, ὁ τόπος εἶναι	Sickness, unhealthiness (said
	νοσώδης.[7]	of places).[8]
βλεπάτωρας .	δραγάτης	. A vine-dresser[9]
βλέπησι .	. προσοχή[10].	. Attention.[11]
βλέπομαι .	. προφυλάττομαι, προσέχω ἐμαυ-	I take care of myself, I look
	τόν.	out.
βοσκήθηκα .	. ἐχόρτασα	. I am satisfied, or have eaten
		enough.
βούργια .	. σακούλι	. A[12] bag.
βουργίδι .	. σακουλάκι	. A small[13] bag.
βυστιριά .	. ἀσθένεια προερχομένη ἀπό	Sickness which comes from
	στοιχεῖα, ἀερικό.	malevolence of ghosts.

Γ.

γέρα . . .	. γηρατεῖα	. Old age.
γαργερός .	. λερωμένος	. Dirty.
γγαλονόμος .	ποιμὴν τῶν προβάτων ἀλμεγο-	The shepherd in charge of
('γγαλο- for	μένων.	milch ewes.
ἐγγαλο-).		
γιαγέρνω .	. ἐπιστρέφω	. I return.
γιοργά[14] .	. ὀγρήγορα, καὶ ἰδιαιτέρως τὸ	Quickly (properly said of the
	ταχὺ βῆμα τῶν ζώων.	brisk pace of animals).
γιότσα .	. ἀποπληξία	. Apoplexy.
γκαύτω[15] .	. ἀναχωρῶ	. I start, quit, go.
γλακηχτής .	ταχύπους[16]	. One who walks fast.[17]
γλακῶ .	. τρέχω	. I run.
γουλέ[18] .	. κομάτι	. A morsel.
γυολίδι .	. κομάτι, κεφαλοτύρι	. A piece of, the top of a
		cheese.

Δ.

δακτυλίδωμα .	ἀρραβῶνα	. Betrothal.
δάμακας .	. ξηρότοιχος	. A bare wall, without mortar.

---

* Literally "vitiated."

Cretan Greek.	Modern Greek.	
δαμάκι[1]	. . ὀλίγο	A little.
δαμινή .	. . σιαγανή[2]	Slow.
δέτης	. . . βράχος μικρὸς[3] εἰς εἶδος τοίχου.	A small rock[4] in the shape of a wall.
δευτερογούλης	ἰούλιος	July.
διαρμίζω	. . βάζω εἰς τάξιν, συγυρίζω . .	I arrange.
διμηνήτης .	. εἶδος σίτου μελανοῦ διαμένοντος δύω μῆνας εἰς τὴν γῆν.	A kind of brown wheat which remains for two months in the ground.
δόμοι .	. . . λωρίον εἰς πολλὰς δίπλας ῥαμέ- νον, καὶ τιθέμενον ὑπὸ τὰ ὑπο- δήματα (κόθορνοι).	A piece of leather thong which is closely folded and used by shepherds for the soles of their shoes against the slipperiness and wear of their mountains.
δροσιά .	. . τίποτε	Nothing.
δῶρον .	. . τίποτε	Nothing. But used by the Cretan sometimes when asking for a present or gift (using the true Greek word instead of the Orien- tal μπαχσίσι commonly used elsewhere).

E.

ἔγγαλα	. . τὰ ἀλμεγόμενα[5]	Milch ewes.[6]
ἐδά .	. . . τώρα	Now.
ἐδιωξε .	. . . μοῦ ἦλθε κατανοῦν, μὲ ἐφάνη νά τὸ κάμω οὕτω.	I remembered it has come into my head, &c.[7]
ἐπά	. . . ἐδώ	Here.
ἐργῶ	. . . κρυόνω	I feel cold.
ἐρωτας[8]	. . δίκταμος	The Cretan dittany, concern- ing which there is much in Tournefort and Pashley.
ἔσω	. . . νὰ κλίνουν οἱ βόες, ὅταν γεωρ- γοῦν πρὸς τὸ γεωργημένον.	Is used in directing the oxen to approach the ploughed part when they are tilling the ground, as ἄνω, to send them to the unploughed.
ἔχνος	. . . ζῶον	A domestic animal, as dog, cat, fowl, &c.[9]

Z.

ζάλο	. . . βῆμα	A pace or step.
ζημιό	. . . λοιπόν	Therefore, however, then.

Cretan Greek.	Modern Greek.	
ζουγλός	ἀνάπηρος (σακάτης)	Lame or disabled.[2]
ζυγόνω	κυνηγῶ[3]	I sport, or hunt.[4]
ζουρίδα	κουνάδι	Polecat or stoat.

Θ.

θές (common everywhere as well as Crete).	θέλεις	Do you wish?
θέσε	πλάγιασε	Lie down, or repose.
θέττω[5]	πλαγιάζω	I lie down to sleep.

Κ.

κεφαλαριά	κεφαλόπονος	A headache.
κακαποδομένος	ἄθλιος[6]	A miserable man.[7]
κακαποδώνω	δυστυχῶ	I am unfortunate.
κακαφόρεσι	ὑποψία	Suspicion.
κακόσορτος (common all over the islands)	κακότυχος, ταλαίπωρος	An unfortunate man.
κακασύβαστος	δύστροπος	A perverse man.
καλουργιά	τὸ πρῶτον γεώργημα	The first cultivation or break-up of land.
καμνίζω[8]	χαμηλύνω, κλείω τὰ βλέφαρα	I look downwards, shut the eyelids.[9]
καμπανίζω	ζυγιάζω	I weigh.
καμπανός	στατέρι	Scales, steelyard.
κανάκια	χάδια	Caressing.
κανακεμένος	χαδεμένος	One who is caressed.
κανακεύω	χαδεύω	I caress, soothe, flatter.
καρφίχτης	καθρέπτης	A looking-glass.
κάσα	λέρα	Dirt.
καταλῶ	φθείρω	To destroy.
καταχανάς	βρουκόλακας	A vampire (see an entire chapter in Pashley).
κατεχάρης	εἰδήμων	A man with his wits about him.
κατέχω	γινώσκω, ἠξεύρω	I know.
κατηγορημένη	ἀδύνατος	A feeble woman.
κατίνα	ῥάχη	Back.
κεντιά[10]	σφάχτης	Acute pain, twinge.
κεντῶ	ἀνάπτω	I light.
κιασουλιάς	καθόλου	At all (ordinary modern Greek, κιόλας).
κοιλιοδρόμι	διάῤῥοια	Diarrhœa.

Cretan Greek.	Modern Greek.	
κοιτάζει	. . κουρμιάζει	(The hen) is sitting.
κοίτη	. . . ὀρνιθόσπητον	Hencoop.
κοκοσάλι[1]	. . χαλάζι	Hail.
κομπόνουμαι	. ἀπατῶμαι	I am deceived.
κοπέλι	. . . παιδίον	A boy.
κοπελιάρης	. ἔφηβος	A young man.
κορμιάζω	. . μουδιάζω	To have a limb asleep, to jar upon the nerves.
κορμός	. . . νεοσσὸς περιστερᾶς, πιπίνι	A young pigeon.
κοῦβος	. . . φραγκόκοτα, γάλλος	A turkey.
κουζουλός(com- ἀνόητος, βλάξ		A silly fellow.
mon elsewhere)		
κουνενός	. . ὑδροδοχεῖον πήλινον	An earthen jug.
κουράδι	. . κοπάδι	A flock, or herd.
κούρταλα	. . χειροκτυπήματα, παλαμάκια	The clapping of hands.
κουτσουνάρα	. βρύσις αὐτόματος[2]	A fountain, or natural spring.[3]
κρεμαστά	. . κάτωθεν τοῦ σημείου, ὑπὸ τὸν	Under the mark or object
	σκοπόν	indicated. (Opposed to σκεπαστά.)
κτῆμα	. . . κτῆνος	A beast of burden or labour.
κτηματσερός	. ὄνος	An ass.

Λ.

λαλῶ	. . . ἐλαύνω	I drive.
λέρια	. . . προβατοκούδουνα	Sheep-bells.
λήξης	. . . γαίμαργος	A greedy fellow.
λιγοψυχιά	. στενοχωρία	Uneasiness.
λιγόψυχος	. στενόκαρδος	Oppressed, fatigued.
λιγοψυχῶ	. στενοχωροῦμαι	I am fatigued, or bored.
λοβιά	. . . ἡ θήκη τῶν ὀσπρίων	A granary.[5]
λογάρι	. . . θησαυρός	A treasure.

Μ.

μαδάρα	. . ὄρος πετρῶδες	A stony mountain.
μαλάκα	. . μυζιθρότυρον	The μυζῆθρα of Greece: fresh cheese made from butter-milk.
μάλαμα	. . ὁ ἀλωνισμένος πλὴν ἀλίχνιστος σῖτος.	Wheat thrashed, but not winnowed.
μαγλινός	. λεῖος	Smooth.
μαλιά	. . λογομαχία[6]	A dispute.[7]
μάλτα[9]	. πορτοκάλι	An orange.
μονάρι[8]	. πέλεκυς	An axe.
μαργόνω (com- κρυόνω[10]		I feel cold, shiver.[11]
mon every-where).		

Cretan Greek.	Modern Greek.	
μάροτον	. . ἀρνὶ χρονιάρικον	A yearling[1] lamb.
μαρουβάς	. . τὸ κρασὶ ἀφοῦ σαραντήσῃ, παλαιὸς οἶνος.	Old wine.
μαρούβισε	. . ἐπάλιωσε τὸ κρασί, πίνεται	. The wine is old, it is drinkable.
μαρτί	. . . ἀρνὶ σιτευτόν	A fatted sheep.[2]
μαρτή[3]	. . . εἶδος κριθῆς σπειρομένης τὸν Μάρτιον, καὶ τῆς ὁποίας ὁ στάχυς εἶναι δίγωνος.	A kind of barley which is sown in the month of March, and the ear of which is two-cornered.
μασέλα	. . σιαγών	Jaw.
μαστόρισσα	. μαμή	A midwife.
ματινάδα[4]	. . τραγούδι[5]	A song, ballad. Apparently a "mattinata" from Italian, like a "serenata."[6]
μελίτακας	. . μύρμηγξ	An ant.
μιγόμι	. . . φορτεῖον	A burden, cargo.
μίστατο	. . μέτρον ρευστῶν[7] δέκα ὀκάδων	. A liquid measure of[8] ten okes.
μιτάτο(properly μητάτα[9]).	μανδρί, στάνη (common in Byzantine writers for a lodging or enclosure, from the Latin metata, castra metata).	A sheepfold.
μονιτάρου	. . διὰ μιᾶς	At once.
μουζούρι	. . κοιλόν	A bushel.
μποτόνια	. . περιδείριον[10]	A necklace.
μπράτη	. . εἰδήσματα[11]	Information.[12]

N.

νάκαρα	. . δύναμις	Strength.
'ντήρησις	. . συστολή[13]	Reserve, shame.[14]
'ντηριοῦμαι	. συστέλλομαι[15]	I am ashamed.[16]
νύχι	. . . τουφεκόπετρα	A gun-flint, lit. a finger-nail.

Ξ.

ξαμόνω	. . σημαδεύω	I aim at.
ξάμου[17]	. . φροντίς μου*[18]	It concerns me, or is my affair.[19]
ξάσου[20]	. . φροντίς σου[21]	It concerns you, or is your affair.[22]

---

* φροντίς μου, if Greek at all, is written Greek, not idiomatic. Probably ξάμου, ξάσου are equivalent to the ordinary Greek ἔννοια μου, ἔννοια σου, meaning, in practice, "never mind," "don't trouble yourself," also "take care," "I'll take care" (lit. "it is my business," "your business"), for which φροντίς μου would be fine Greek.[23]

Cretan Greek.	Modern Greek.	
ξεμύγησῃ . .	. φυγὴ ἔντρομος καὶ βιαία[1] . .	Hurried flight.[2]
ξεμύστευσῃ[3]	. σωτηρία, ἀπαλλαγὴ δεινῶν	Escape or safety from dangers.[4]
ξεμνστεύω .	. ἀπαλλάττω, ἐλευθερόνω	. . To deliver or set free.
ξεπαραλῶ .	. ξυλόνω.	. . To undo, cut the seam.
ξερά . .	. τὰ καλάμια τῶν ποδῶν .	. . The shin-bones.
ξερονόμι .	. χόρτον ξηρόν	. Dry fodder.
ξέσυρε . .	. παραμέρησε	. Get out of the way.
ξετρέχω .	. ἀκολουθῶ, τρέχω κατόπιν τινός[5]	I follow, I run after some one.[6]

O.

ὄμπανε. .	. ἀπόψε	. . To-night.
ὀργιά (ὀργυιά, σπάγκος		. Twine.
a yard measure).		
οὔγια . .	. ἀλοίμονον	. . Alas !!

Π.

παῖδα[7] . .	. βάσανον	. Trouble.[8]
πεδουκλόνουμαι	ἐμπερδεύονται οἱ πόδες μου[9]	. My feet are hampered. (It is usual Greek.)[10]
παιδομή .	. βάσανον	. Trouble, grief.[11]
παντέρμος .	. πάντι ἔρημος	. Entirely barren.[12]
παπούρα .	. γήλοφος[13]	. A ridge of earth.[14]
παραβολή .	. ὅταν γεωργοῦν οἱ βόες καὶ φθάσουν εἰς τὴν ἄκραν, νὰ ἐπιστρέψουν	Word used when the oxen are ploughing the ground, and reach the end of the furrow.
παρασύρα .	. σάρωμα[15]	. Sweepings.[16]
παρασύρω .	. σαρώνω	. I sweep.
πάσπαλα .	. κόνις	. Dust.
πασπατεύω	. ψάχνω, ψηλαφῶ. . . .	. I touch, search by feeling.
πεδοῦλι .	. κομμάτι πετζίου	. A piece of leather.
πηλά . .	. λάσπη	. Mud.
πηλώθω[17] .	. στιβάζω	. I pile up.
ποθές . .	. πουθενά, εἰς κανὲν μέρος	. Somewhere (anywhere, nowhere).
πορίζω . .	. ἐξέρχομαι	. I come out.
πόρος . .	. δίοδος	. Passage, transit.
ποταμίδα .	. ἀηδόνι	. Nightingale.
ποῦλο . .	. φάσκελο	. The middle finger stretched out in cursing an adversary, as if imprecating blindness.

Cretan Greek.	Modern Greek.	
πρᾶμα . . .	τίποτε	Nothing.[1]
πρᾶσσω . .	μανθάνω[2] . , ...	I learn.[3]
πρίκα (com-mon everywhere).	πίκρα, λύπη	Sorrow or grief.[4]
πρόδωκα . .	παρεδόθην εἰς τὸν ἐχθρόν . .	I surrender or have been betrayed to the enemy.
προσκάδα . .	ἔνεδρα[5]	An ambuscade.
πρωτογόνατος[6]	πρωτότοκος	Firstborn.
πρωτογούλης	Ἰούνιος	June.

P.

ῥάσσω[7] . .	δράττω	To reap, bind in sheaves.
ῥέμπεται . .	ἐπαίρεται[8]	Is taken, seized.[9]
ῥοξονάρω . .	ὁμιλῶ	I speak (It. ragionare).
ῥούκουνας .	ἀγκονή, γωνία	A corner.

Σ.

σακάζω . .	ἀποκόπτω τοῦ γάλακτος . .	To wean.
σάρακας . .	πριόνι	A saw.
σίβια . . .	ὅλως, διόλου	Altogether, entirely.
σιμοσάτωρας[10]	σύντροφος κατὰ τὸ ἥμισυ . .	A partner of halves, an equal sharer.
σκεπαστά . .	ἄνωθεν τοῦ σημείου, τοῦ σκοποῦ	Above the mark or object pointed out. See κρεμαστά.
σκευρώνω . .	κάμπτω, στραβόνω	To bend.
σκιάς . . .	κἄν	Even, if even.[11]
σκλόπα . .	γλαῦκα	An owl.
σκολινός . .	χοῖρος	A pig.
σκοράρω . .	διαβαίνω	I go, pass through.
σωμίλιγκα .	λοιμική	Plague.
σώπατο . .	ἐπίπεδον	A plain, on a level.
σοῦρο[12] . . (It. súghero.)	φελλός	Cork.
σταμόνα[13] . .	(στάσου μόνος) ἡσύχασε . .	Be quiet, stay still.
στοῦπα . .	χιόνι	Snow.[14]
στειρονόμος .	ὁ ποιμὴν τῶν στείρων προβάτων	The shepherd of the barren ewes.
συβάζω* . .	συμφωνῶ	I make an agreement.
σύβασι* . .	συμφωνία	An agreement.
σύγκλησι[15] .	χείμαρρος	A ravine, torrent.

* Common everywhere.

Cretan Greek.	Modern Greek.	
συγκόκαλη	. ἡ ἀποκρέω	. The carnival.
συργουλιστά	. κολακευτικά	Flatteringly.
σφάκα . .	. ἡ πικροδάφνη	. The bitter laurel.
σώχωρο .	. τὸ περιφραγμένον ἐκλεκτὸν χωράφι.	The well-fenced inner field or enclosure.

T.

ταγή . .	. βρώμη	. Oats.
τάξε . .	. ὑπόθεσε	. Suppose.
ταρός . ' .	. ἄνεμος	. Wind.
τάρταλα .	. λάφυρα	. Spoil, plunder.
ταὒτέρου .	. αὒριον[3]	. To-morrow.[3]
τσινιά . .	. κλοτσιά	. A kick.
τσινῶ . .	. κλοτσῶ	. I kick.
τσίτα . .	. σουβλὶ ξύλινον . .	. A wooden spit.
τσίπραγά[4]	. δίδυμα	. Twins.
τουπί[5] . .	. κατήφορος	. A steep descent.
τουρλῶ[6] .	. γλυστρῶ[7]	. I slip, or slide.[8]
τουπιά . .	. τυροδοχεῖα	. Skins for cheeses.
τριτάρης .	. σύντροφος κατὰ τὸ ½ . . .	. A sharer of thirds.

Υ.

ὑστεροβύξης .	ὑστερότοκος	. The lastborn.

Φ.

φαμέγιος .	. ὑπηρέτης	. A servant.
φθαρμίζω[9]	. βασκάνω[10]	. To bewitch.
φθαρμός[10] .	. βασκανία	. Sorcery, evil eye.
φιοῦ[11] . .	. ὅταν βρωμᾷ τι, ὕβρις . .	. Exclamation of disgust at a bad smell.
φουντούλης .	ὑπερήφανος	. A conceited man, coxcomb (Turkish fodol).
φρασκιά .	. μελισσοδοχεῖα, κυψέλια .	. Beehives.
φρύον . . .	. κράμβη[12]	. Cabbage.[13]

X.

χαλέπα .	. πετρόλοφος	. A stony hill.
χαμήλωσε .	. κάθισε	. Sit down.
χαντῶ . .	. νομίζω	. I suppose.
χαράκι . .	. λίθος	. A stone.
χαροκόπος *	. ξεφαντωτής	. Pleasure-seeker.
χαστουκιά .	. σβερκιά[15]	. A blow.
χαυτοῦμαι[14]	. τρώγω	. I eat.

---

* Common everywhere.

Cretan Greek.	Modern Greek.	
χουρχούδα	. ῥόπαλον	A club.
χρειασίδι	. . πήλινον ἀγγεῖον, γαβάθα .	. An earthen vessel.
χῦμα[1]	. . . κατήφορος	A hill (looking down, as ἀνή-φορος is a hill looking or going up).
χυτά	. . . κατηφορικά	Downhill.

Ψ.

ψακί	. . . φαρμάκι	Poison.
ψακόνω	. . φαρμακόνω	I poison.
ψεγάδι	. . ἐλάττωμα	A defect or fault.

NOTES.

ἀγκοῦσα, *i.e.*, " the strangler."

ἄγομαι. In the original the words stand ἄγωμε, πήγενε, which seems impossible, as a present ἀγώμω cannot be conceived. Perhaps it should be ἄγωμεν, ἂς πᾶμεν, *i.e.*, "let us go," "come along," " *allons.*" The root is extinct everywhere, just as the Latin *ago* in modern Romanic tongues.

ἄθος. For ἄνθος.[2]

ἀνάδια. Probably a corruption of ἐνάντια.

ἀπόγι. Lit. " earth-radiation."

ἀπορόχια. I do not know the Greek explanatory word, and cannot find it in any of the dictionaries. It must be remembered that these last have hitherto made it a point of honour to suppress or ignore the so-called " vulgar " Greek. βρουβο- is doubtless from βρύον.

ἀποσταχυάς. *Lege* ἀποσταχειᾶς: interesting as preserving the Hellenic use of ἀπό with a genitive.

ἀργατινή,[3] *i.e.*, " the late," like τὸ βράδυ, or the Spanish *tarde.*

βούργια, βουργίδι. The Latin *bulga*, of Gaulish origin, as we are told; *Bulgas Galli sacculos scorteos vocant.* The Irish affinities are well known. It is our word *bellows.*

γιότσα. From the Italian *ghiozzo*, "drop." Compare the Turkish *damla*, "drop," and " apoplexy."

δόμοι. *Bands* ; from δέω, doubtless, though the accentuation δομοί might be expected in that case.

ἐπά. Ἐδεπά, *i.e.*, ἐδά[4] + ἐπά, is common in most of the islands instead of ἐδώ (an inversion of ὧδε rather than from ἔνδον).

ἐργῶ. Perhaps[5] from ῥιγῶ.

ἔσω. A word which is retained nowhere else, being supplanted by μέσα.

ἔχνος. Apparently formed from ἔχω, on the analogy of κτῆνος, a " possession," " chattel," " cattle."

ζουρίδα. *Zorrilla,* properly "a little fox," is used in colonial Spanish for a variety of skunk or polecat, Buffon's "zorille."

θέσε, θέττω.[1] Here given as neuter, but in the Greek play used as actives —"μὰ τὰ πάσπαλα τοῦ θὰ θέσω στὸν Ἅιδη," "by the ashes I shall lay in the grave."

καλουργιά. The vernacular form of the now common word καλλιέργεια, which, however, is a revived word, brought in from books, or rather constructed on ancient principles. The good Cretan family name of Kalerges, in the sense of "a farmer," is more likely to be from this indigenous source than from any vague meaning of "doer of good deeds."

κάσα. Found elsewhere in the sense of "scurf," "head-grease."

κοπέλι. Perfectly common everywhere; also in the Wallachian *copil.* The derivation from κόπτομαι can hardly be admitted. Κόπελος is used in Byzantine writings for a bastard. On the whole the word is more probably of Greek than of Romanic or barbaric origin.

κούρταλα. From κρόταλον. Κουρταλίζω is common everywhere, and as old as the twelfth century.

λήξης. Probably λείξης or λείξιος, from λείχω.

λιγοψυχῶ, &c. These words are used elsewhere, like the more usual λιγοθυμῶ, λειποθυμῶ, in the sense of fainting rather than mere oppression.

λοβίδ. From Hellenic λοβὸς, "peascod."

μαλάκα. The word μυξήθρα is probably expressive of the straining or squeezing process, calling to mind Virgil's "*pressi copia lactis.*" Μαλάκα seems to be a form of the old word for *milk,* common to most of the Indo-European languages, which has run together or formed an etymological confluence with the word μαλακὸς, itself ultimately from the same root, much as *mulcere* and *mulgere* in Latin. The Cretan word reappears at the other end of Europe, among our own islands: "*mulcán* (gloss glassia, *i.e.* γαλαξία? a kind of milk frumity) is O'Reilly's *mulachán,* 'a kind of soft cheese.'" (Whitley Stokes, "Irish Glosses," No. 243).

μασέλα. From the Italian rather than the Latin stage of *maxilla.* The Latin stage is preserved in μυξιλλάρι, "a pillow." Compare Chaucer's *Wanger* and the Arabic *mukhadda* (whence Spanish *almohada*), both meaning "cheek" or "jawpiece."

ματινάδα.[2] Pashley spells the word μαδινάδα. The oldest work in the Brescian dialect (1554) consists in part of a "canzone villereccia," entitled "*Matinada, id est Stramboggio che fa il Gian alla Togna.*" (Biondelli, "Saggio sui dialetti gallo-italici," 163.)

μίσταρο. Perhaps from an assumed ἡμίσταρον in Hellenic.[3] Compare the Latin *dimidiana,* whence our *demi-john, dame-jaune,* &c.

μουζούρι is not from *modius,* nor even the It. *misura,* but rather from the Byzantine μυσούριν, a confluence of the Latin *mensura, mensa,* and *missus.* It is a dry measure containing 15 okes (the oke = 2½ pounds) of wheat, or 12 of barley. Its half is a πινάκι, its quarter a πρατικό,[1] and its sixteenth an ἀξάγι.

μονάρι.[2] Query μανάρι, It. *mannaja.*

μποτόνια. A neuter plural. Properly pendants, or *button*-shaped ornaments. It. *bottone.*

μπράτη. Compare below πράσσω (μανθάνω), *i.e.*, "to work for information," "strive to learn." The formation seems irregular, unless the word is for ἐμπράκτη. Πράσσω and ποιῶ are generally extinct, the latter, however, being retained in common use in the Trebizond country.

ξεμυστεύω. But in the "Vavilonía" it means "to set free soul from body," "to kill," "smash," "*écraser.*" "Τὸν ἐξεμύστευγα δεδίμ, τὸν ἔπεμπα στὸν "Ἀδη," "I say that I have smashed that man, and sent him down to Hell, Sir."[3]

ξεπαραλῶ. In this word -λῶ is from λύω: in καταλῶ (φθείρω), given above, it is probably from ὄλλυμι. The present λῶ for λύω is a natural consequence or suggestion arising from the aorist ἔλυσα. As a general rule in vernacular Greek, all verbs whose aorist is -ησα, -ισα, -υσα, alike pronounced -isa, can form a present in -ῶ upon the model of the contract verbs, whatever it may have been in the ancient, or may also be in the "revived" written language. Thus, as ἐφίλησα is from φιλῶ, and ἠγάπησα from ἀγαπῶ, so ἔσβυσα has suggested a colloquial present σβῶ[4] by the side of σβύω[5] or σβύνω: ἔπτυσα has φτῶ[6] as well as πτύω: ἐκόστισα, κοστῶ[7] (*constare, costare*) as well as κοστίζω. It may be seen by this how the grammatical modifications of the ancient language which constitute modern Greek have arisen naturally out of changes in pronunciation. Ἐμεῖς and ἐμᾶς, and ἐσεῖς and ἐσᾶς, must have arisen from the impossibility of working the language in daily life, as soon as ἡμεῖς and ὑμεῖς came to be pronounced in exactly the same way; and so with many other instances.

προσκάδα. It. *imboscata.*

πρωτογούλης, *i.e.*, "the fore July," as δευτερογούλης is "the latter July." The other variant names for months in Greek are *the Reaper, the Thresher, the Vintager* (θεριστής, ἀλωνάρης, τρυγητής), peculiar to the Ionian Islands. These names remind us of the ancient English and the Slavonian sets of names. Γούλης for Γιούλης (Ἰούλιος), if not a misprint, exhibits the Rhodian and Cyprian peculiarity of hardening a *y* sound after liquids before *a, o, u,* as καμμγὰ σαρανταργὰ for καμμιὰ σαραντάρια, *une quarantaine,* *a lot of forty.*

ῥέμπεται. It is impossible to say whether this means "it is raised," or "it is seized," owing to the author's use of high polite Greek instead of real Greek. Ἐπαίρεται is good ancient Greek in the former sense. Παίρνεται, its legitimate derivative, is good modern Greek in the latter sense. No such word as ἐπαίρεται exists in the modern Greek language, properly speaking. But it has become, as I have said before, a point of honour to revive ancient forms, letting them take their chance as regards embodying modern idiom ; and the confusion thus occasioned to philological work is great. So, below, χάρακας (γιθος) may be stone or may be marble ; we cannot tell which, because the author uses an ambiguous and dead word instead of his own living words, πέτρα in the one case, μάρμαρον in the other. So, above, μύρμιγξ, explaining μελίτακας. Μυρμήκι or -μήγκι is good modern Greek for "an ant," and μύρμηξ is good ancient Greek for the same ; but μύρμιγξ is a jumble of a misspelling and a dead and withered case-ending. In the present case, moreover, it is most important to know which is which. If the word be παίρνεται ("it is seized"), ρέμπεται must be one of two things—either a very old vernacular cognate of the Indo-European word which we possess in the form *rob*, or else the Albanian "*remb*" (rembéñ, "I seize") which has passed over into Crete.[1]

ρούκουνας. Arabic *rukna ;* as this word is not used in ordinary Turkish, the Cretan must be from Arabic direct—a very rare occurrence.

σιμοσάτωρας. Probably for ἡμισάτωρας, or from εἰς + ἥμισυ + -άτωρας. This last form, which is from the Latin *-ator*, is common in Byzantine and modern Greek.[2] Compare βλεπάτωρας above.

σκοράρω. Apparently from It. *scorrere*.

ταγή. Properly "a ration" or "allowance" (from τάσσω), thence specially one of horse-provender, thence oats generally. In this sense it is used by Byzantine writers. From it, further, comes the modern verb ταγίζω, "I feed" (active). Compare the converse process in the Latin *cibus* becoming limited in the Spanish *cebada* to the meaning of *barley*.

ταυτέρου. Can this contain the lost ἕτερος in any way ?[3]

τουπ̣d. Perhaps from τύπος, with the common retention of the old sound of υ : *types, moulds*.

ὑστεροβύξης. Hence the family name of Sterovizi.

φθαρμός is probably to be referred to ὀφθαλμός, elsewhere lost.[4]

χαροκόπος. The common word for "a spendthrift" or "free-liver."

[Mr. Antonios Jeannarakis, a native of Crete, editor of "Kretas Volkslieder" (The Popular Songs of Crete), Leipzig, 1876, and author of a Grammar of Modern Greek for Germans, published at Hanover in 1877, kindly undertook the revision of the Modern Greek in this volume. We are also indebted to him for the following suggestions and emendations, the numerals of which correspond to the numerals which appear on pages 112 to 129.]

PAGE 112.
[1] lege ἀρίς
[2] lege ῥοδαμός, from ῥο- δαμνος or ῥάδαμνος
[3] doubtless
[4] lege βεντέμα
[5] πονοκέφαλος
[6] κεφαλαριά
[7] lege φταρμός

PAGE 114.
[1] lege φταρμόν
[2] φταρμέ
[3] lege ἀπού τσ' ἑβδομην-ταδυὸ φλέγες
[4] χασμουριέται
[5] ἐλούστηκ'
[6] κερά
[7] ἐχτενίστηκε
[8] lege στὸ θρόνον τση ἐκάθισε or ἔκατσε
[9] κ' ἐφταρμίσασίν τηνε
[10] τσῆ
[11] lege ἤντά 'χεις μάνα, ἤντά 'χεις or rather ἴντά 'χεις μάνα, ἴντά 'χεις
[12] ἐλούστηκα
[13] στὸ θρόνο μου
[14] χτενίστηκα
[15] φταρμίσασί
[16] ἀλικιά

PAGE 117.
[1] rather ἀγκούσια
[2] conversation, mention
[3] ἀγνάντια
[4] λάμψις
[5] gleam, brightness
[6] ἐγείρομαι, ἀναβλέπω
[7] to rise, to look up
[8] ἀπομενάροι
[9] (?)
[10] ἀργαδινή

[11] rather ῥοδαμός
[12] (?)
[13] (?)

PAGE 118.
[1] (?) σπουργίτης
[2] also γρῦ
[3] syllable
[4] (?)
[5] βεντέμα
[6] βλάτος
[7] βάλτος
[8] morass, marsh, mire
[9] keeper
[10] ἐπιστασία
[11] inspection
[12] leathern
[13] leathern
[14] γοργά
[15] γκαύγω
[16] δρομεύς
[17] runner
[18] (?) μιὰ οὐλέ or μιὰ οὐλιά
[19] ὀλίγον τι
[20] a little
[21] (?)

PAGE 119.
[1] (?)
[2] σιγανή|
[3] μικρὸν ὕψωμα
[4] rising ground
[5] ἀλμεγόμενα πρόβατα
[6] milch-ewes
[7] it struck my fancy, it struck me
[8] (?)
[9] a cattle

PAGE 120.
[2] cripple
[3] διώκω
[4] I pursue

[5] θέτω
[6] δυστυχής
[7] wretched
[8] καμνυῶ, or rather καν-νυῶ
[9] I close my eyes
[10] (?) σφαγή and σφαή
[11] σκιαουλιᾶς

PAGE 121.
[1] κουκκοσάλι
[2] ὑδρορρόα
[3] gutter
[4] λοβί, or rather λουβί
[5] a pod, a capsule
[6] ἡ ἐπίπληξις
[7] a censure
[8] μανδρι
[9] (?)|
[10] παγόνω
[11] I freeze

PAGE 122.
[1] female
[2] lamb
[3] (?) μαρτάκι
[4] μαντινάδα
[5] δίστιχον
[6] a distich
[7] ὀκτὼ ἕως
[8] eight to ten
[9] (?)
[10] περιδέραιον
[11] πράγματα, σκεύη
[12] chattels
[13] σεβασμός
[14] respect, regard
[15] σέβομαι
[16] I am regardful
[17] lege ξά μου, commoner ξιά μου
[18] ἐξουσία μου, δική μου δουλειά

19 my authority, *i.e.*, my business

20 ξά σου, commoner ξιά σου

21 ἐξουσία σου, ὅπως θέλεις

22 your authority, *i.e.*, as you like

23 ἐξουσία μου, ξουσία μου, ξσία μου, ξσιά μου, or ξιά μου

PAGE 123.
1 τρόμος, ταραχή
2 alarm
3 lege ξεμίστεψι
4 deliverance
5 διώκω, ἐπιδιώκω
6 I pursue
7 (?) παιδωμή
8 torture, torment
9 ἐμπλέκομαι
10 I entangle myself
11 torture, torment
12 entirely abandoned
13 κορυφή, ἀκρώρεια
14 a mountain-ridge
15 σκοῦπα, σάρωθρον
16 a broom
17 (?)

PAGE 124.
1 anything
2 συχνάζω
3 I frequent
4 bitterness

5 lege ἐνέδρα
6 (?)
7 (?) ἀράσσω, Modern Greek ὁρμῶ, I storm
8 ἐπαναπαύεται
9 he relies
10 lege συμμισάτορας, commoner συμμισιακάτορας
11 at least
12 σοῦρος
13 (?)
14 snowflakes
15 lege σύγκλυσι

PAGE 125.
2 early, in the morning
3 τὸ πρωΐ
4 oftener συμπραγά
5 (?) χύτης
6 (?) τσουρῶ
7 κυλίω, κυλίομαι
8 I roll
9 φταρμίζω
10 βασκαίνω
10 φταρμός
11 lege φυοῦ, or oftener φτυοῦ, from πτύω
12 ἀνθοκράμβη
13 cauliflower
14 χαύτομαι
15 πάτσα

PAGE 126.
1 (?) χύτης

2 (?) αἴθω; αἰθάλη, soot, ashes; ἀθός = bloom
3 ἀργαδινή
4 (?) ἐδῶ
5 doubtless

PAGE 127.
1 θέτω
2 μαντινάδα
3 from It. mestato

PAGE 128.
1 oftener ἡ κάρτα
2 lege μανάρι
3 ξεμυστεύω or ξεμιστεύω means ἀπαλάττω, to deliver
4 (?)
5 (?)
6 φτυῶ
7 (?)

PAGE 129.
1 ῥέμπεται means "he relies," apparently from ῥέπω
2 lege συμμισάτορας, oftener συμμισιακάτορας, from the common adj. συμμισιακός
3 apparently from ταχύτερος
4 lege φταρμός, apparently from φθείρω

58 GREAT CUMBERLAND STREET, W.,
January 17, 1865.

MY DEAR FREEMAN,—I have been owing you a letter this many a day, and have written it on the tablets of my mind more or less every Saturday morning; but as there is no such thing as inter-mental telegraphy as yet, and as I am lazy and irresolute like the Turks, I have never yet managed to come to the writing point. I say every Saturday, because I always find something of yours to set me agoing. The Saturday before last you flurried me with a vengeance. As for the Zamzummim, I give them up to you, and you may dance on their grave as long as you like, if you can find it. But the Kaukones—my own Kaukones, whom I value next in the world to the Lithuanians—what makes you step out of the way merely to murder them, or, at least, summarily clap an extinguisher over them, when they are burning out of themselves, and just at the last flicker? Why didn't you instance Myrmidons, or Dolops, or Pisidians? But the whole point of the Kaukones is that their name survives to this day, as applied to the only dialect now extant which can be called co-ordinate with the ancient Greek dialects—which, at all events, is no dialect of modern Greek. Finlay (who, by the way, is not a philologist), in treating of the Tzakonians, incidentally compares their name with that of Laconia; so did Leake, who was the first Englishman who drew attention to them; so did, I think, the Venetians. But the Germans have quite given this up, and Okonómas (a very safe and good Greek, a Cyprian, professor at Corfu, whom I met there, and who warmed my heart by pronouncing his doubled consonants as an Italian or Arab would) points out very clearly that the letter change of *l* to *tz* is quite unwarrantable, while that of *kā* to *tza* (a Greek's nearest approach to *cha*) is regular enough; compare κακίζω, κακόνω becoming τζακίζω, τζακόνω.

As for the *υ*, that also disappears in combinations like αυκ in common speech, though of course retained in conscious speech and book work; compare καμηλαῦκι, the priest's cap, commonly pronounced *kamiláji*, or else *kamiláki*. This arose, of course, from the nature of things after *-αυ -ευ* had lost their diphthongal sound, and become *αv, εv*. When εὔμορφος came to be awkward and uncomfortable to pronounce, as written and in theory, it got the easier sound of ὄμορφος in spoken language—if, indeed, that last has not been spoken all along. As for the dialect itself, it is queer stuff, and dreadfully corrupted; but it has plenty of Doric traces: moreover, they have got a perfect, all right:—ὡράκα, I have seen. The pronouns are unlike anything in the Romanic above, or the Hellenic beneath, or the older Aryan, which is under the Hellenic. Bopp himself would be puzzled to account for such forms as ἐκιοῦ, τί, νί, κίου, for σύ, σου, σοι, σέ. But I've no doubt it is merely a sub-dialect of Spartan Doric run wild, and left by the schoolmasters to take care of itself. They had a settlement in Crete, where there is a village Tzákonas. I have written a very brief essay on Cretan, to be published in Captain Spratt's forthcoming book on that island, which I should be very glad to show you. But I cannot get the proofs sent me, though they are in the printer's hands for more than a fortnight. I have given, as concisely as possible, my view of the origin of modern Greek, and accounted for the absence of true dialect in it. On the whole subject, I can only say that if E. A. Sophocles were a little fuller, he would be to it what Diez is in Romanics, and Zeuss in Celtics, and Grimm in

Teutonics—the father of true philological method and criticism.

Talking of Greeks, I see by this day's "Times" that Finlay's friends, the Logiotates, or Kalamarádes, have massed their artillery, and have written all at once, either by concert or inspiration, to compel us through the "Times" to say Πηληιάδεω their way and not our way at school and college. And of course we shall have the old Reuchlinian and Erasmian war waged day after day, after the fashion of what the Germans call "der silly season," without a single new argument, or a single reference to Sophocles, or any acknowledgment of the one fact that the whole theory of the Hellenic sound-system becomes order and harmony only when viewed by the light of comparative philology—unless, indeed, Max Müller takes up the subject and writes peremptorily. I do firmly believe that a common modern English or German strong verb throws more light on certain points of Hellenic *Lautlehre* than anything modern Greek can tell us. As seen by a modern Greek, there is no vowel change at all in λιπ-, λείπω, λέλοιπα; and the change in spelling is caprice or nonsense, or it "growed so." What would he make of Fιδ-, Fείδω, Fοῖδα, or φυγ-, φεύγω, πέφευγα (for πέφουγα)? Our *wot* and the German *biegen, bóg, gebogen*, retain traces of each change, which is perfectly exhibited in Gothic—*wit* and *bug* being the root-forms, with the simple vowel *weitan* (preserved in *in-weitan* and *bingan*) for the first *steigerung* or diphthongation; and *wáit* and *láng* with the second; the series being $\left\{ \begin{matrix} i & ei & ái \\ w & iw & áu \end{matrix} \right\}$ in Gothic, and $\left\{ \begin{matrix} ι & ει & οι \\ υ & ευ & ου \end{matrix} \right\}$ in Greek, the Sanskrit being the same absolutely; though I don't venture to give that without a book of reference. Our *wot* is by regular change from the older *wát*, which has the regular old-English superscription of iota, as in *stains, stán, stone.*

I find I have sacrificed the world and our common friends to the Kaukones, and have no more room, so I must remain, ever yours truly,   STRANGFORD.

58 GREAT CUMBERLAND STREET,
March 4, 1865.

MY DEAR FREEMAN,—It is only ten in the morning, and I have but just taken up my Saturday. The article I first see is naturally the one headed "**Armenian** Popular Songs," and **there** the first words that **meet my** eye are "**The Armenians** were, **and for** the most **part** still **are, members of the** Greek communion." Well, **it isn't much in** England, **but to a** πολίτης, or Constantinopolitan **like** myself, it **reads** like saying that **the** Ultramontanes **are still members of Mr.** Spurgeon's congregation. **You were** good **enough to be nervous and** appeal to my **silence about your Kaukones; but** what do you say to this? **I was not** astonished **at all after** that to find the reviewer **compli-** menting the author **on the "accuracy of** his translation." The first sign **of decadence in a paper** like the R——— is the abandonment **of special subjects to** commonplace **general men.** As for **the editor, be it mine to burn** his **father and** break his windows.

I see by your friend the Emperor **that the reason of the** disappearance **of all** knowledge **about the Roman kings** was because "their mission was fulfilled." **I hope you are now** satisfied **about** Ancus Martius.—Ever **yours truly,**

STRANGFORD.

———

58 GREAT CUMBERLAND STREET,
April 15, 1865.

MY DEAR **FREEMAN,—You** have held **the stirrup and** mounted **me in the saddle, but I don't think** you **will** succeed in getting **me** to ride my **hobby to** much purpose, **or on** a straight road. Your **main points I** take to be **these** two—whom in the **ancient world do the** Albanians represent? and how near does **Albanian stand to** Greek? Now at the very outset, **and before** attempting to give a precise answer to either **question,** I begin by saying **that**

whatever may be the name of the people who spoke
ancient Albanian, modern Albanian, in my opinion, differs
from its former stage, or mother tongue, as much as the
speech of Ludovicus Cæsar differs from that of Julius
Cæsar—his French I mean, not his Corsican—and differs
much in the same way. Or, to take another illustration,
it represents it as modern Welsh represents the splendid
Latin-like speech of the pre-historic Celts, such as we just
manage to see in Celtic inscriptions, and can reconstruct
to some extent by legitimate induction. In Albanian we
have no literature, no archaism, no staple of language, and
consequently cannot reconstruct in detail; but we have
enough means to enable us to conclude that the modern
language is phonetically degraded and grammatically
changed from the old tongue, in the same way as the
modern languages I have instanced are changed from
their respective mother tongues—by great phonetic corruption, and by the progress of grammar from synthesis
to analysis. Old Albanian can thus be shown to have
been a true synthetic speech, like all other old Indo-
European languages. In this style it is a probable conjecture, which I do not think it safe to state as a certain
conclusion, that it stood nearest to archaic Greek among
the extra-Hellenic dialects of Europe, but not nearer than
some languages in Asia Minor, such as Phrygian. Furthermore, that it so stood, not, as now, alone, but as one
of a group. Whether this group included Thracian,
Macedonian, and the like, whether it was subordinate to any one of them, or whether it was co-ordinate with any of them, I hold as beyond the limits
of such conjectures as those to which I now wish
to restrict myself. All I can say is, that the true
Albanian part of the language, such as we are forced
to take it, after precipitation of the foreign elements,
is distinctly Indo-European, and is more closely connected
with Greek than with any other Indo-European language
existing or recorded. Of missing languages of that stock

I can take no count with safety. This position of special
affinity with **Greek**, moreover, would be assigned to it
under any geographical circumstances, and wholly irre-
spective of its neighbourhood to Greece. But, whether
it be the modern of ancient Illyrian, of ancient **Epirotic**,
or ancient Thracian even; whether it be transitional between Greek and any or all of these rather than their continuation, I cannot say, for I have no means of saying;
nor has anybody else. All I can do is to try and guess
sense instead of guessing nonsense. My own conjecture
is that the ‘language in its present’ diffusion is quite
modern, that is to say, of the Roman Imperial times; that,
at the time of the first-mention of the name, Ptolemy's
Albanopolis, it was confined to a comparatively small
area in the Central Pindus, one probably of many other
dialects of something either Epirotic or Illyrian (which,
for aught I know, may be the same), and that the modern
Greg and Toshk and Ljap and the rest are sub-dialects of
this central nucleus spread forth by conquest, rather than
continuations of the elder dialects. This is tame work
after Hahn and the people who make **Achilles and Deu-
calion** speak modern Albanian, and who interpret **Peleus
and Thetis** and everything you choose by it in a way not
a bit better than Vallancy and the little pig book, nor
half so amusing. There is, to be sure, a coincidence about
the name of the swift-footed Achilles which I quoted from
Fallermayer in a note in my wife's book [1]—Ἀσπέτε in
Plutarch being his Epirotic epithet, and τσπέτε being
Albanian for swift; but I do not think this is more than a
coincidence. If more, it involves the assumption that the
language was always phonetically the same, which is out
of the question. No attempt to treat Albanian will succeed which treats it as the Welsh treat their language—
one in the category of Basque or Hebrew instead of one in
the category of modern English or French. And even the
best of philologists are but men; they cannot resist temp-

1 "The Eastern Shores of the Adriatic."

tation, and will persist in over-knowing their subject. To
my mind Albanian is the one speech which is the best
example and type of languages dangerous to the philologist. Foreign elements in its vocabulary, and even
foreign influence on its grammar, are at the maximum;
and I would not trust Bopp and Pott themselves to deal
with it unless they had an anteroom full of Klephts,
Cadis, and demogerontes to be called in and consulted on
points of vernacular usage at a moment's notice. Grammar and vocabulary are, of course, full of later Greek.
Then there is some distinctively earlier Greek, but not
much of it. For instance, *istrèmbere*, crooked, represents
the old meaning and old *beta* pronunciation of στραβός,
now meaning blind, not crooked. Turkish also, of course,
is not one whit less abundant than late Greek. Then
there is some Slavonic. But the one language which has
absolutely saturated Albanian, and ·has more affected it
than any of the others, or perhaps all put together, is
Latin in various ages and forms. The German philologists, over-estimating the originality and value of Albanian, are disposed to ignore and shirk this last point,
and have not worked it out in detail. They constantly
treat rank Latin words as genuine Albanian. Now there
is Latin of the classical period—late republican or early
imperial, evinced by the retention of an older pronunciation, in such words as *kiél*, heaven, *kjepą*, onion, *fkin*,
neighbour (*ą*, a graphic sign for an obscure short ă or ĕ),
and many other such which keep the old *k* sound of *c*
before *e*, &c. There is Romanic Latin from their neighbours the Southern Wallachians—a great deal of this,
which must have been going on for a long time,[1] though
I have never seen it observed; and there is Romanic
Latin from the Italians of the Middle Ages and the Venetian period in a small quantity. These two last can be
distinguished in some words. The Latin *integer* in Italian

---

[1] *E.g.*, sąndós, sound = Modern Greek γέρος, in Wallachian sąnitosw
(sanitosus), sound, strong, healthy.

is *intiero* and in Wallachian *'ntrégw.* In Albanian one
form, *iterą*, is supplied by Italian, in the sense of *entire;*
another, *ndrék*, by Wallachian, in the sense of straight,
downright, complete, ταμάμ as a modern Greek would
say with the Turkish word, half adjective, half inter-
jection.

There is a considerable amount of its grammatical
mechanism taken from Latin and Greek of different ages,
which, again, the Germans won't look in the face : such as
oñ for the derivative verbs, surely the late Greek *-όνω : -ime*
in nouns from verbs, from Wallachian, where it is very
common (crimen, discrimen, &c.): *afąr* (near), *mafąr*
(nearer), merely *ma* from *magis*, as in South Wallachian
multu, ma multu: let for our *let* (*let skruañ*, let him write);
which is a compound of *le + te – le =* Greek ἄς for ἄφες,
from the South Wallachian *la*, from *lasdre* (framed probably on the model of ἄς), and *te* being equivalent to the
Greek *va.* In this last instance the identity of idiom
which pervades all these languages is exemplified. Bulgarian, Wallach, Greek, and Albanian have all lost their
infinitive mood, and cannot say, like a Hellenic, γραφέτω,
or like an Italian, *lascia scrivere;* so all say ἄς γράψῃ (for
ἄς νὰ γ), *la si scria, lete skruañ,* and whatever the Bulgarian
may be. This cast of one mould as it were, has given rise
to a prevalent German theory that Albanian, *such as we see
it,* is the survivor of one family—say Thracian—spread
over the whole Peninsula at one time, which was the mould
in which the other languages were successively cast upon
contact with it. This I don't believe at all ; holding that
this special character proceeds partly from each, and as
much from one as from the other of them ; and that one of
its most important features (not found in Greek, moreover),
the suffixed definite article, is certainly not Albanian
originally, but, in my opinion, Slavonic (Proto-Slavonic):
in Max Müller's Romanic, it being equally open to a
Roman to say *dominus ille* and *ille dominus.* This theory,
as expounded by Miklosich, I think, I shall notice in full

some day. I know nothing of Albanian vernacularly, nor do the German philologists; they have the advantage over me in being themselves, I being only myself; but I have the advantage in a vernacular knowledge of Greek (which matters less) and of Turkish, which matters a great deal, and saves much trouble in determining the nature of words at first sight. Now, what more can I say for certain? I cannot say anything about Epirotic or Thesprotian, or the like, because I know nothing positive to say. In looking at Albanian, I am in the position of one looking as it were across the Channel at barbarian Frenchmen with no historical or literary record of their language, calling water ô, which, by my hypothesis, I have no resource for writing down other than phonetic spelling. How am I to know that that has anything to do with *aqua?* An Albanian calls water ύγε (ούγιε). I declare I have no means of deciding or guessing whether this be a phonetic corruption from the root of the Achelous, let us say, or from an old cognate of ὕδωρ. Ἀσπέτε, above mentioned, is positively stated by Plutarch—whatever the statement may be worth —to be Epirotic for πόδας ὠκύς. I have said before that I think the modern τσπέτε is only an accidental likeness to it; but if I might obtrude my own guess at what it really is, I can do so without straining by comparing Ἀσ with ὠκυ-, Sanskrit âçu—and πετε with ποδ—Sanskrit pad, so as to be = ὠκύπους, âçupada. I do not press this in the least, and indeed don't believe it, for I don't want to stop gaps with guesses.

To sum up, what I think we may venture to say is briefly this: Pre-Hellenic Greek was specially connected with one or more groups of dialects more or less standing in an intermediate and transitional position, impossible now from want of means to define in detail between it and the Italo-Celtic group on the one side and the true Aryan, or Iranian, on the other. The Albanian is the modern representative of one of these dialects; and its own dialectic variations, as we now see them, are of modern

rather than ancient origin, because their **difference is not**
such as would have **been caused by the lapse of three**
thousand years, and their mutual **unintelligibility in their**
extreme forms arises from the variety **in foreign influences,**
not from change in the native element.

The languages of **Northern** and Central **Asia** Minor,
which include **the** Thracian, were certainly transitional
between Greek **and** Aryan, and adopted with **equal ease**
Greek or Persian names, and, I suppose, language. **I should**
like to make one group of this. It is hard, perhaps, **to**
separate Macedonian and Illyrian by a special **line from**
Thracian, but I do not suppose it to be a strong separation,
and I make another group of that with Epirotic; **more**
particularly transitional to Italo-Celtic, as the first **is to**
Aryan proper. **This makes my view** of the whole **Pan-**
Aryan class to stand **thus,** *omissis omittendis.*

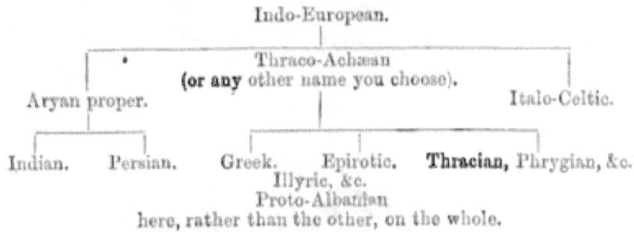

Macedonia, I cannot help thinking, must in the very old
times have actually belonged to the Greek group after all,
rather than to any other, but this I put in an uncertain
way. They must all have **been** very like one another in
Homer's day, to judge by the likeness in such extremes **of**
time and space as Themistocles's verbs in $\mu\iota$, and Xerxes's
verbs in *mi.* What complicated the matter in the way of
obliteration of some dialects, change of **type in** others, extension of others, **must have been the constant** maritime
migrations and **settlements going on between all** the three
peninsulas **side by side with the land work.** This has
Grecised the **Italic vocabularies, and made** the languages
look more Greek than **they are.** Of the head of the Adriatic

I don't like to talk; as it is, I have conjectured more than I intended to have allowed myself to do at starting. On reading what I have written, the only point where, I think, I have said too much is where I said that Albanian would be assigned at sight to a nearer affinity with Greek than with anything else. This I feel to be over-stated; for, as it stands, it is very unlike anything. It stands both to the eye and in reality as near to Greek as the phonetic Irish of a modern hodman, taken down without regard to traditional orthography, &c., stands to the language of Cicero, its nearest extra-Celtic ally. This parallel is as nearly exact as the case admits. Practically, modern Albanian is almost as far from modern Greek as Turkish, and their being influenced by the modern Greeks I do not think has anything to do with language or affinity of race. The Wallachs, whose language is unwritten, are equally influenced, and to much better purpose. The Albanians have given Greece as much as they received from her. The curse of Palikarism, encouraged by Otho, did more harm to the kingdom than words can describe; and when this lasted the town population was distinctly better off in Turkey, and the island population no worse off. In ancient times I have no doubt it was as you say. Indeed, had it not been for the Assyrian Empire and the Semites, and the unfortunate geographical position, the speakers of Cyrus's language might have been Hellenised or Europeanised through kinship of speech and race.

What I can do in a small way more than this is to give you a list of undoubted and manifest Albanian affinities of the old period. But I have not got Hahn, and Leake's grammar and vocabulary are hardly enough. However, something can be done with that.—Very truly yours,

STRANGFORD.

58 Great Cumberland Street,
April 18, 1865.

My Dear Freeman,—The best summary of opinions on the Albanian question is found in a treatise of Fallmerayer, published in 1857. I did not consult this when writing to you, preferring to do so out of my own treatment of the materials afforded me by Leake, all I had, Von Hahn not being as yet in my library. Fallmerayer says, and perhaps believes, that Hahn is very clever and methodical. I considered his book a disorderly chaos when I last saw it. But Fallmerayer's own statement of Hahn's conclusions, and his defence of them against some very silly and presumptuous criticism by a Greek, may really be called lucid and satisfactory. These take up most of the aforesaid treatise. Two parts, in continuation, have since appeared, which I have not got. The Greek critic, whose essay I happen also to have, is one Nicocles of Kozani, in Macedonia, a man of some little learning and much pretence, who studied in Germany. His little book is written in perfectly good and most creditable Hellenic, so far as I can judge, without any κατ' ἐμὴν ἰδέαν idioms in it. But it is full of inept sneering at the good Dutchman, who, though clearly cock of the Albanian walk, is by no means given to crowing; and it is all of a glitter with that barren tinsel wit locally called "*l'esprit Grec*," which all Greeks have, and none have more or less than another—such as takes in all superficial observers or visitors, but makes old resident observers sick, melancholy, hopeless, or Mussulman, according to their dispositions.

His view is that Albanians were Tauro-Scythians (pray don't ask me to explain), who came in from Tauro-Scythia about the seventh century, and that the proof of this lies in the word *Skipetar*, which is Σκυθίβηρος, also in the name of ἀρδαῦδα, said by the author of an anonymous Periplus to be the native name of the Tauric town Theo-

dosia, the present Kaffa, which is obviously the name
Arnaut used by the Turks. Fallmerayer seems to think
a man who writes like this should keep a civil tongue in
his head. The *Ur-Albanese*, in his own representation of
Hahn's conclusion, belonged to an "Urvölkertrinität," of
which the *Ur*-Romans and *Ur*-Greeks were the other
members, or, as he calls them, consubstantial elements.

So far so good. But when it comes to limiting and
defining, I venture to differ from Hahn in some points.
Epirotic, Thracian, Macedonian, Illyrian, everything,
whether gloss or local name, to be found in any ancient
author touching these countries, is made Albanian at once.
All is Albanian, and Albanian is each and all of them,
not even excepting pre-Hellenic Greek, such names of
which as are not explicable in Greek are so in Albanian.
In general, and with certain explanations and reservations,
Hahn's result is good enough, and there is fair evidence
wherewith to obtain it. But his philological method is
unsafe, as well as unnecessary, to say the least. Fancy a
man, and a Dutchman, sitting down to tell us that *Atlas*
is from the Albanian *Natle*, "what is placed on the
rafters to support the tiles;" and *Ceres* from *ntsjéres*,
"bringer forth;" and *Etruria* from *vjeterure-ia*, "the old
place." This last is capital for us, because demonstrably
vjéter, "old," is simply the Latin *veter*, one of my early
set of words borrowed from Latin, like *kiel*. Had it been
later, it would have been *vechin, već́lw*, as in the two
Wallachian dialects. *Ure* is merely the Latin *-ura*, so common in Romanic Latin, especially Italian and Wallachian;
compare κλεισούρα as a termination. I don't see why
Von Hahn deserves more respect in his philology than
Sir William Betham or the Duke of Roussillon.

This is the superfetation of my former letter, which may
be of use to you in reading it.—Very truly yours,

STRANGFORD.

58 GREAT CUMBERLAND STREET,
April 18, 1865.

MY DEAR FREEMAN,—Superfetation No. 2. But I think I have made a real philological discovery, though I dare say some German will turn out to have made it ten years ago. As you know, Albanian suffixes the definite article; and I think my first letter will have given you a fair idea of the amount of speculation and theory on the same. I think, however, that I have discovered the remains of a prefixed article in an earlier (not the *earliest*) stage of the language, very likely suggested by the Hellenic one, and cognate with it when both were demonstrative pronouns.

Now *mir* is "good," whatever that may be related to. Here are its inflections, masculine and feminine, in the singular; first without, then with, the regular suffixed article :—

No. 1.

Masculine.		Feminine.	
Nom.	imira	*Nom.*	emira
Gen.	miri	*Gen.*	samira
Acc.	tamira	*Acc.*	tamira

No. 2.

Nom.	imiri	*Nom.*	emira
Gen.	tmirit	*Gen.*	samirasa
Acc.	tamirana	*Acc.*	tamirana

Now what can all these initial changes possibly be other than the stiffened, dead remains of a prefixed article, once a separate word? Bopp, who has written on Albanian, cannot have missed this, and it is clear that I must get his essay at once. But is it not queer stuff?—Very truly yours,

STRANGFORD.

58 GREAT CUMBERLAND STREET,
May 13, 1865.

MY DEAR FREEMAN,—I owe you a letter, and am incited
to pay the debt by much in your revilings of to-day. You
are quite right, working on a small scale, not to discuss Albanian matters. My Phrygian evidence I find in
glosses, in, so far as I remember, direct statements, and
in inscriptions—the Doghani inscription, somewhere near
Angora, I think, ending in *MIΔAI FANAKTEI*, being
the chief. It is not archaic Greek. I have been waiting
for Von Hahn and Bopp, but they have not been sent to
me yet. As regards the Celts and Latins, or rather Pan-
Italians, they must have been very near indeed. But the
more we go back among the European Aryans (a word I
only use for shortness' sake, and would fain keep for the
true Asiatic Aryans exclusively), the more difficult does
it seem to classify clearly and decisively. Thus much is
certain, that the Germans *plus* the Litu-Slaves form one
certain group. But some Germans are inclined to assign
the Celts here rather than to the Italo-Greek group. I
look on the Italian as transitional between Celtic and
Greek. Much of special lexical affinity between Latin
and Greek, I suspect to be simply early borrowing, which
one would expect from the known history of civilisation—
e.g., one of a thousand, *pœna*, and its derivative *punio*, are
surely not of native Italian evolution, but bodily transferred from ποινή.

Coulthart of Coulthart is one of those things that make
one religiously thankful, as for daily bread. It is incomparable, especially the *Leucophibia*, or white lie, as I interpret it. Bonar I remember to have been pointed out to
me by my father. There should be a saint in it, and a
great many Polish kings of the Piast period. This last is
a very good and original element, much beyond Sir Ber-
nard's own power of invention.

Now for Vretos. Your Bulgarian Vretos is Papadopulos Vretos, who sat for Santa Maura as a Rhizospast deputy, turned his coat in my time, and wrote fulsome articles in praise of Sir Henry Storks. By this time I presume he has inked the lining sufficiently to look like the original cloth again.

What am I to do about the transliteration of modern Greek names? You are ultra-classical, to which I have no objection as for you; but the acquisition of modern Greek is, for the educated public at large, a process not of learning, but of unlearning; and I want my spelling to help them in this. But the sailors and merchants cry out at me as being too classical, and would fain treat Greek like Oriental phonetics.

You would call Mount Ida, or the Cretan upland valley, respectively Psêloreitis and Lasêthê (or Lasêthi— I don't know whether it is feminine or neuter). The sailors want Lasethee and Psceloreetee, and protest against my newfangled Italian spelling " Psiloriti " and " Lasithi." Balancing all the pros and cons, I should always spell as Leake, on the whole, as the best compromise between the ultra-classical and the ultra-vulgar. I *could* willingly yield to you on the point of ê for η, provided it be in Hellenic words alone.

Now *Karpenisi* is the word which has led me into this train of writing, and it may be news to you that it is not a Hellenic word, and has nothing to do with fruit or islands, though it has much to do with ash-trees. Its rural dialect is Wallachian, even yet " carpinu;" Italian, " carpino," French, " charme," is the real origin.

Ἄνθρωπος τῶν γραμμάτων is surely as good as my πλοῖον τῆς γραμμῆς.

Φιλολογία, I must tell you, is (or was) not philology, but, generally, literature. The want of a word for our " philology" may have changed this since my time.

There is no such word as ληστής in true modern Greek, truly speaking: that is, it is a modern Greek word, as *progenie* is a modern Italian word, and the distinction between *le'st* and *klepht* is audacious trash. Not that I blame the Greek for trying it on, any more than I blame air for rushing into a vacuum. Here, at all events, is a genuine voice from the Pindus, which says the direct contrary to Vretos: I take from the "Lexikòn Tetrá-glosson."

Οἱ κλέφταις	Φ οὐρ ᾽λι
κλέφτουνε	φούρα
τὴν νύκτα	ντε νοάπτε
οἱ λῃσταί (*sic*)	χαραμίσ᾽λι
εὐγαίνουν	ἔσου
τὴν ἡμέραν	ντζοῦα
καὶ πατοῦνε	ὄτι κάλκα
τὰ καρβάνια	κερβάνελε

I have never heard a common man, or any man talking simply, say λῃστής, for all this. I suppose you can guess at my second language. *Dzúa* for *dzi-oa*, north of the Danube *zi-oa, i.e., die-illa.* Κλέφτης is as comprehensive as "thief" in English, and it alone is used for all: κλεφτουριά being the vernacular for a thieves' rookery, whether in the city or the mountain.

Brigandage within the limits of Greece is as you say. On the frontier it has disappeared for two or three years from the parts about Epirus or the Pashalik of Janina. On the Thessalian frontier it is the same on one side as on the other, but not very bad just now on either. On the Greek side of Epirus it is bad, but there is nothing to rob in particular, except sheep. The patriotic Klepht is a pure fiction of modern Greek *logiótati* and poets; and, as Finlay says, has been, so far as he really existed, ante-dated. I do not *quite* despair of the Greek kingdom, and certainly not of the Greek race—a very different thing; but if ever I heard a Greek thief say "Τὸ Βαλάντιον ἢ τὴν ζωήν," I should indeed despair. Fancy Cipriano la Gala saying, "Aut crumenam aut vitam," and making it his point of honour to suppress "Faccia in terra!" What a Greek

Klepht does say is " Stondópo "—στὸν τόπον—" Stay where you are."

I got a book the other day for which I have been long looking, and which I cannot resist sending you that you may read the true vernacular of late Imperial Rome. It is so obviously what Claudian *must* have talked when at his ease. I think you will enjoy it.—Very truly yours,

STRANGFORD.

58 GREAT CUMBERLAND STREET,
June 13, 1865.

MY DEAR FREEMAN,—I intended to have come down to Oxford on Sunday to meet you and the Prussian caliph, or whatever he may best be called. But my wife, who has been ill for some weeks past, had a return of fever that day, and I did not like to leave her. As you are coming to town so soon, I am content to wait; but please let me know when to expect you, and how long you are likely to stay. W—— gave me a very good account of the humours of Oxford on Saturday and Sunday last, which partly made up to me for not having been there.

What I wrote to you, after a somewhat desultory manner, about Greek transcription, was put into my mind by the sight of Captain Spratt's book on Crete. I may say here, that I contributed to this an appendix on modern Cretan, which I understood would have been printed separately in a few copies to be sent to friends; but this has, most unfortunately, through somebody's oversight, not occurred. It is a nuisance to me. Spratt phoneticises his Greek anyhow, and writes *Nίδa*, *Neetha*, frankly and artlessly. . . . As between Leake's and my *Italianics* and your Hellenics, I think the preference must be determined by the subject treated. If treating Greece continuously, keep to the Hellenic method. If modern Greek matters

alone, then I say transcribe after the Italian fashion.
There is inconvenience in either case when followed out
rigorously : on one hand, it is hard to have to write *Milos*
and *Tinos* (I would never leave out the *s*, because no Greek
ever does in talking Greek, nor in transcribing into Frank,
except in personal names), when it is so necessary to make
people unlearn that stupid talk about " Tenos," now
" Tino," or " Tenedos," now " Denetho " (!). On the other
hand—your hand—some line must be drawn so as to exclude the mass of foreign names ; otherwise you transcribe
all sorts of un-Greek sounds according to a mere makeshift orthography, which is what the Greek is : *Karpenêsi*
is unobjectionable ; but what would you do with Μπαλταν-
τζῆς and Κατζῆς, or even Βουντούρης (Budúris—the Greeks
seem to be giving up μπ for *b*, except when they cannot
help themselves), or all the ten thousand Slavonic feminine and neuter adjectives in -*ova*, -*ovo* ? I would
never write *Socrati*, or, if ever, in careless writing only,
and recognised names like Coletti. Sokrátis with *á* accented I should insist on, in order to make the Dons, who
read me, unlearn Sŏcrătĕs. If writing of Greece compre-
hensively, I might spell the modern name with *ê* for η.
To tell you the truth, I want us to be taught two pronun-
ciations. I want us to keep to our own Dons' pronunciation for everything classical, or meant to be such ; and the
Klephts' pronunciation for everything Christian and later.
Of course, I put Lucian, Longinus, and the Anthology in
the first class ; and I do not hesitate to put the New Testament in the last. Meanwhile I should like to accustom
Dons' eyes to a transcription which forces them to keep in
sight accentuation, and to bear in mind the change of
vowel sounds. As for Frankifying their own names, the
Greeks do it worse than we do. I once had a card left on
me bearing the superscription " Socrate Homère." This,
you will see, is the Greek way of assuming " Norfolk
Howard."

I would draw a wavy and an elastic line, and make it

exclude names which, un-Greek originally, would, if transcribed from Greek, present an unsightly appearance. But when the modern Greek is Hellenic, I would stick to Hellenic, which is what you do; all I want you not to do is Metzobon. As for the choice between ι and ê for η, I have no rooted preference for one over the other; and I feel that I write it ι against the grain in words that have come down unchanged.—Ever yours truly,

STRANGFORD.

P.S.—I must further say, as a part inducement to you to soften the absolute rigidity of your ê for η, that the termination -ης has no more right to be ης in most modern proper names than to be ις, nor so much. Ις for ιος is the natural phonetic corruption which has befallen what the comparative grammarians call the -ια stems in the language of *oc* (*glazi* for *gladius*), in Queer-Welsh (*evangeli, misteri*), and pre-eminently in Lithuanian (*perdis* for *perdias*, genitive *perdjo*—I leave you to guess the meaning from Greek and Grimm's Law in English—compared with *ugnis*, genitive *ugnês*, the true *i* declension). In modern Greek neuters in -ιον it is universal. The colloquial declension is—

σεγρετάρης	σεγρεταρέοι
———ρη	———ρέων
———ρην	———ρέους

(but final ν goes for nothing, and is dropped or not at pleasure), the genitive plural being hardly ever used in talking, except in phrases like πόσω χρονῶ εἶσαι, "How old are you?" by the mere untaught.

58 Great Cumberland Street,
July 26, 1865.

MY DEAR FREEMAN,—I am sorry to say that I am in the hands of a doctor. . . . I read in the "Pall Mall Gazette" of last night these words, beginning a leading article :—

" Roumensch, we believe, is a curious jargon, composed of Arabic words engrafted on a corrupt Roman patois."

What is a jargon, what is a patois, what is an uncorrupt patois, and what is belief in etymological matters ?—Ever yours truly,   STRANGFORD.

———

. . . . . 1865.

MY DEAR FREEMAN,—I owe you a letter, but have preferred to put off the payment thereof until my return from Brighton, where I have been staying for a fortnight. As for your letter, its items have been driven into remote corners of my mind, if not bodily exterminated, by two successive weekly waves of invasion from the same quarter—on kindred subjects, too. Firstly, Prendergast. I had read the book with special interest as bearing on the inquiry how far the old Irish race has been altered or obliterated in Ireland. I agree with every word you say about it in the uttermost degree; and as for your parallel between the Klephts of Greece and the Rapparees, I had not only made it my own, but had done so independently from the literary or philological side by means of the Irish κλέφτικα τραγούδια, of which there exists an immense mass unknown in England—not that I can read a line of them without a crib. One thing is certain, that the English nation of a hundred and fifty years ago did wilfully and deliberately murder, in a national sense, the old Gaelic nation. Perhaps it did so for self-preservation, but at all events, it did so as a matter of fact ; and the modern English-speaking Irishman has not yet had time enough to outlive the memory of the fact. All the reason in the world will not account for modern Irish discontent and sentiment, so long as we, in our English way, persist in neglecting to consider the unreasoning and sentimental element in our own dependencies. As for Prendergast's fact, I do not believe the obliteration to have been complete, or, at all events, permanent. The proof of this is to be found in one of the most curious books I have ever read, which you would read with deep interest, in spite of the intolerable Gaelic names of which it is made up. This is O'Donovan's edition—preface, notes, and translation— of a topographical Irish poem of the early part of the fourteenth century, by one O'Duvegan; the first line of which was thus paraphrased by Lynch, the author of "Cambrensis Eversus:" "O socii, pulchræ fines obeamus Ternes." The arrangement is, of course, nothing more than the enumeration of clans and sub-clans, with rivers, mountains, and the like; and the notes give their identification. Now, in extra-Connacian Ireland, you constantly meet with the observation that representatives of the clans O'Jack, and O'Tom, and O'Harry are to be found *in situ*, and *iis nominibus*,[1] and generally in abject poverty. These, therefore, must either have been overlooked by the Cromwellians, or have wandered back again. These names are to be found in every page. Ireland is made up, in fact, of these details; and in the face of this the "Times" talks of there being no consciousness of a difference, or power of detecting a difference, between "Saxon" or "Celtic" descent in modern Irishmen; and not only the "Times," but all Englishmen, wonder why the Irish should be so fractious and perverse under the nursing of our good and reforming generation of English. The Gael has become an Englishman or Briton with a brogue, and the national aspiration has become a republican aspiration, and America has taken the place of France as the promised land; but whatever type the feeling may take, its direction will for

[1] Or their so-called English translations, such as Norton for O'Neachtan.

the present be anti-English, and for some time to come,
even if no priests existed to foster such a feeling for political purposes.   Time alone can make the two bodies grow
together, not tenant-right, nor the abolition of the Irish
Church.

Now for a much more serious business, one which
irritates me like sandflies, and on account of which you
must prepare for bad language on my part.   I allude to
the last new manifestation or dodge of Scotch provincialism, which is to me one of the most aggravating
and pestilent nuisances of modern times.   Cold-blooded
wretches, they never go wrong grandly and genially, like
the noble Welsh, or Gloucestrians, but vex you with a
perverse show of argument and a virtuous arrogance of
logical treatment when their premisses convict them of
the most utter ignorance and backwardness.   You say
you don't see why Robertson's book was written.   *I do.*
It was written to MacBuncombe, or Clan Buncombe,
if I may allow myself to use, for convenience of illustration, words which would never have been heard east of
St. George's Channel in that form, had not certain Irishmen brought them there.   It must have come to be
written on this wise : Scotland is a geographical term, or
a political term, but not an ethnological term, except
under certain limitations, excluding all reference to ultimate descent.   It may become one in the future, as may
Switzerland; and this analogy of yours is one which has
long struck me.   Ethnically, Scotland is simply made up
of Northumbrian English and Scotian Gael; to these must
be added, as elements historically known, certain people
called Picts, and certain true Cambrian Britons.   But as
these people were all politically united for hundreds of
years, their descendants want to reduce them to uniformity of race as far as they can do with safety, and without sinning in the light of day.   The Picts are taken up as
the stalking-horse of this theory, as alone furnishing the
necessary obscurity.   The Irish connection is disliked in

Scotland, as the Lappish connection is disliked in Hungary; so that when Skene was the first to proclaim the identity not only of the Picts with the old Caledonii, but the direct representation of these by the modern Highlanders both in blood and in language, he was crowned a prizeman, and met the wish of the national mind so exactly, that he founded a school in the long-run. Of this school Mr. Robertson, on whom I have had my eye for a year or so, is the noisiest member. Its doctrines are now almost a fixed article of faith north of the Tweed, so far as I can see. You do not contradict them, but I do not believe a word of them. They stultify the whole application of comparative philology to Celtic; and, whatever may have been the case at the time Skene wrote his treatise, there is no excuse for them since Zeuss and Whitley Stokes.

For every philological purpose, except the merest modern delineation of dialects, Scotch and Irish Gaelic must be considered absolutely as one language. But the one is oral only, the other is literary; it has records, by means of which its history and its modifications can be traced. Now the oral forms of the one island are meaningless and inexplicable by themselves, but are quite clear when confronted with the older records of the other island. Thus, both the modern Highlander and the modern Irishman say *robh me, eram*, "I was." By itself this may be Basque, or Semitic, or anything. But in old Irish the word is regularly *robu*, or *robbu* = Sanskrit *prababhuva*, Greek $\pi\rho o + \dot{\epsilon}\phi\omega$, or Lithuanian *prabuvo;* containing the regular Aryan root *bu*, *plus* the preposition always used for other Gaelic preterites, just as we used *ge* in *gefuhton*, "they fought." [The Celtic loss of initial *p* is very curious and all-pervading.] It is this history of their own language of which the modern Scotch are so perversely ignorant when they treat it as though it had always existed as it now stands. No attempt is made to show that the Albanic Scotch vocabulary or grammar differs from the

Hibernia; but appeal is made to the local names of the known Pictish district as betokening a so-called high-Gaelic language, distinct from its cognate low-Gaelic of Ireland. This appeal you will find in a paper of Skene's in the "Archæologia Cambrensis," entirely prescientific in character. Whatever these local names may really indicate, the language of the people themselves is either Irish of the Scotch settlement, or is so thoroughly Hibernicised that its original difference has been made completely to disappear.

Assuming Skene's view to be true, the Edinburgh antiquaries must accept the latter alternative willy-nilly, for, things English apart, they must either have been Irishmen, or been mastered and moulded by Irishmen.

I believe Picts were Britons with a difference of dialect, primitive and *un-Romanised*, and this difference may have made it nearer to Gaelic, as was certainly the case with the Romanised non-Cambrian British of Cornwall and Armorica (see the article, for instance). I believe these Picts *were Scotised*, or *Gadelised*, from Ireland alone, but that in blood the modern Highlanders *partly* represent them. And, finally, I believe that no Celt will ever do anything with his language until he has seen that it is in the category of modern French rather than in the category of Basque. But is it not wonderful how those reiving loons north of the Tweed have reft Ireland of the name Scotia to begin with, and are in a fair way of monopolising the word Gaelic as well? I have not seen Robertson's new book.—Ever yours truly,

STRANGFORD.

58 GREAT CUMBERLAND STREET,
Wednesday, October 1865.

MY DEAR FREEMAN,—I was going to answer you on Saturday, but I preferred to wait until I had taken in

and digested your **revilings of Dasent, of** Gladstone, and
of the military **road man, who indeed** seems but a **well-**
meaning **poor** creature, **entirely** insignificant. But **he**
should have **left** bookmaking **alone. As** for Gladstone,
all comparative philologists should **combine to present**
you with a gold medal for speaking out **in the way you**
have done about his crudeness and haziness. **But as**
for Dasent—for I suppose **it** is Dasent—no punishment
can be too severe for him and his absurd Scandinavian
slop.

The idea of Scandinavians at all in Herodotus's time
must be utterly wrong. I believe that the geographical
Scandinavia must then have held nothing but Lapps and
Fins, and that the ethnic Scandinavians were as yet un-
born as a separate Teutonic family. It is more than **I can**
stand to **be told** of a deity Thor, *co nomine*, in the fifth
century B.C.; it is quite as **much as one can do to** admit
him in the fifth century A.D. When did the Scandinavians lose their initial *w*'s **and throw out their** medial
n's, **so as to** turn **the real form, Wodan, into Odinn** (the
second *n* here being the assimilated *s* of a nominative
case), and Thunor into Thor? I believe that it was at
a late period rather than an early one, and I am confident
that the distinctive points which constitute **Scandinavian-**
ism as opposed to Teutonism—as regards grammar, **at**
least—arose from their conquests or settlements or other
relations being among my friends the Lithuanians mainly,
who gave them **the idea of** their passive voice and their
suffixed article.

This leads me to the important point of your letter, the
relative age of High-Dutch and Low-Dutch. I don't
think there is anything more difficult in all philology
than the exact classification **of the** Pan-Teutonic or All-
Dutch languages. It is easy **enough to take** an extreme
form and make that the type **of a class, but I** do believe
that the mass of the languages **are more or less transi-**
tional, or got more or less mixed up, and affected by one

another, taking them as we find them. Take the spell found by Grimm on the cover of a book for instance, beginning—

> " Pul endi Wodan
> Vuorum zi holza."

The *z*'s here are clearly High-Dutch, but the general language of the spell is Low-Dutch, and the *v* in *vuorum* seems even extreme West Saxon, or mere Somersetshire. Even the language of the Heliand seems to have High-Dutch, or at least un-Saxon, in it here and there, as the omission of *h* in the oblique cases of *he*, as *vio* for *hira*, &c. The extremes are clear enough, certainly; and the early transitional or undefined dialects all tend to grow up in one direction or the other; but as to relative archaism, I am only disposed to go with you as regards the system of sounds. This, I think, is clearly older in the Low than the High. But in grammar it seems to be the other way, at any rate nowadays. There are things in the High, if you go back far enough, older than anything in Ulphilas, such as the first person plural, *hepamês*, older than *habam*. And the Low seems, so far as I know, to have begun early to lose its inflections in its articles and nouns.

I never could make head or tail out of *dog*. I once heard that Latham, who in his wild way occasionally hits the mark, compared it with *dachs*. A badger is not a dog, certainly, but I have an impression that a brock is, in some Celtic county or other ; not that Latham knew that. However, your Toggenburg, *plus* Doggenburg, seems to settle the matter. But is the word originally Dutch, and how comes it by its *o* ? Was *o* long or short ? Long Dutch *o*'s are the successors of original Ur-Dutch *a*'s, and short Dutch *o*'s are modern things altogether. I suspect that the word must have been once *dog-Latin*.

I never cared much for the Wends, having always given my warm heart to the Wits, though Weonodland managed to hold its own better than Witland. Is there anything known in a full way about the ancient Wendish gods, for

there is next to nothing about the Slavonian gods generally? Zernebock and Bielibog are not half enough.

Do you know one F. N.? He has been writing an
article about cuneiforms in the last number of " Fraser,"
being instigated thereto by his chief, than which I never
read more intolerable and aggravating stuff. He finds a
Frenchman, who treats King Darius's Persian in a way
that my friend the little pig-man treats King Howel's
Welsh; he then pits him against Rawlinson, and pre-
tends to adjudge between the two by a modified alphabet, determined by the application of *Greek;* he having
no knowledge whatever either of Sanskrit or of Zend,
or of modern Persian, nor any idea that such knowledge
was necessary. The wretched man has no idea that if
Rawlinson had never been born, and the big Behistun
inscription never been carved, our knowledge of the language would simply have been deficient by one letter,
occurring in two words only; for that was the whole
amount of Rawlinson's actually new contributions to the
alphabet, worked out co-operatively in Germany by the
help of comparative philology from the Persepolitan inscriptions. Sir Cornewall has a great deal to answer for
in regard to the backwardness of philological study in
England, and I fear I shall find myself some of these days
speaking disrespectfully of him. As for his theory of
Latin being broken up by German invasion, I read it
exactly the other way, and am disposed to think that it
was the loose and disintegrating spoken Latin which broke
up the well-knit Old Dutch.

I have been in Ireland for two months, among Fenians
and rumours of Fenians; but I was just a year too late to
see a real old original Fenian bard—the only one left in the
country—who died at the reputed age of 120. This man
would recite Fenian poems for hours on end, with a
chant, I was told, which must have been like an Oriental's
recitation, and did really wander about like an ancient
ἀοιδός; but nobody cared twopence about him and his

Ossianic poems. Why do we not send "an illustrious Ossianic scholar" to settle the Fenian and other Irish difficulties? The judgment of an ordinary common-sense Irishman on such an appointment would give the exact counterpart of the judgment of an ordinary common-sense Ionian—say Lascarato—on the famous Homeric scholar despatch.

With best regards to Mrs. Freeman, I remain, ever yours truly,   STRANGFORD.

———

Wednesday, December 20, 1865.

MY DEAR FREEMAN,—Firstly, of my Arabic monogram. It is merely Strangford with a prosthetic *i* marked *alif*, without which it cannot be pronouned in Semitic countries. Now pray admire the way I am going to connect this with the Picts. This very same characteristic has been supposed to have always belonged to Welsh, or rather to Cymmric, because it belongs to modern Cymmric; and I know not what has not been said about the "Turanian character of Welsh phonology." Now it is not found in Cornu-Armorican, nor in *Old* Cymmric. Here I must ask you to grant me the full and free use of the word "initiality," on the analogy of Lord John's "finality." I want it in order to define the condition of identical existence, as we see them now attributed to languages, which are thereby held to be virtually or absolutely unchanged from all time. If we have no record of an older stage of a language, we must take it as we find it; if we have such a record, we must make use of it. Now the fallacy of initiality is one into which all Scotch Gaels without exception fall, through their provincialism; and Jones and even Guest, so far as I have seen of his writings (which is very little), fall into it as regards Cymmric. [Don't mind my two *m*'s; I'm coming to them.] But no one who has properly mastered the principles of

Zeuss and the details of the large post-Zeussian literature should fall into it. Thus Jones says the Romans made Venta out of Gwent. This is equivalent to saying that the Greeks made Artaxerxes out of Ardeshîr and Mithridates out of Mihr-dâd, or that the Romans made Catti out of people who called themselves Hessen. There was no harm in saying so in days when nobody knew, or thought it possible to know, any **Persian** or German older than current Persian or current German. But it cannot be said now without flying in the face of comparative philology in points absolutely and scientifically settled. The Greeks and Romans took the prototypes of modern Aryan words in a pure old Aryan form, sometimes identical with their own form, and always lending itself to it and falling naturally into it. It became stereotyped in Latin and Greek, but in the original language had to stand or fall with the main body of living speech. Welsh is not an *initial* language, any more than French, or German, or Persian, or English; Basque is, or anyhow must be treated as such.

Jones's local names are the best part of his book, but they altogether fail to convince me that they belong to Proto-Gael. I do not believe in the word Gael as a general and primeval ethnic term at all. The Cymmry took Gwyddyl from the Irish Goedel, which, with Gaidel, Gaidil, is the oldest accessible form of the word, and prevailed in the era of confusion, if one may say so; the fifth and sixth centuries. *Wy* in Welsh is the etymological equivalent of $\bar{e}$ in its former stage; sometimes of $\bar{o}$ (as Clywd = Clôta), and if representing anything else, does so orally and not etymologically. This shows it was borrowed at a period when the word was the same as in the fifth century. Had it been borrowed from the Proto-Gael, assuming them to have used it at all, it would have been stereotyped in a different form, for Irish words of the fifth century are themselves in a late and corrupt stage. But I am convinced the Proto-Gael did not use the word in this

L

comprehensive way. Such generalizations are very rare in rude nations; and as for the Gael, when they first appear, they do so with two or three alternative names—Scoti, Trar, Iberionaces, quite as comprehensive as Gaedil. One side of the question has been entirely overlooked by Jones. This is the distinct record of long and lasting invasions in the Irish annals. Twenty-five years' permanence would account for a settlement by a band in *any* part of Wales; and such an invasion did once occur. Manx is much too near Irish to be Proto-Gaelic, and is certainly the result of such an invasion. If you have anything so positive as a recorded series of invasions, concurrently with the *à priori* weight of philological argument, I think it is necessary to show cause why these words should not belong to this period more positively than by conjecture, and presumption of what would have been and might have been, which is all that Jones does. But, after all, he states his theory in a perfectly undogmatic way, and as one quite open to the other view. Broadly, I myself would say that no Gael, or trace of a Gael, exists on this side of the Irish Sea which is not directly derived from Ireland since the downfall of Roman rule.[1] The worst of Jones's book is his trying to make anything out of the wretched Triads, which are simply not worth the paper they are written on. The only thing certain about Cuneddaf is the Latin and Ogham bilingual of "Sagrani fili Cunotami;" and Ogham is as post-Roman as Latin is Roman. The only firm ground in Old Welsh is upon the "Liber Landavensis," the "Laws of Howel," and the Oxford and Luxemburg-Glosses, with the lines in Juvencus; to stand upon the Triads is standing on a wet bog.

As to the Picts, I do believe they got that name from the Roman colonists in Britain, as being wild, untamed, or tattooed, distinct from the tame and clothed Britons. The Spaniards in Mexico distinguishing their Indian neigh-

---

[1] The word *Albion* may possibly be one exception to this, though it need not be so for certain, for it may be Britannic.

bours on the north as Mansos, or tame, and Bravos,
or wild, illustrate this view. I suppose they were wild
Britons. There *may* have been Proto-Gael among them,
but this is one of those things which do not appear. How
Gael got to Ireland, and when, I cannot tell, and had
rather not guess. One would think it was from Britain,
with Wales for choice; yet it is curious that the grammatical and lexical affinities of Gaelic are much more distinct
with South-British (including Armorican) than with Cambrian. Then the persistence of the Spanish tradition *plus*
the resemblance of Iverio (the oldest form of Erin) and
Iberia may possibly be worth consideration, though full of
difficulty. Then Gaul, the Veneti of Brittany, compared
with Venedotia, Gwynedd, and Fened, the probable Irish
source of Gwynedd, and oldest form of our Fenian friends
on record. But the Scotch Highlands I put quite out of
the question. Edward Lhuyd, an admirable philologist,
far beyond his age, made the Picts quite Cymmric, and
even called the lines in Juvencus, which he could not
translate, Pictish. The main authority for this view is
Chalmers, in his great work "Caledonia," which is most
excellent, though very long-winded. Till Skene appeared,
Pinkerton was the only serious holder of an opposite view.
I think Skene very poor compared with Chalmers, and
now, since Zeuss's school, worth little. His recent attempt at analysing local names is mere sleight-of-hand,
doing pea-and-thimble work with Inver and Aber. Local
names are utterly fallacious unless, firstly, you have the
whole of them, and, secondly, you are master of the language to which they belong; he answers neither condition. I have read somewhere—perhaps in him—of there
being no Bens in Ireland, while every hill is a Ben in the
Highlands. This is true on a small map; but for all
that, I was at a place in Ireland the other day overhung
by three Bens, and from ten minutes' walk of which you
could count twelve more.

I would rather use Britannic than your Cymric, for indicating the whole group, or the type; though, of course, both mean the same thing; keeping Cymric or Cambrian for the sub-family, as opposed to the sub-family of the Corn-Welsh, or West-Weal as ·*plus* the Armoricans. Welsh should be what it really is, the equivalent of Britannic, not of Cymric. This last word I would spell with two *m*'s, because it is so spelt in Old Welsh systematically, and because it points out its etymology from *cyn* and *bro*, *i.e.*, Combroges as opposed to Allobroges; showing clearly, at the same time, that it has nothing to do with Cimmerians, or Cimbri, or Cambria either, in all likelihood. Bret-Welsh is a very good word; as I suppose it is impossible to restore Welsh by itself to generic honours in common talk after so long serving to mark the species. Rum-Welsh and Gal-Welsh I fear are too strong meat for babes as yet. But are you going to leave out the Wallachs in the cold—the Wallachs, "who are now learning," according to the "Guardian" of this week, "to call themselves Roumains"!

I do not know whether you ever see the "Athenæum." Some weeks ago Professor —— actually wrote therein a long letter, worth its weight in gold, maintaining that the Welsh are or were Belgæ, because that word must have been pronounced Weljæ or Welshæ by Cæsar, one reason for which last, among others, being that at Cardiff he actually saw a modern Greek word over a shop with β doing duty for a *V*. Morologically speaking, the production is no richer or sillier than your prize-fool from Gloucestershire, or my little pig Welshman, but it is really of serious importance as coming from a real man of science, who must know what science is, and who thus manifestly shows that he has no idea of any philological science. The thing would be impossible abroad; a Berlin man would not dream of dashing into etymology without consulting Bopp, any more than he would dash into chemistry or geology without consulting the chief respective heads of science; but here there is no school of philology, and I do not quite hold M. Müller guiltless for not having founded one, instead of going off into comparative mythology.

To return, finally, to Jones. I should like to know whether, when he wrote his book, he had not previously assumed, tacitly and as a matter of course, that High-landers and Manxmen were actual Proto-Gael, and not Irish or Hibernicized Gael, or Hibernicized something else. I am sure this must have been his impression. But the philological evidence is conclusive. The two forms of speech were absolutely identical in the twelfth century, as proved by the entries in the "Book of Deir," and the corruption or divergence thenceforward took place chiefly in the province, not the mother state. The lan-guage in its oldest form is far gone in disintegration. If the Highlanders had been præ-Roman-Proto-Gael, the di-vergence of their speech from the Irish during the Roman dominion, when they had no common literature, and no intercourse with Ireland, would have been infinitely greater —great to mutual unintelligibility. Skene would fain claim the Fenian songs as an old stock of poetry common to both—songs with Lochlan (originally Loch*land* in oldest MS.) and modern Danish names like Oscar in them (Oscar was Auskar at first). I cannot comprehend Skene's repu-tation, at least on other than Scotch grounds.

The man whom I am disposed, in this question, to put above all others in learning, criticism, and breadth and calmness of view, is *Reeves.* Don't be astonished; I mean an Irish Reeves, whose chief work is his edition of Adam-nan's "Vita Columbæ." Modern Irish writing on Scotian matters is wonderfully *metropolitan*, and his is the best. O'Donovan is very good, but contrasts with Reeves just as a very learned Arabian sheikh would contrast with De Sacy.

I devoutly trust Goldwin Smith will hold on awhile. The only way I can help you meanwhile is to break ——'s head for his astonishing fatuity and folly in getting F. N. to write his cuneiform nonsense in "Fraser."—Ever yours truly,   STRANGFORD.

December 1865.   Monday.

My Dear Freeman,—What here follows is superfetation over and above my Hibernian outbreak of Saturday. What I want to say is that I have never seen Basil Jones's " Vestiges," though I am aware of his general theory, and know the book, though chronologically and therefore unavoidably pre-Zeussian, to be a good and valuable one. I do not know whether the Gaul whose vestiges he finds in Wales are in his eyes Gael from Ireland and of the Christian period, or Proto-Gael left behind after the others had gone to Ireland. If he maintains the latter view, I should indeed like to see anything like a proof of it. I cannot, as yet, admit it in Wales; for I doubt very much whether the names of Gaedil and Gwyddel (observe that the Welsh form, taken down by ear and not by eye, retains the old pronunciation of the Gaelic medial lost in latter days) are of true primeval antiquity. I have no positive proof of this, but as the ascertained outswarming time of some Gadhelians *eo nomine* was Christian and Columbian in South Britain, I think the onus probandi lies on those who are bound to bring positive proof of the contrary, and to show that the Gwyddel were not Irishmen of 500 or 600 A.D. in the present case. Positively, I believe we know nothing, absolutely nothing, of the original peopling of Ireland. But those who maintain that it was peopled by a race of whom the Scotch Highlanders left behind in Britain are the descendants, seem to me to be the same or worse than those who maintain that the Armoricans are descendants, judged by language, of the ancient Gaels.

Do not reprove my word Proto-Gaelic. It is very convenient, and necessary if we do not use the German *Ur*, and have lost our own *Or*.—Ever yours truly,

STRANGFORD.

LETTER TO MR. MAX MÜLLER.

January 11, 1866.

MY DEAR MÜLLER,—I don't know whether you ever see the " Pall Mall Gazette." In that of last night I wrote a little note about the *Church* controversy—I did not write with much sense of responsibility, as my chief object was to make game of Dr. Cumming and his dogmatism, and to warn readers against too ready adoption of Mr. Ferguson, whose book about river names is very silly. Not being sufficiently careful, I fear I overstated the unanimity of German opinion in hesitating to receive κυριακὸν; but I referred Mr. Arnold to Diefenbach *sub voce* "*kêlikn.*" After writing the note I consulted Sophocles—not the playwright, but the Greek who made a Yankee of himself—as to the use of κυριακὸν, and found some seven or eight distinct references to passages where it is employed for the building. Then I looked at Miklosich, whose etymologies are generally quite sound, under the Slavonic form *tszkv-,* which is certainly taken from the German, though its initial letter-change and its *v* are curious deviations.

He adopts κυριακὸν as the origin of the German. Wackernagel, *sub voce* "*chirihha,*" does the same. So I reluctantly made up my mind on the whole in favour of the Greek as the ultimate origin. Your letter of this morning quite confirms me, as you have come to the same conclusion by the same process, *plus* the argument from *Dominicum.* I should hardly think however that *kêlikn,* though doubtless an un-Dutch word, is κυριακὸν. If anything, it must be *cœnaculum,* a word which it actually represents in one passage ; and it never translates anything but tower, house, or upper chamber, without the least idea of the Lord attaching to it. Possibly it may be in the same category as *andbahts = ambactus, i.e.,* neither Latin nor Greek, but old Celtic ; for the word distinctly occurs in an old Gaulish inscription ending (I quote from memory) *icuru sosin celicnon,* on, I think, a circular plate or rim. This surely is too like the Gothic word to be accident. I believe in confluent etymologies, and think it not improbable that the similarity of sound in the Latin word may have rendered the attribution of its meaning the easier to the already existing Gothic word, taken from the Celtic —there being no generic repugnance in the two meanings.

Freeman will never give up the original Teutonism of the word, I fancy, after having actually heard the Swiss say *chilche.*[1]

I observe you transcribe the Anglo-Saxon *w* or *p* as a *v,* as do most modern Germans; but you did not in your books. I own that I feel something like a modern Greek in this matter—that we are right in the matter of pronunciation, and the Germans—unless they mean it for a conventional sign—are wrong; though I hope with more reason than a modern Greek.

Can you tell me the exact title and publisher of the book you quote as " Historical Proofs," &c., by a Mr. Robertson ? I only know of it from a review by Freeman which I cannot find. I believe the book maintains a pestilent provincial Scotch heresy, that the Gael of Scotland are co-ordinate with, and not subordinate to, the Gael of Ireland; that their language, at any rate, descent apart, is Proto-Gaelic, not transplanted Irish. I paid much attention to this when in Ireland last year, and am sure that there is not a single form in the whole language which is not either actual Irish or decayed Irish. Such a view simply stultifies the whole work of Zeuss and his school. Scotch Gaelic is merely good as Yankee English is good. But is it not astonishing how the dwellers in Scotland have robbed the Irish of the word *Scot* in old days, and have all but succeeded in depriving them of the word Gaelic for their language ?—Ever truly yours,

STRANGFORD.

---

[1] Mr. Freeman states that he does not remember to have said this or heard this ; but he has seen some such form as *cilch* somewhere.

LORD STRANGFORD'S NOTES CONTRIBUTED TO
"THE STUDY OF CELTIC LITERATURE," BY
MATTHEW ARNOLD, LONDON, 1867.

Mr. Arnold says :—

" The poor Welshman still says in the genuine tongue of his ancestors, *gwyn, goch, craig, maes, llan, arglwydd,*" &c.

Lord Strangford remarks on this passage :—

" Your Gomer and your Cimmerians are of course only lay figures, to be accepted in the rhetorical and subjective sense. As such I accept them, but I enter a protest against the 'genuine tongue of his ancestors.' Modern Celtic tongues are to the old Celtic heard by Julius Cæsar, broadly speaking, what the modern Romanic tongues are to Cæsar's own Latin. Welsh, in fact, is a *detritus;* a language in the category of modern French, or, to speak less roughly and with a closer approximation, of old Provençal, not in the category of Lithuanian, much less in the category of Basque. By true inductive research, based on an accurate comparison of such forms of Celtic speech, oral and recorded, as we now possess, modern philology has, in so far as was possible, succeeded in restoring certain forms of the parent speech, and in so doing has achieved not the least striking of its many triumphs ; for those very forms thus restored have since been verified past all cavil by their actual discovery in the old Gaulish inscriptions recently come to light. The *phonesis* of Welsh as it stands is modern, not primitive ; its grammar,—the verbs excepted,—is constructed out of the fragments of its earlier forms, and its vocabulary is strongly Romanised, two out of the six words here given being Latin of the Empire.

Rightly understood, this enhances the value of modern Celtic instead of depreciating it, because it serves to rectify it. To me it is a wonder that Welsh should have retained so much of its integrity under the iron pressure of four hundred years of Roman dominion. Modern Welsh tenacity and cohesive power under English pressure is nothing compared with what that must have been " (pp. 5, 6).

Here again, says Mr. Arnold, let me have the pleasure of quoting Lord Strangford :—

" When the Celtic tongues were first taken in hand at the dawn of comparative philological inquiry, the tendency was, for all practical results, to separate them from the Indo-European aggregate, rather than to unite them with it. The great gulf once fixed between them was narrowed on the surface, but it was greatly and indefinitely deepened. Their vocabulary and some of their grammar was seen at once to be perfectly Indo-European, but they had no case-endings to their nouns,—none at all in Welsh, none that could be understood in Gaelic; their *phonesis* seemed primeval and inexplicable, and nothing could be made out of their pronouns which could not be equally made out of many wholly un-Aryan languages. They were therefore co-ordinated, not with each single Aryan tongue, but with the general complex of Aryan tongues, and were conceived to be anterior to them and apart from them, as it were the strayed vanguard of European colonisation or conquest from the East. The reason of this misconception was, that their records lay wholly uninvestigated as far as all historical study of the language was concerned, and that nobody troubled himself about the relative age and the development of forms, so that the philologists were fain to take them as they were put into their hands by uncritical or perverse native commentators and writers, whose grammars and dictionaries teemed with blunders and downright forgeries. One thing, and one thing alone, led to the truth: the sheer drudgery of thirteen long years spent by Zeuss in the patient investigation of the most ancient Celtic records, in their actual condition, line by line and letter by letter. Then for the first time the foundation of Celtic research was laid; but the great philologist did not live to see the superstructure which never could have been raised but for him. Prichard was first to indicate the right path, and Bopp, in his monograph of 1839, displayed his incomparable and masterly sagacity as usual, but for want of any trustworthy record of Celtic words and forms to work upon, the truth remained concealed or obscured until the publication of the 'Grammatica Celtica.' Dr. Arnold, a man of the past generation, who made more use of the then uncertain and unfixed doctrines of comparative philology in his historical writings than is done by the present generation in the fullest noonday light of the 'Vergleichende Grammatik,' was thus justified in his view by the philology of the period, to which he merely gave an enlarged historical expression. The prime fallacy then as now, however, was that of antedating the distinction between Gaelic and Cymric Celts" (pp. 17, 18).

"Professor Bergmann's[1] etymologies are often false lights, held by an uncertain hand. The Apian land certainly meant the watery land, *Meer-umschlungen*, among the pre-Hellenic Greeks, just as the same land is called Morea by the modern post-Hellenic or Romaic Greeks from *more*, the name for the sea in the Slavonic vernacular of its inhabitants during the heart of the Middle Ages. But it is only connected by a remote and secondary affinity, if connected at all, with the *avia* of Scandinavia, assuming that to be the true German word for *water*, which, if it had come down to us in Gothic, would have been *avi*, genitive *aujôs*, and not a mere Latinised termination. Scythian is surely a negative rather than a positive term, much like our *Indian*, or the *Turanian* of modern ethnologists, used to comprehend nomads and barbarians

---

[1] Les Scythes les Ancêtres des Peuples Germaniques et Slaves, par F. G. Bergmann, professeur à la faculté des Lettres de Strasbourg: Colmar, 1858.

of all sorts and races north and east of the Black and
Caspian seas. It is unsafe to connect their name with
anything as yet; it is quite as likely that it refers to the
bow and arrow as to the shield, and is connected with our
word to *shoot, sceótan, skiutan,* Lithuanian *szau-ti.* Some
of the Scythian peoples may have been Anarian, Allophylic, Mongolian; some were demonstrably Aryan, and
not only that, but Iranian as well, as is best shown in a
memoir read before the Berlin Academy this last year;
the evidence having been first indicated in the rough by
Schaffarik the Slavonic antiquary. Coins, glosses, proper
names, and inscriptions prove it. *Targitaos* (not *-tavus*)
and the rest is guesswork or wrong. Herodotus's $Ta\beta\iota\tau\grave{\iota}$
for the goddess Vesta is not connected with the root *div*
whence Dêvas, Deus, &c., but the root *tap,* in Latin *tep*
(of tepere, tepefacere), Slavonic *tepl, topl* (for *tep* or *top*),
in modern Persian *tâb. Thymele* refers to the hearth as
the place of smoke ($\theta\acute{\upsilon}\omega$, *thus, fumus*), but *familia* denotes
household from *famulus* for *fagmulus,* the root *fag* being
equated with the Sansk. *bhaj, servira.* Lucan's Hesus or
Esus may fairly be compared with the Welsh *Hu* Gadarn
by legitimate process, but no letter-change can justify his
connection with *Gaisos,* the spear, not the sword, Virgil's
gæsum, A. S. *gár,* our verb to *gore,* retained in its outer
form in *gar*-fish. For *Theuthisks, lege Thiudisks,* from
thiuda, populus; in old high German Diutisk, Diotisk,
popularis, vulgaris, the country vernacular as distinguished
from the cultivated Latin; hence the word *Dutch, Deutsch.*
With our ancestors *theód* stood for nation generally, and
getheóde for any speech. Our *diet* in the political sense
is the same word, but borrowed from our German cousins,
not inherited from our fathers. The modern Celtic form
is the Irish *tuath;* in ancient Celtic it must have been
teuta, touta, of which we actually have the adjective
toutius in the Gaulish inscription of Nismes. In Oscan we
have it as *turta, tuta,* its adjective being handed down in
Livy's *meddix tuticus,* the mayor or chief magistrate of

the *tuta.* In the Umbrian inscriptions it is *tota;* in Lithuanian *tauta,* the country opposed to the town, and in old Prussian *tauta,* the country generally, *en Prusiskan tautan, im Land zu Preussen"* (pp. 79, 80, 81).

"The original forms of Gael should be mentioned— Gaedil, Goidil: in modern Gaelic orthography Gaoidheal, where the *dh* is not realised in pronunciation. There is nothing impossible in the connection of the root of this with that of Scot, *if* the *s* of the latter be merely prosthetic. But the whole thing is *in nubibus,* and given as a guess only" (p. 82).

"The name of Erin is treated at length in a masterly note by Whitley Stokes in the 1st series of Max Müller's lectures (4th ed.), p. 255, where its earliest *tangible* form is shown to have been Iverio. Pictet's connection with Arya is quite baseless" (p. 83).

"Our word *gay,*" says Mr. Arnold, "it is said, is itself Celtic." Lord Strangford remarks:—"Whatever *gai* may be, it is assuredly not Celtic. Is there any authority for this word *gair,* to laugh, or rather 'laughter,' beyond O'Reilly? O'Reilly is no authority at all except in so far as tested and passed by the new school. It is hard to give up *gavisus.* But Diez, chief authority in Romanic matters, is content to accept Muratori's reference to an old High-German *gâhi,* modern *jähe,* sharp, quick, sudden, brisk, and so to the sense of lively, animated, high in spirits" (p. 101).

"Modern Germanism, in a general estimate of Germanism, should not be taken, absolutely and necessarily, as the constant, whereof we are the variant. The Low-Dutch of Holland, anyhow, are indisputably as genuine Dutch as the High-Dutch of Germany Proper. But do they write sentences like this one,—*informe, ingens, cui lumen ademptum?* If not, the question must be asked, not how we have come to deviate, but how the Germans have come to deviate. Our modern English prose in plain matters is often all just the same as the prose of 'King Alfred' and the 'Chronicle.' Ohthere's 'North Sea Voyage' and Wulf-stan's 'Baltic Voyage' is the sort of thing which is sent in every day, one may say, to the Geographical or Ethnological Society, in the whole style and turn of phrase and thought" (p. 117).

"The Irish monks whose bells and books were found in Iceland could not have contributed anything to the old Norse spirit, for they had perished before the first Norseman had set foot on the island. The form of the old Norse poetry known to us as Icelandic, from the accident of its preservation in that island alone, is surely Pan-Teutonic from old times; the art and method of its strictly literary cultivation must have been much influenced by the contemporary Old-English national poetry, with which the Norsemen were in constant contact; and its larger, freer, and wilder spirit must have been owing to their freer and wilder life, to say nothing of their roused and warring paganism. They could never have known any Celts save when living in embryo with other Teutons" (p. 143).

Written in 1866, 1867, *and* 1868.

Tuesday, January 2, 1866.

MY DEAR FREEMAN,—Firstly, I send you a reviling, which I wrote off in a rage yesterday morning, about Mr. —— I should have done it long ago, and stood by with a hot iron to sear the place when you cut off his head at first: in that way we might kill off a good deal of trash between us; but it is not very noble work. I wish I could write a book; but I can't, because I sympathise with a thousand subjects, instead of knowing any one subject as a master. If I could keep to Turk exclusively, let us say, or Greek exclusively, I might do it, but I sympathise much too actively with both to stick to either. When I go right, it is sympathetic instinct that leads me right rather than real critical faculty. If I were twenty years younger, I should get to work, and boil down Grimm's "Deutsche Gram.," so as to make a standard English work of it: this I take to be one of the greatest wants of the age. I shall end, I suppose, by doing something in Lithuanics, our un-Dutch next of kin.

I have an indistinct impression, which is not so very indistinct, of having seen Earle at Constantinople, in a hotel window, some twenty years ago, and of our having then discoursed upon Turkish verbs. His letter is very complimentary, and his approbation valuable, as coming from a master. I had no idea it was he who reviewed Zeuss in the *Arch. Cam.*, and am sorry to hear it. This seems a very ungracious thing to say; but what I mean is, that when I read the paper, as I did about eight months ago,

I rejoiced overmuch in the thought of its being by a really wise and strong Celt at last, one who not only would walk straight himself, but would know the reason why if his countrymen did not do likewise. And of course my joy has become damped upon hearing that it is by a mere Englishman after all. Norris, who did not know much about the matter, told me he thought it was by Longueville Jones the editor. But I think it is much above the strength of any Celt going, except Whitley Stokes.

I think that I am doing right in giving you and him a memorandum of Stokes's work so far as known to me. (1) A book called "Irish Glosses," 1860; (2) Cormac's "Glossary," 1861 or 2; (3) a Cornish play, recently published; (4) Essays, not many, which I have not seen, in Kuhn and Ebel's "Zeitschrift;" (5) and these are the chief things — Adamnan's "Vita Columbæ," *Sat. Rev.*, September 5, 1857; Latham's "Celtic Philology," August 7, 1858; "Taliesin and Ossian," May 22, 1858; "*Gaulish Inscriptions*," March 5, 1859; "The Indo-European Unity" (not specially Celtic), November 19, 1859; "The Book of Deir," December 8, 1860. This last, and particularly its closing words, I beg you will recommend to Jones. It is a sin and a shame that these articles are not collected. There is a translation of Ebel's German papers, with a preface, by a Dr. Sullivan, called "Celtic Studies," which is well worth reading, or rather necessary to read, though as obscure and slovenly in style as nine-tenths of such High Dutch papers are. Glück's "Die Keltischen Namen bei Cæsar," reviewed, I forgot to say, by Stokes, December 26, 1857, is, however, as clear and strong and savage as Goldwin Smith, having been stirred up by an abortive little school of Celtomaniacs who sprang up in Germany at the time, and went on about Hu Gadarn in the real old Helio-Arkite style. I shall send you this.

It is possible that I may underrate Skene. And I certainly should not have dwelt so wholly upon what I considered the inefficient side of his workmanship without giving him credit for anything else, had I thought that my letter would have fallen into **the hands of a** friend of **his**. Worse still, I may say the same **of Jones, whom, though** I hope not reviling in words, **I yet fear the** tone of my letter **may have** not been sufficiently crediting. What made **me kill** Skene I cannot conceive, but I have the impression that I saw his death a few months ago in some **paper.** But I stick **to** my point, that Skene is inefficient and pre-scientific in **his purely** philological work. **His** High Gaelic and Low Gaelic notion I hold to be one **of** the utterest delusions that ever were started. I **do not** see **a trace of** acquaintance in anything he **has written with** Zeussian and post-Zeussian literature, and with the principles therein laid down, whether universally acknow- ledged or as yet under discussion among authorities. The language held **by him** in his notes **to** the book of the **Dean** of Lismore about O'Donovan **is too** bad, especially when accompanying a poor statement of the differences between Scotch and **Irish Gaelic, in which he seeks** to show, or rather to convey **the impression, that the absence** of nasalisation and *eclipsis* **in the Scotch is a true** *initial* **differentia,** which has always existed. **It is merely a pro- cess of** further simplification in the language. **Of Scotch Gaelic,** Zeuss says, "In vetustâ Hibernicâ fundamentum **habet."** Let Skene read for himself the grounds on which **Zeuss** says this, and let him disprove it if he can. It will **not do** merely to manipulate the local names. In a word, **Scotch Gaelic** is as modern Armorican, **and not as the** Gaulish of Cæsar's Veneti.

What puts my back up against Skene is this. **To an** Englishman nothing is more **curious than** the shift **of** national consciousness which **has** taken place among **the Scotch** Highlanders. The Fenian poems which **we,** misled by an impostor, call by the name **of one** author, Ossian, are the genuine link and **symbol of their** former unity with Ireland in the ethnic sense. It is very striking, and it calls out all **the sympathy** in one's nature, to hear that

M

the genuine oral tradition of Mayo and the genuine oral
tradition of Ross-shire are word for word the same for
hundreds of lines together, and that old women in Caith-
ness are to this day singing songs about the O'Driscolls
in Cork after a political separation of a thousand years.
Fancy people in Yorkshire and people in Sleswick, barely
conscious of each other's existence, singing and handing
down songs about Huæf and the Hocings and Scyld
and the Scæfings, and all our real old English traditions
and heroes, down to this day.   Yet this, or little less than
this, is the Gaelic case.   But, since the wretched Macpherson's time, the Scotch think it the proper Scotch
thing to do to speak up for "Ossian," and to defend Macpherson wherever they can.   As against Ireland, their
attitude is one of provincial self-defence.   The Irish, on
the other hand, warmly adopting the doctrines of the new
school in philology, hold a position, it seems to me, of
sound criticism and of hearty concession where concession
is due, not of carping vindication.   Now Skene, though
not ultra-national, as Scotchmen go, is ultra-national, or at
least national when read from a non-Scotch point of view.
And when he had an excellent opportunity of putting the
whole Fenian case in a very striking light before English
readers in his edition of the Dean of Lismore, he did
nothing but poor and petty vindicatory criticism.   He is
the victim of his old book, I fear, to which he seems incur-
ably wedded, and which has made him indocile.   But, as
in the case of Cato and his Greek, it is not too late for
him to read Zeuss and Stokes.   I must further, in justice
to myself, mention that in his translation of the "*Duan
Albanaich*," or poetic list of the kings of the Scots down
to Malcolm, contained in some old Irish collection, and
edited by one of the Dublin scholars—Todd, I think—he
has been shown up as a blunderer in almost every line;
and having fallen into all, or nearly all, the blunders of
previous translators, Innes and Pinkerton, he manifestly
uses their translations for his crib.   He is, in fact, no

Gaelic scholar, nor anything like a Gaelic scholar. Of course I am not one, but I know what it takes to be one. And when they are on common ground, it is not to his advantage that one contrasts him with Reeves, whose erudition and references are first-hand, and who is thoroughly sound and large-minded in everything he writes. Then fancy a man writing in these days such loose criticism as this, "This poem is written in very old Gaelic with obsolete expressions." I have not got the exact words, but I have got the idea.

There is no such thing as an undefined antiquity in Gaelic except to those who cannot lift their eyes off Scotch soil. The whole point of modern teaching is the manner and the necessity of defining such alleged antiquity— "very old English, with obsolete expressions," might mean Layamon or Maundevile or Shakespeare; and would not go down unrebuked in an English critical essay.

The mischief done by Macpherson is quite incalculable. He is thoroughly incorporated into Scotch national vanity, and I suppose even the most liberal Scotchmen can hardly be got to say anything stronger of him now than of Wallace or Mary. Try Finlay. To be sure, Macaulay does—but then he has always been unfilial towards his "ancient mither." Some of these days I shall throw up house and home and go north, and preach to the Scotch how much nobler truth is than Scotland; how, properly speaking, there is no such thing as a Scotchman; and if I am martyred and lapidated, as of course I shall be, I shall say with my dying breath to the foremost of my persecutors (who will probably be called Blackie):

> " Majorum primus quisquis fuit ille tuorum,
>   Aut *Anglus* fuit, aut illud, quod **dicere nolo**"

—which last is a very pretty expression for an Irishman. Strathclyde Britons and Norsemen are too few to go for anything.

The Scotticizing of the Picts is, of course, very curious.

But, after all, the Scots had a long time to do it in; and, on the one hand, one cannot assign any limits to the power of assimilation exercised by a freshly literate and freshly Christian people upon a wild and not very numerous race of white heathens—while, on the other hand, there were no ethnologists in those days to tell us how long the old speech may have held on in holes and corners: though Henry no doubt gives us a fair estimate for its entire disappearance.   Who would have thought that people were talking pre-Ottoman or Tartar Turkish in Hungary (Cumanian) in Maria Theresa's time?   And for the assimilative power, the work of the Slavonians in Russia, Slavonizing and Christianizing Ugrians on end as far as they could go, and thus forming the great bulk of the modern Russian people, seems to me an exact parallel. By the way, fancy Dean Stanley reviving the old idea of Ezekiel's Rosh being Russia!   It's like saying Meshech was a Mexican, or Tubal a man of Tobolsk.   He should at least have known how to translate $P\omega\sigma\sigma\iota\sigma\tau\grave{\iota}$ $\mu\grave{\epsilon}\nu$ $\beta\alpha\rho\text{ου}\phi\acute{o}\rho\text{ος}$.   Has he been talked over by Dr. Cumming?

With every deference to Jones as a critical Welshman, who would not prefer Wales to truth, I do not think that I, that is to say, the consensus of the Continent, assume "*too decidedly*" the non-initiality of modern Welsh.   His generality about the spelling of a language not being absolutely good for anything beyond its written form, or necessarily exhibiting its spoken form, is all very true under certain conditions and limitations.   But a special argument is what is wanted for the present case, not a general one.   The sounds of the Latin alphabet are known to us with quite sufficient accuracy for philological purposes, though not with absolute and minute accuracy.   The first application of that alphabet to Welsh as to other Aryan languages can but have been a very few centuries older than the oldest existing Welsh records.   And when first applied it must have been applied to a vernacular speech, for there was, broadly speaking, no other to which to apply it. But sounds alone are but a small part of the case. *Venta* may have been *Gwenta* as regards minute pronunciation, in a British mouth: I do not take my stand on the *gw* alone, though I believe it to be late: what I maintain is that it was not Gwent with an *a* tacked on, but that at one time, however *v* may have been sounded, the word was distinctly *Venta* in the nominative, Ventas in the genitive, Ventai in the dative, Ventau in the accusative, and so on; and this time I believe to be as late as Cæsar, for I cannot suppose that his "sermo haud multum diversus" meant a difference *in stage* as well as a difference of dialect from Gaulish; and the stage of Gaulish is an ascertained fact. It was first restored by scientific process; and the forms so restored were *subsequently* verified by their actual discovery in inscriptions. After that, it seems to me that nothing remains to be said, unless people choose to say that the dative plural in, for instance, *matrebo namausikabo* were brought in from Latin. Except the recovery of old Persian, I declare I know no greater triumph of comparative philology than its work in Celtic. My belief is that it was the 400 years of Roman rule which broke up old British, and helped no doubt at the same time to break up the Latin which must have been spoken here, and which *we* extinguished: these things being generally give and take, more or less. *Gw* occurring in Armorican where it does in Cambrian is a strong reason in favour of its being older than the English conquest; but that is a long way off Cæsar. Of course there are hitches, or places where the theory does not run smoothly. The initial-letter changes in Gadhelic are the same in principle as in Britannic, and to meet this objection we must assume *in moderation* an inherent tendency of analogous or parallel decay. This is mysticism; but we can hardly do without it here, as in the similar parallel of Italian and Wallachian, the *common* post-classical or Romanic elements of which are much too advanced in decay to represent the real spoken Latin of Aurelian's date, the time of their final separation: here we must admit a principle of analogous decay. In Celtic the character in question is merely phonetic originally, and has been raised to grammatical value by the art of writing, which fixed it. An Irish eclipse is merely this: Suppose modern Greek unwritten, and taken down for the first time as Irish was once taken down, τὸν τόπον, τὴν πόλιν, tondópo, timbóli, or todópo, tibóli, if you choose, for no Greek conceives the alternatives to be other than the same thing. Literary fashion may separate them when first written, as *to ndopo, ti mboli;* and grammarians, improving on it and seeking to show the original letter and the pronunciation at once, may write *to d-topo,* and *ti b-poli:* thus people would ultimately cease to recognise the *d* and *b* as part of the article. This is a pure genuine Irish eclipse. So in Welsh, you may call *pen* a head, *fy mhen* my head, grammatical permutation; but it is really merely phonetic in origin, *min* or *mim mhen* for *min pen* (meina penna): which *min* I believe is actually found.

If I said the loss of *p* at the beginning of words was all-pervading, I used too strong a word. But it is something more than dialectic, for it seems to occur in Welsh and Gaulish. *Etn* for a bird is probably connected with the root *pet,* "the flyer," and there seems no other way of accounting for the preposition *ar,* Gaulish *arē* (Aremorica), which would otherwise stand alone, but which the Germans take to be παραί. Ebel has a special paper on the subject.

If I were you, I would not be disquieted about *ou.* The diphthongation or guna of words like *hús, wíf,* both in English and German, is certainly very curious: I believe Grimm has written specially on it; I do not know where. The French or Gal-Welsh seem inherently to hate this as much as the Dutch inherently love it—and keep the two sounds as separate as they can; hear them say "Aic am going aout:" if they can shirk the diphthong they do. I take it that is at the bottom of Schaffhouse and Mulhouse: for these I do not know whether there are any really old forms, but I do not think it would have altered the case if there were, as the Gal-Welsh would have made them *ou* whether or no. When the *u* and *i* sounds are original, of course the Swiss are right: but when the *y* and *ou* represent *ei* or *áu* in Ulphilas, of course theirs is the late and the wrong. *Uff* and *uss* (not *ouff* or *ouss*) are very good, and book-Dutch wrong, as their Gothic has *up* and *us*. No doubt *ou* was then as it is now. But *ou* in the real old High Dutch may really have been, as in modern English, the graphic sign of *aú*. *Houpit = haubith* may have been *ou*, as in modern Ober-deutsch; but *poum* for *bagms must* have been once pronounced *paum*, otherwise there would be no reason or nature for it.

I don't oppose your theory of waves one bit. Only I look nearly at your waves, as waves in a gale of wind; there they are and must be, but each wave taken by itself may be broken into a thousand crests and undistinguishable. I don't say Ireland was not peopled from Britain: the choice of difficulties makes me believe it was, on the whole; but I hold there is not a direct vestige of it.—
Ever yours truly, Strangford.

58 Great Cumberland Street,
May 14, 1866.

My Dear Freeman,—You have been on my conscience for months past, and I have been finding it uphill work to keep it quiet; besides, I had plenty of things to write to you about. Not articles, because you seem to have been reviling very little of late. Firstly, let me say that though I cannot make you a history professor, you have made me a judge in Wales. About two months ago I received a letter from one Prydderch Williams, indited upon notepaper inscribed "Yr Eisteddfod," wherein I was invited to be one of three judges to decide upon the merits of the prize essay on the amount of British blood in the modern English. As the competing essays were

allowed to be written in Welsh, I declined to have anything to do with them; but on hearing that that was
somewhat of the nature of a patriotic flourish, and that the
really competing essays would certainly be in English, I
accepted, although much against the grain.   My colleague
should have been judge single-handed, or judge in concert
with you, for he is no less a man than Guest.   It is
ridiculous to join me to him, for I know nothing whatever
of the details of the subject, and all I can do is to see
where the writers go wrong and where they keep steady
in the philological part of the inquiry.   But it is most
unquestionably your exhibition of my Pictish letters to
Basil Jones, who was a judge last year when the prize was
withheld, which has brought this honour upon my head—
an honour of which I am sensible in the highest degree.
I do not know Guest, nor do I know whether, in cases like
these, concert between the judges is allowable : in cases of
difference of opinion I suppose it must be.   But at all
events I think I shall ask you to be kind enough to give
me a letter of introduction to him, which I can make use
of any day by just running down to Cambridge.   As
things stand, I should be disposed to adjudge the prize to
the few lines in your "Fortnightly Essay" which immediately bear on the subject.   You are the first man who
has ever put Rowena to a useful purpose—that of showing
that Hengist's Englishmen must have brought their wives
and families over here, which is all Rowena is good for.
As for the main question, it seems to me that the common
sense of it can be said in two words; that what is true
of Kent and Norfolk is not true of Salop and Devon.
Between you and me, the prize, or rather the animus
which led to the foundation of the prize, looks horribly
like a bribe to prove that we are all half Welshmen; but
for goodness' sake don't go and let out that I say so.   Last
year they seem to have been a pack of fools who wrote,
one and all; but as the prize is well worth trying for, I
am in a state of dread lest I should be called upon to

decide among **half-a-dozen** German *Gelehrten*, each no better and no **worse than the** other, and all knowing and saying the same things.

I ought to say that the Eisteddfod paper is headed thus /ı\. This delightful symbol, I am told, is said by Mr. Williams ab Ithel to be the utterance God made when He created the world, being the first three letters of the Welsh alphabet, after which it became three sticks or divining rods. I believe, morologically speaking, this is purer nonsense than the little pig-book, but it is not so amusing.

I write pretty constantly for the "Pall Mall," a paper which so far suits me that I can write at any length in it I choose, and need not beat out a single idea beyond ten lines, if I have nothing more to say about it. I have done two good things by writing in it. I have gone some way to make people apologise for using the word Anglo-Saxon, and I have quite succeeded in extirpating the word Schleswig from the "Pall Mall" printing office. In the note whereby I achieved this I quoted you and Latham as the only two men of the day who really cleave to our own form, Sleswick. . . . If I were more of a historian, my idea would be to write a special parallel between the "Roman and the Teuton" and Bryce's "Holy Roman Empire," for the purpose of distinctly showing the nature of your school, and that it is your school. But I should break down in detail I fear. Have you read "Hereward the Wake," and are you going to review it? It is very good fun to think how Kingsley has turned you upside down. The popular delusion being that there were no Englishmen before 1066, Kingsley goes and says there were none *after* 1066, at least such seems to be the meaning of "the last of the Englishmen." But what is Goldwin doing, and why does he not speak up? By the way, if you do review "Hereward," pray don't let him off for bringing in a Lett, and making him talk a harsh, or rugged, or barbarous jargon—I forget the exact words—but my exact words are "Confound his impudence." What angers me

about Kingsley at Cambridge is from the Ottoman point
of view.   Those poor Turks are abused up hill and down
dale for taking a tobacco-boy and making him a Lord
High Admiral, but nobody has a word to say touching the
joke of taking an ardent novelist and making a history
professor of him.   It may be sport for him, but it is death
to the undergraduates. ·

The Klepht telegram was utterly absurd.   I have just
seen a consul from Dodona, whose sayings, therefore, must
needs be right, who says that his part of the country has
been dead asleep for two years.—Very truly yours,

STRANGFORD.

LONDON, *August 7th*, 1866.

MY DEAR FREEMAN,—I return your proofs, which are
not in as good condition as they should be, because I read
them in an express train going to the country on Saturday.
I have no remark to make, only I am very sorry that you
are so brief.   I quite agree with you about the Proto-
Saxons (why on earth cannot we revive *or*—or introduce
it as *ur* from High Dutch?   I want Proto or something
answering to it at every step) of the fourth century, coming
as they did by driblets, becoming Romanized at once;
and have come by this opinion independently.·   I think
you understate the Romanization of Britain somehow,
though I grant it may be called superficial compared with
other Roman provinces.   I fancy British nationalism was
but a poor sort of feeling in the late days of Roman
dominion: and when it appeared again above the surface,
say in 300 years' time, as stiff and stubborn as Jewish
nationalism, it was the result of compression by English
conquest.   Cambria was the Welsh Montenegro, in fact.
I wish you had found occasion, or rather made occasion,
to say that it was the 400 years of Roman rule which
broke down old Celtic and made modern Welsh of it,

putting it into the category of modern French, more or less.

I must testify against your use of Cymry to denote the Britannic genus as well as the Cambrian species. Keep it for contrasting Cambrians with West Welsh or Armoricans, and use Britannic to include the whole genus contrasted with the Gaelic genus. There is always a risk of confusion if one word has to do duty for genus and species at once. But there is actual danger in the present case of leading people to believe that there were such people as Cymry before the English conquest. I hold their very name to be a proof of their expulsion from divers parts of Britain ; *Uskoks* or fugitives, *conterranei*, people who come to the same land and there form a new people. I think the point so far of importance, because, if strictly observed, it would be of great help towards unteaching the pestilent heresy of Cimbri and Cimmerii, and suchlike.

What is Old-Rum-Welsh ? Is there any Rum-Welsh older than Dante, broadly speaking ? or do you mean the Old-Sard-Welsh of the eighth century ? But that is hardly Rum-Welsh at all. Or do you mean Latin, neither more nor less, or is it Old-Gal-Welsh ?—Very truly yours,

STRANGFORD.

August 11th, 1866.

MY DEAR FREEMAN,—All I mean about *Cymry* is that it is a late word, a post-Roman word, applied to one branch of the British people alone in consequence of recent political circumstances, and that as it bears this specific sense, it is inconvenient to use in a generic sense. There is nothing exactly wrong in it, nor indeed is it exactly wrong to call the ancient Spartans Moreotes. But the word, over and above inconvenience, should be unlearnt or disused forthwith, as regards anything pre-

English, on account of Gomer, the Cimbri, and the Cimmerii. So I am very glad you follow Zeuss and use the word Briton.

The Scotch bishop. Give me his name at once; I am ravening for him like a wolf, or rather like a young wildcat—for my humour is much more feline than canine towards the latest school of Scotch writers on Celtic matters; I am perfectly playful, bitterly cruel, and wholly relentless towards them. A man Ossian, indeed! And Iona too. I think I once wrote to you that, according to Whitley Stokes or rather to William Reeves, it is simply a misreading of the Latin *Iona insula, Iona* (or Iova) being the adjective of Hy or I, the true name of the saint's island now and always: there being doubtless some contact with the idea of a dove and the saint's name in the minds of those who first used it. The parallel case is that of Hebrides for Hebredes: a pure misreading.

Guest's letter I return, as you may need it. I am very glad to learn the origin of London at last. I never believed in the old story about the "place of ships," because *long* for a ship must of course be *navis longa*, and therefore not pre-Roman. Half the vocables in Welsh are merely Latin in disguise, if Welshmen only would acknowledge it—not that it matters much if they don't.

By the way, I remember that in one of his philological papers, Dr. Guest explains Anderida sylva, Andredes leah, by the modern Welsh *andred*, from *an* and *tred*, the uninhabited place. Now I would be much inclined to doubt whether the euphonic change of modern Welsh initials, like that of τὸν τόπον into ton dópon, existed in the Welsh or Britannic of Cæsar's time—seeing, moreover, that the language of the Welshman who wrote his verses in the "Cambridge Juvencus" in, say, the ninth century, had not crumbled down so far as that. But, without discussing the matter *à priori* or by analogy, I think it is possible to analyse the word Anderida as it stands. *Ande*— the German *and* and Greek αντι, is *ind*—in the old Irish

MSS.; and occurs in old Celtic in andecamulum, Andecavi, anderitum (the place on the ford), and several others given by Zeuss and Glück. Rida on account of the *d* I would hesitate to connect offhand with the wheel-and-chariot set of Celtic words, which must have a *t* in the elder language—no, by the way, there is *rheda* itself given as a Gaulish word. It is fair to suggest the connection, however, with the root signifying course or locomotion (found in modern Welsh *rhedu*), because I find on reference to Zeuss that he says *non certo patet consona originaria, num* d *an* t. *Sed hod. cambr.* rhedu (*currere*) *non* rheddu *monstrat originariam* t. Be all this as it may, I am really sure about the *ande.*

Does Dr. Guest actually believe that the Romans found people over here who called a place Gwent (*sic*) without any termination or anything, and that they Romanised it by putting a Latin termination to it? Surely no more than Herodotus Grecized the terminations of Darius and Xerxes. Yet it might be fair to say that he did, if we had nothing to help us but modern Persian. I declare that I am somehow the only man left in England to preach the doctrine of the Proto-Celtic: Whitley Stokes is gone, and Norris is past work.—Ever yours truly,

STRANGFORD.

What a wonderful talent you have for finding out men who haven't read Guest! There is something worse than that, though: men who say they have read him and have never seen a line; and of such is my biggest prize essayist. On the other hand, there is an humble-minded publican essayist who makes a formal apology for not having had time to fish up his scattered papers. I am sorry to say that, if possible, his philology is worse than the Pharisee's.

1866.

My Dear Freeman,—I take it that Cookworthy and its substantives Cookworth and Cookworthiness do not so much denote worthiness of contributing to Cook, but of coming under Cook's hands, or being treated by Cook. But either sense will do, no doubt. In the negative, we can distinguish Uncookworthy from Cookworthless, and so keep a word for each sense.

—— is a poor provincial creature. I could have written his letter *verbatim et literatim* to be put in the mouth of any given Scotch scholar of the modern school. It is half true and wholly MacBuncombe.

I suppose —— may be taken as an old English euphemism for Lamb, which will account for his lack of force. I think I have heard his family name before in that quarter, and will go and look. Here it is, sure enough:

> " Witta weold Swæfum
> Wada Hælsingum
> Deódríc weold Froncum
>
> .   .   .   .   .
>
> Billing Wernum
> Oswine weold Eowum."

And I sincerely hope Oswine did not spare them, if they talked in a narrow-minded way about the Scotch.

To talk of the "labours" of Skene and O'Curry in one breath is to me much as talking in the same way of the "labours" of Beale Poste and Dr. Guest would be to you. Skene's history and archæology I feel and know to be very good, but his philology is quite worthless, and all the worse because he has read all the recent books without taking them in. And his "labours" as regards the Dean of Lismore's book simply consisted in his getting a Highlander, a good Gaelic scholar, Maclachlan, to transcribe and translate it for him, being a poor Gaelic scholar himself. Besides this, he wrote a preface to the book, and an

appendix, wherein, by taking the initial euphonic per-
mutations of the Celtic languages for their permanent
characteristics from the beginning, he stultifies all his own
references elsewhere to Zeuss and his school.

No one ever doubted the genuineness of Ossianic poetry
(if the word must be used) within the last two generations.
But the genuineness, &c., of *the* Ossianic poems, which
your friend says is settled past all controversy, is a very
different thing; and it is necessary to say clearly that
Macpherson's Ossian has nothing to do with the question, before admitting that as it stands. It would therefore be much better to disuse the word Ossianic and substitute Fenian in its place, in order to keep Macpherson
out of the general reader's mind.

The idea of calling the vast mass of Ossianic remains
found in Irish MS. of the twelfth and thirteenth centuries
"copies of the originals," meaning Scotch originals, is
one of the most delectable pieces of provincial coolness I
ever read. The whole local scenery is Irish exclusively
as regards its *headquarters*—there is much exclusively
Irish, but nothing *undoubtedly* Scotch exclusively, except
avowedly modern poems in the collection. And this very
book of the Dean of Lismore, cited so triumphantly by
your friend as though it were a new thing of which he
alone has heard, is actually filled with purely Irish poems
which Skene does not print because they do not refer to
Scotland! "The purely Irish poems of the O'Huggins, the
O'Dalys, &c., are not given in this work, the only object of
which is to illustrate the language and literature of the
Scotch Highlands at an early date." Now the fallacy in
this is to suppose that these had any appreciable separate
existence at that date apart from Irish. The language
and literature were the same in each, and Ireland was the
metropolis. No Scotchman has done anything for his
Gaelic, nor ever will do anything, if he looks at it from a
solely Scotch point of view: which is wholly inadequate to
explain any single one of its phenomena. If he wants to

explain it he must go **to the Zeussian or Stokesian Irish**
of the eighth and ninth centuries, or else sit down content
with **the old** pre-scientific **belief that it is** now more or
less such as it always was; in which last case he simply
remains out in the cold—out of the philological running
altogether, like a mere Welshman of the old school . . . .
indeed, because he simulates reason and criticism.

The one thing which should have been done with regard
to the Lismore book **is** the one thing which has not been
done—to **note down the points** where the language, phonetically written, and therefore pure vernacular of 1514,
differs from modern Gaelic **of to-day, and** to explain and
illustrate **these archaisms. But the fact is** that this
could not be done properly except **by an Irish** scholar.
It is an *immense* misfortune that Whitley Stokes left England before the book was published. **The idea** of assign-
ing the Fenian legends **and poetry to the** Proto-Gael,
assumed to have existed from **the beginning** concurrently
in Scotland and Ireland, which **is the theory** of Skene's
introduction, would have been shown up in all its absurdity
if Whitley Stokes had reviewed the book. Gaelic **never**
was spoken at all in Scotland till **it came from Ireland; it**
developed itself on Irish ground just as French developed
itself on Gaulish **ground;** and if primevally spoken in the
larger island, as it probably was, it was spoken when it
could only have differed slightly and dialectically, if at
all, from the contemporary Britannic or Proto-Welsh—in
other **words, was** not distinctively Gaelic any more than
the language of Ennius is distinctively French. You will
know, at all events, that I have proof of some sort for these
assertions.

I believe, in **short,** and testify, like a Mohammedan in
his profession of faith, that **when** Himilco came here (if
he ever came), he **heard the Latin of "the** tombs of the
Scipios;"—that when **Cæsar came, he heard,** say, Trajan's
vernacular; that when Hengist **came, he** heard "Pro deo
amur et pro Christicin poblo," and thence forward the

analogy is not conjecture, but fact. **Modern Bret-Welsh is modern French, simply. Gaelic is better—say modern Queer Welsh.**

What dreadful thing is this you write me back on the authority of the bishop about Iona being a mistake? Why, of course it is, and the one which I expounded myself to you in my own letter—telling you how it arose by a misreading of the *u* in Ioua insula as an *n*; Ioua being a Latin adjective made out of I or Hy. You have been taking my own thunder and making use of the episcopal arm to launch it back at me.—Ever yours truly,

STRANGFORD.

1 HOLLAND ROAD, BEORHTHELMESTIEN,
October 20th, 1866.

MY DEAR FREEMAN,—Don't talk to me of ——, for I can't bear it. It is disgraceful in every respect. I have the sense of what is right and what is wrong in your subjects, or some of your subjects, just as you have in mine; and I therefore see what rouses your wrath against him. But he is worse to me than he can be to you. It is extraordinary and hardly creditable presumptuousness on his part to volunteer the most outrageous philology with a flourish in your face, and then coolly tell you that it is what Max Müller would say. His Celtic philology is more deserving of punishment than the honest old wild outbreaks of the mad Welsh and Irish, because he has no excuse for not knowing better. His German is but modern High Dutch, just as you say of the Westminster man, whom I did not attempt to read beyond the first page. The idea of treating the modern High Dutch sound of *sch* as an original and constant fact in all Dutch everywhere and at all times! But the worst to me is the bit about the Oxus and the Jaxartes so coolly put into Max Müller's

N

mouth : it is so bad morally, because it shows how utterly
reckless —— is, or how ignorant of the one rule which
is the sheet-anchor of etymology. Has the word under
treatment any history within its own limits, or can any
history be made for it by authorised scientific rule ? No ;
perhaps the worst is the batch of Greek and Welsh par-
allels. For twenty days I have been lying fallow in an
atmosphere of ——, as it were ; absorbing Coctian elements wherewith to fertilise the crop of my vengeance,
which, if late, will be-bitter. I will so manage that I will
burn and consume my —— on the 5th of November.
Where and how does Green answer him ? We should
mass our artillery on him. No ; the worst of all is, I think,
the Maxolatry of ——, and utter misconception of M.'s
position ; taking him as the sole master and the type of
modern philology, when he is but a pupil, one in the
second generation, one among several who form its first
class. It is especially bad in Celtic matters, where M.
says next to nothing, and what he does say is but the
acceptance and endorsement of Whitley Stokes.

To leave out all mention of Guest in his account of the
English conquest, and to leave out all mention of Zeuss in
his account of the character and relations of the ancient
British language, that is what he has done. We shall
next have him tell us, as Professor Airy, the Astronomer
Royal, told the world last autumn, that the Belgæ of
Cæsar's day must have been Welshmen, because the word
was in all probability pronounced Welshæ.

I have never supported the Turks in this business, though
I should, on the whole, be inclined to do so as long as I
see their hands tied behind their backs by the consuls.
Indeed, I have said that the Cretans in the field are fine
fellows, as they certainly are. What I have done is to
criticise the telegrams as they turn up. The joke of these
is that they are all brought by one and the same steamer
from Canea to Syra, whence they branch off. I hope you
appreciated Heraclea when interpreted as Herculaneum,

and understood that Heraclea meant Megaló-Kastron. I
wish I could reduce the question to the simple issue you
do. But the fact is that the present movement, with the
determining causes of which I am unacquainted as regards
immediate details, is not a spontaneous but a factitious
movement, the result of direct propaganda carried on from
a monastery on the south-west coast ever since 1858, under
the superintendence of the Russian consul, and with the
connivance of the French consul. This monastery being
under foreign protection, could not be touched by the
Government. By propaganda I do not mean the μεγάλη
ιδέα only, but powder and rifles. I must go in more to
the French position, for that is the key to the whole thing.
From the Crimean peace onwards they co-operated steadily
with Russia in the Levant, partly out of mistrust of our
supposed selfish objects, partly out of a wish to conciliate
a late adversary. In 1858 the result of this co-operation,
working with the Hellenic propaganda as its instrument,
was seen in an armed outbreak of the Sfakiots and mountain Cretans, who cajoled or bullied the lowlanders to join
them. No fighting took place, and the matter was calmed
down by the sacrifice of the English consul and the Turkish
governor, an active man, who was doing much good in the
island, and had succeeded in creating a real good feeling
between the two classes. This threw the island back half
a century, and has created a permanent ill-feeling, on which
anti-Turkish diplomacy has of course been working ever
since. But the French have at last had their eyes open to
the fact that to parry English selfish aggressiveness in the
Levant is to parry the blows of a man of straw, and that
they have probably been merely acting as a tool or cat's-
paw of Russia in pulling Turkey to pieces at once, and
actively. To precipitate matters would only serve to un-
mask their special game, which is Suda Bay, in plain
English. If the island is once annexed to Greece, a
Christian power, the French have lost their chance of
getting it, unless in a general smash. They want it to

become Egyptian again by purchase, knowing that their relations with Egypt are such that they can get it handed over to them at any moment as a pledge, or a forcible transfer, or somehow, so as to make sure of the most commanding naval position in the Levant. Hence the sight of the French turning their back on themselves all of a sudden, bidding Moustier rate King George, protesting against the American occupation of what seems to be Suda Bay, and generally taking up the supposed Palmerstonian policy in Greek Turkey with the utmost vigour, after having spent ten years in picking Greek Turkey to pieces. That Crete will end by becoming French I am very sure; and the Cretans may thank those vainest and silliest of men, the modern Athenians, for it. Their own wish was to grow off Turkey on to a large and ideal Greece; and if France and Russia would but have let these countries alone, this they would have done; attaining perfect independence quietly through the stage of semi-detachment. They never sought, any more than the Ionian islanders sought, immediate annexation to the small real kingdom; nor do they do so now, unless it be in hot blood. It is ludicrous to suppose that the Athenian Government, unable to protect industry in Attica, would protect it in the Cretan lowlands. The Sfakiots and mountaineers, who are the arms of the present movement, would simply continue to be a dominant caste, as at present, only with much more lawlessness. Do not compare them to Montenegrins. These don't rob and murder Christians, but the Sfakiots do. As for the Athenian bureaucracy, no words of mine can give you an idea of their worthlessness, nor would you believe me; but I live in hopes of your seeing Finlay before he is out of print, as I fear he soon must be, at his age. I see that his knowledge of Crete is general, not special; but it is better than other people's special knowledge. The one thing to get at is the '58 and '59 movement: the —— will never publish this, for it is not creditable to us, and there is a personal scandal in it about . . . .; nor does anybody know anything about it really, that I know of, except one man, a civil engineer, employed by V. P. to make a road between Canea and Retimo [observe the vernacular retention of the old pronunciation of η in Ρήθυμνος], which was stopped by the consuls and the Sfakiots before the row began.

I hardly care to relieve you about Iona, nor am I in a writing mood just now. Brighton may have been a decent place when Beorhthelm first saw it, but to me now it is a mockery of nature, worse than London a great deal, because there you have nothing to remind you that there is such a thing as nature, except perhaps day and night.

For the last two months I have thought of the 14th; nor was I free from a dreadful idea that your friend L. N. B., a man who loves such combinations and coincidences, might think fit to repeat the experiment. He has got something to avenge on the 21st, however.

But young people nowadays no more remember what happened on the 21st than they read Walter Scott.—Ever yours truly, STRANGFORD.

———

1 HOLLAND ROAD, BRIGHTON,
November 17, 1866.

MY DEAR FREEMAN,—I send you back Finlay's letters, as I ought to have done long ago. They are as good as sunlight in all that regards Greece; but all that about M. Gobineau and the cuneiforms is such a muddle and a tangle as could only proceed from the brain of a French diplomatist who had begun official life by intriguing among Persians and ended it by intriguing among Greeks. I know all about the soul of the matter, and may as well set it right for you to tell Finlay. The article whereof Gobineau complains was written by F—— N——, and so far from being Rawlinsonian in spirit, it appeared to me a most presumptuous and ridiculous attempt to un-

settle the *universally*-admitted principle of interpreting
the old Persian texts by substituting pre-Hellenic Greek
for Sanskrit, Zend, and modern Persian as the chief
instrument of interpretation—the writer ignoring these
languages altogether. Thus the word which everybody
recognises as *abavam*, I was, Sanskrit *abhavam*, he reads
as *ebum*, unsettling the established value of the letters in
order to suit the Greek word ἔφυν. In this article Gobineau, whose work I have not seen, is represented as
making the whole thing purely cabalistic. If he merely
does this over and above the ordinary literal version of
the Behistun text, he has a right to complain of misrepre-
sentation; Jews do the same thing to the Bible; but if
he means to exclude all meaning save the cabalistic one, he
has been treated only too leniently. I was very angry at
the article. . . . —— by no means shared my indignation
at the utter violation of the first principles of comparative
philology, but actually spoke up for Gobineau's cabalism.
This he seemed so thoroughly convinced to be in itself a
probable thing in the occult writings, of Eastern castes
and priesthood that he lost, comparatively, the sense of
the absurdity in detail of Gobineau's special application
of his principle. I do not think Finlay in his own remarks is sufficiently aware that it is now thirty years
within one since Lassen established the Persian cuneiform
alphabet with precisely the same values for each letter as
those assigned independently by Rawlinson working by
himself in the East, with two or three exceptions alone;
and that, since the simultaneous discovery in 1847 by
Hincks in Ireland, Oppert in Paris, and Rawlinson at
Baghdad, of the diphthongation or guna of *i* and *u* by
means of an inherent *a* in certain consonants, there has
never been one single doubt raised, not one of any kind,
as to the validity of the restoration of the old Persian
alphabet and grammar. How, *à priori*, could any one be
expected to fail in deciphering an ordinary alphabetic
cipher of thirty-six letters, with all the words separated,

containing a language in high grammatical preservation almost identical with Sanskrit, and with a modern descendant still existing, which hardly differs more from it than modern English from old English of King Alfred? If Rawlinson had never been born, we should have still been just where we are now in *Persian* cuneiform interpretation, only with an infinitely scantier vocabulary, because we should not have had the great Behistun inscription. Rawlinson's discovery was thoroughly his own all the same, and his glory greater than that of any other single worker; for he had no one to show him the way till he had half done his own researches, and found it out himself long before, indeed.

Bishop Julius of Iona is not a Greek, nor a Syrian, nor a Scotian, nor a Scotchman, nor a Culdee, nor yet a Chaldee. He is a Frenchman, and his name is F. What he wants is altogether beyond me. The only thing I ever heard of him is that he once fell among Bedouins somewhere in Padan Aram, and was stripped of his clothes then and there, being fain to make his way to Aleppo or Damascus in that plight. I suppose a man who starts naked has the right of choice between vestments ecclesiastical and vestments lay; but that by no means explains his going to a Scotch island. Perhaps he is a judgment sent to vex Bishop Ewing for his Ossianic heresies and injustice to Ireland.

Whitley Stokes has just printed a grand Celtic book at Calcutta, with the full text of the Book of Deir in it, which ought to be a matter of shame to the Scotch philologists—not that there are any such. The point is that it is genuine Aberdeenshire Gaelic vernacular of the twelfth century, and that it differs from Irish Gaelic of the period just about as much as written Massachusetts English from written Middlesex English. You see now that disposes of the Proto-Gaelic theory and the co-ordination of Highland Gael with Irish Gael. I have got to be amused rather than angry at seeing Scotch Highlanders struggle against the fact of their being merely Irish Yankees. I have not done . . . but he is merely a thing for all time rather than a topic of the day, and will keep. He must be **bracketed** with Professor —— and the Belgæ being pronounced Welshæ by Cæsar.—Very truly yours,

STRANGFORD.

———

LONDON, *December* 29, 1866.

MY DEAR FREEMAN,—I have been owing you a letter for some time past, but having been backwards and forwards between this and Brighton rather than settled in either, I have not thought myself able to come up to the scratch, either to write to you or to anybody or thing else. Now, firstly, of your names. Where on earth did you find them, to begin with ? That I should really like to know. Wyrtesleof may be Wladislaw, but I should think was most probably Wrastilaw. It seems to take as kindly to its old English form as Wrastilaw to its new English pronunciation. Gotteschalk must be merely a translation, if he be a **Wend**, as you say. How Wyrtgeorn can be a Wend I cannot possibly tell, for it is quite beyond me. Before a Wend of Weonodland within the historical period could have got an English name he must have had a Dutch one, from which the Engle must have taken it. Now what can have been the Dutch form of Wyrtgeorn ? Surely the chronicle must have written Weonod by mistake for Wealh. There cannot have been any Wyrtgeorn, surely, but the man who called himself Vortigern in his own Bret-Welsh modernised into Gwrtheyrn [observe that this is spoken defiantly, and against those who will go on believing that Welsh was at all times such as it is now]. Whether such a word as Wratihran would be good Wendish I must leave to special Wendish scholars to settle.

I was at one time **Dutch rather than** un-Dutch in the matter of *church*, yet **by no means** with mind made up.

The more I think of it now the more I am convinced that it is a case of confluent rather than of single derivation. Whether the Goths ever had the word in any way or not we cannot possibly say, nor do I think it matters *essentially.* I believe the Germans borrowed the word *circus* from the Romans at as early a period as they took the name of Cæsar; the early date being shown by the retention of the original sound of *c* before *i*, and that this word afterwards coalesced or ran together, as it were, with the word κυριακὸν taken by some German race—I strongly suspect the Engle —either directly or indirectly from Greek. So long as the Gothic language only comes down to us in fragments, and so long as we are without anything to show for colloquial Latin in the period, say, A.D. 300–600, we are not in a position to lay down negative statements about those languages with absolute authority, or to say the Goths never had the word from the Greek, if they had it at all, or the speakers of Latin never had *cyriacum.* The Wend forms are undoubtedly from Dutch direct, and not *urverwandt.* That is proved by the initial *ts*—a derivative and secondary sound. As for Earle's *cylch*, and all the Gaelic and Welsh, it seems to me to have got off the rails somehow, and likely to get bogged in a swamp. *Cylch* is probably connected originally with *circus;* probably derived from *calyx;* probably descended from the old Celtic *celicnon* for a bowl or plate in the Gaulish inscription, which again is, as regards form, the identical Gothic *kélikn,* a tower. But it cannot be all three, and Grimm's law makes a real difficulty in connecting anything German with any one of them, except in the way of actual derivation, which last most likely is the case with *kélikn.* That, however, may be *cœnaculum*, which it translates in two places, I think. I wish the word church could be fairly made Dutch, as far as wishes go.—Ever yours truly,

STRANGFORD.

P.S.—Æolus at the Tuileries has been fiddling for years

past with the fastenings of the windbag which holds the south-easterly gales, and now he is in a state of mind because it has got loose at last. I do not see how Turkey is to survive this year. The Greek difficulty is nothing compared with the storm brewing in Servia, which is loaded to the muzzle, and *must* explode. The whole of the Austrian Militärgrenzer regiments are determined to join her, and can now force Austria's hand. Then will come Russia to Constantinople when she likes, and France in Crete and Egypt.

———

WEDNESDAY, *April* 3, 1867.

MY DEAR FREEMAN,—The fact of the matter is that you must look on my letter as so much blow off of waste steam or priming of boilers which have long lain idle and fôul, rather than as an objection or protest to your names. What I was really driving at was the mixed or composite nature of all Low Dutch *eo nomine* as we have it. Dutch is not strictly accurate as a descriptive name for the Pan-Teutonic class, nor is it quite convenient as a conventional name, but there is none other which has not tenfold greater objections against it, and thus I have no business nor wish to debar you the use of it. The word which should be used is the word which cannot be used, because no one knows what it was—the native name by which all speakers of German called themselves in Cæsar's time. What on earth was it? Until we know it, your Dutch is certainly the best popular name for enforcing a correct idea, even though especial philologists may take exception to it as a descriptive name.

There were no people who *eaten* and *drinken* (allow me a confusion of past and present in setting forth my illustration) before Karl. In the oldest Germanic days represented by Ulphilas (whom, away in Mœsia apart from other Germans, I take to be in the category of modern Icelandic, *i.e.,* older than any contemporary kin-speech) the people *itand* and *drinkand.* Later on these one became two, Saxons and Dutch, or rather North Germans and South Germans, the one set, ourselves in fact, *etath* and *drinkath,* the other *ezzent* and *trinchent.* The children of the former never got to *eten* and *drinken* until they were Teutonized and Christianized by Charles, and were made to forsake diabolum and allum for his wordum and wortum—a thing for which I find it hard to forgive Charles, but for whom people would be speaking English in North Germany now. But I quite agree with you in your position as expositor; it is only in the strict and minute philology that I criticised.

I shall certainly deal with the special point of the "Anglo-Saxon" name - question before long, but I am just now driven to distraction at the effrontery and impudence of people in philology. You remember sending me a letter of Finlay's about Gobineau, whence it appeared that Gobineau had been grievance-mongering about the inattention of people to his cuneiforms. Well, the present number of "Macmillan" contains an article half apologising for Gobineau and making fun out of the "Rawlinsonian" (!) system, and treating it as if it were a sort of matter for inexperts and all men to discuss as they would discuss dual voting. . . . I hope you will never desert what King Darius calls "pathim tyām rāstām"—it is hardly necessary to translate "the right path," for it speaks for itself—in philological matters.

—— I know of only dimly as an ancren riwle, or a hali meidenhad, or an ayenbite of inwit, or suchlike, with an evil turn for cockney facetiousness. He is not much of a man, so far as I know. Who was it who first created the Semi-Saxons? You will never unteach them I am afraid. Edward Geoffrey Smith-Stanley, Earl of Derby, I take to be the most prominent Semi-Saxon going just now. It is a wonderful expression. I suppose Tricoupi is Semi-Hellenic and Lascarato Middle-Romaic.

Eyre was the piano-wire, and poor old Mustapha Pasha's

back smarts for it—one of the kindest-hearted and most blameless of human beings, who has done everything in his power to prevent bloodshed, whereof, indeed, there has been marvellously less in Crete than on like occasions elsewhere. The Mussulman women and children took refuge in the towns, and suffered disease rather than distress. The Christians had no towns to go to, and were starving out on the open; it was quite right to take them off.—Yours very truly,

STRANGFORD.

———

April 13, 1868.

MY DEAR FREEMAN,—Beware of ——; he is just like ——, and will repine equally, whether you hit him hard or hit him soft. In '65 he wrote a huge essay signed " Multis Unus," for which I refer you to Basil Jones. In '66 he sent in the very same essay, as I was told by Arthur Johnes, whom I consulted about the question of withholding the prize. And he is now bringing it out as a book. He actually wrote to me at the end of '66 to ask me to become a subscriber: I tried to reason with him about one or two points, but he is dogmatic, indocile, and as obstinate and perverse as King Pharaoh or the deaf adder. His philology is indescribable, but it seems to me that everybody goes wrong in philology.

In Zeuss, vol. i. p. 226, the derivation of Cymry is given at length. The oldest recorded form of the word is in the MS. called by him Codex Legum Venedotianus, where it appears as Kemro sing. masc., Kemry plural, masc. fem., Camraüs, Camaraüs: other and modern forms being Cymro, plural Cymry, whence Cymraeg, Cynmraeg, for the language, Cymru and Cymmru for the country. The word is derived from can, in composition cyn = Latin con-, and bro, previously brog = terra, and signifies *conterraneus, eandem terram habitans indigena*—" vetustissima

forma fuisset (si e.gr., Romanis audita; sed ortum procul
dubio nomen post invasionem Saxonum), Combroges, cui
significatione oppositum est vetustum nomen gallicum
Allobroges, i.e., alienæ terra incolæ." After this he proceeds to support this by philological comparisons, and to
disprove Owen's suggestion that the *cym* is from *cyn*, *pri-
mas præeminens*, *cyn* being originally *cynt*, as shown by
the superlative *cyntaf*.

No one in any way cognisant of Zeuss's work has
attempted to raise any objection to this, or to any other
part of Zeuss's teaching for that matter, though all the
Welsh and other insular students of these things over
here—all, that is, with four or five exceptions—choose to
ignore it, or are really ignorant of it. It is accepted by
the school of comparative philology as established doctrine,
and those who object to it must show cause for doing so.
There can be no doubt that all Britain was thoroughly
Romanized, excepting, of course, the far North: and that
the Welsh are not the descendants of unsubdued Britons,
but of Britons who had undergone hundreds of years of
Roman rule, and who were what it may be assumed that
the Kabyles of Mount Atlas will become if the French
hold on in Algeria three hundred years longer. I take the
word Combroges to indicate the rally of the Brits west of
the Severn against the conquering English as a general
camp of refuge from all quarters. Wright is excellent
in so far as he shows the thorough Romanization of South
Britain, but his notion of Wales being re-Celticized from
Armorica is portentous.

Welsh *y* is modern all through; a secondary and a
derivative sound; when, therefore, found in a word, it
must not be associated with an original *i* any more than
a Greek *υ* with a Greek *ι*, &c. The Cimbri may have
been Celts, and probably were; but then *i* has nothing to
do with the *y* of the modern Cymry. What the Cimmerii
were nobody can tell; probably something that has vanished utterly, and is irrecoverable. I do not believe

Llocgwr has anything to do with Liguria, though it is tempting on account of the coincidence of the meaning in Welsh with the geographical position of the Ligurians. *g* in *gwr* is secondary; the old Celtic word for man must have begun with a *v* according to modern philology, whereas the *g* in Liguria must be treated as primary until shown to be otherwise. Then its *r* does not exist in the Greek forms. Λιγυες may be Λιβυες for aught I know, but there is no safe ground in this sort of work. I do believe, however, that there was a *vast* deal of Iberian blood about all these parts, and, so far as I can afford an impression on the subject, my impression is that the Ligurians were Basques rather than anything else.

I congratulate you on your Macedonian madman in the last ——. But he is too good for belief. I would not, however, put him above the Duke of ——, and certainly not above ——. I have not seen Mr. ——'s book, unfortunately. But the best of the joke is that he has a school. There is a Mr. —— who writes in the " Fortnightly," and who reviewed Mr. —— there with entire belief and animated support. Are the Cuthites the same as the Cushites? This kind of writing, I think, ought to be taken up by the doctors as an obscure form of mental disease; a determination of morbid etymological thought to the brain: it should be called *etymites*, or *etymorrhœa*, or some such name, and then medically treated. Something has got to be done to ——. I am beginning to know that sentence with Sigurd, the Nibelungen, and the Shah Nameh in it by the mere look of the page. It has got to be a public nuisance.—Very truly yours,   STRANGFORD.

58 GREAT CUMBERLAND STREET,
May 5, 1868.

MY DEAR FREEMAN,— . . . Did I say that the Romans thoroughly Romanized Britain? If so, I meant, of course, that they must have made it altogether their own property, and have swept away every native political and social institution that stood in the way of their dominion, rather than that they completely obliterated everything, language and all : which last, indeed, as the Welsh tongue would have to be accounted for, necessarily makes me talk Wrightism, and maintain Cambria to have been re-Celticized from Armorica—a monstrous view. I take the simple view to be the true one ; that Gaul, being on the Continent and close to Italy, had, say, one or two centuries' start of Britain in the path of Romanization, and that if the Romans had held on that much longer here, and the English stayed at home, the Bret-Welsh would have talked Romaic as much as the Gal-Welsh. The right linguistic analogy for Bret-Welsh I take to be, as you say, Basque, the vocabulary of which is one mass of Romanic ; or better still, and much less known, Albanian ; in spite of what is said by many of the new school who want to bring back even its most evident Latinisms to the old Aryan connection, calling them Pelasgic and what not.

It is very hard and unjust that we should take up the parable against the little pig-man and the Macedon man and Mr. Lysons, and spare the people who quote you that pestilential stuff about *Deffrobani* being on the site where Constantinople now stands as a real Cymric tradition. —— is sure to have it in his book; I remember he made much of it in his essay in connection with the country of Pwll, which always seemed to me as a Welsh echo of Poland : it is my hope that you will have slaughtered him well outright.

I have had the most frightful row with ——, who has been reproving me for speaking with scorn and contempt of the exploits of Mr. Farrar, our great new philologist in divers foreign tongues !—Very truly yours,

STRANGFORD.

58 Great Cumberland Street,
December 12, 1868.

My Dear Freeman,—I can hardly bring myself to look
you in the face after such long silence, but it must be done.
The spirit has been urging me to do it, on at least five
special occasions. I suppose you heard that in the summer I was taken ill. . . . With regard to the elections,
I am inclined to say that the select band perished by the
visitation of two things which I have been in the habit
of believing to work with the evil eye, one being the
personal visitation of —— ——, the other being the lau-
dations of the "Spectator." These two personalities are
known to me as uncanny, and their admiring glance is
bascantic. In Cretan the evil eye is called φθαρμὸς,
which may be, and probably is, ὀφθαλμὸς, but it has a
nasty touch of φθείρω in it. I have no doubt you forgot
to spit over your left shoulder when you read the "Spectator" on you, and that will account for anything. As for
——, I take it to be a matter of course that he visited
your nomination—may be visited the electors, and was not
understood by them.

Well, about ——, I saw his book and list when the said
book was first published. But afterwards, just before I
fell ill, I had lent to me a most villainous hysterical pam-
phlet by the said ——, who appears to have been put by
your review into a state as of a sheep gone giddy, com-
pounded with the state of the cat gone mad. Heaven
forgive me for the comparison, but it seemed to me
exactly what —— would have written under similar circumstances. —— is no better than an unmanly ass. I
did so want to be at him for this: nor have I forgotten it.
As for his list, I fancy it is a subject to which I am never
without the faculty of reverting at any time. A better
list, if I remember rightly, is to be found in Cootes' book
on English origines. The fact of our old English borrowing from Latin is certain enough, but allowance must

be made for such words, few enough no doubt, which we took before leaving the Continent through such Germans as were neighbours of Romans there. As for the real old words of affinity as demonstrable through Grimm's law, words whereof —— is fool enough to cite several in support of his proposition, he only establishes his own incapacity to treat of philology at all.

But I must say that such ill-treatment of philology by men who claim to treat it as masters, merely on the strength of their accepting its general results in a second-hand way, has actually become the curse of the country. I shall never forget ——, any more than I shall forget Professor —— proving that the Belgæ were Welshmen because Julius Cæsar probably pronounced Belgæ as Welshæ : the point of which last undoubtedly lies in its coming from a really scientific man. . . . —Very sincerely yours,

STRANGFORD.

FUGITIVE PIECES.

Reprinted from the Pall Mall Gazette.

CHURCH OR KIRK.

January 10, 1866.

A FEW days ago the celebrated Dr. Cumming wrote a letter to the "Times" about English and Scotch liturgies, and wound up with a postscript upon the etymology of the words *church* and *kirk*, this last being expressed with much dogmatism, such as is natural to one who has the ear of the public, and not unbecoming to one who "explored" the Latin and Greek tongues with "intense energy" for fifteen years. We thought something would come of it, and something has come of it. Mr. T. Arnold writes from Oxford to controvert the great Doctor's authoritative statement. Now the fact of anybody really knowing anything about the matter thinking it worth while to treat Dr. Cumming *au sérieux* upon philological subjects is in itself sufficiently remarkable to call for attention. Mr. Arnold writes sensibly; but somehow it is a very long etymological lane which has no crooked turning in it. Mr. Arnold has diverged at a tangent out of the straight path in pursuit of the merest *ignis fatuus* held out to him by a Mr. Ferguson, the author of a book on local names in Westmoreland and another on the river names of Europe. Mr. Ferguson is typically a half-learned man, without any fixed principles in his work; and such are more unsafe to follow

than even the wholly unlearned, as those who have pro-
fited by the masterly archæological and historical articles
of a weekly contemporary know well by this time. Referring to a point of Teutonic philology without consulting
Grimm or Diefenbach, or any one in the enormous host of
German investigators, is as though an undergraduate were
to undertake to decide upon some point of Greek without
ever referring to see what Liddell and Scott had to say on
the matter. To assign the precise Teutonic position of the
word is not easy. But Mr. Arnold, whose *general* opinion
is that of all German scholars of weight, will find what he
wants in Diefenbach's " Gothic Lexicon," under the word
kêlikn. The best thing in Dr. Cumming's letter is his
outcry against our Southron word *church* for its guttural
sounds. This he says, not having the least idea what a
guttural sound is, but because he thinks it the proper
Scotch thing to do to crow over us from a presumed
Scotch vantage-ground. It would, indeed, be hard if we
could not find some amusement in anything written by
the author of " Sebasteapol "—like " teapot "—and " *Rem
quomodo rem.*"

IRISH ARCHÆOLOGY.

January 1866.

DR. PETRIE, who stood at the head of the native Irish
archæological school, or at least shared that position
with his eminent survivor, Dr. William Reeves, is just
dead. The mention of a native Irish school of archæology
probably conveys no idea to the English " general reader "
beyond that of a dreary muddle of unsorted details, fitfully
lighted up by flashes of declamation and comic outbreaks
of extravagant national claims. Yet the modern Hiber-
nologists, if we may be allowed such a word, stand not
only foremost, but stand unapproached as a co-operative
and working body of archæologists among the antiquarian

societies of the Empire. It may be strange, but is no less true, that they are equal to the best Germans in massiveness and depth of erudition, in width of view, and severity of criticism. This is true of Protestant and Catholic alike—of Reeves and Todd as well as of O'Donovan and O'Curry; and if there is one thing that gives more unmixed satisfaction than the method and result of their work, it is the spectacle of Protestant and Catholic here labouring harmoniously together upon the common ground of their country's past. There is nothing like them in any other Celtic country, and there is nothing like them in England, where there is no school, and where antiquarians work piecemeal and separately. Dr. Petrie's domain of research being obscure and special, with no practical issue, he, of course, only came in for a pittance of biographical notice at his death, and this is the sort of thing he got. He got patronage, and he got contemptuous shoves out of the way; but he nowhere—out of Ireland, that is to say—got appreciation. One paper owned that he really had antiquarian merit. Another commented upon his great work on the Round Towers—a work both exhaustive and final, such as Jacob Grimm might have written—in a pooh-poohing tone, the coolness of which is something indescribable. "All very well," it was said, but people of "real learning" are by no means disposed to acquiesce implicitly in its conclusions. This contrast, in disparagement of Dr. Petrie's "real learning," is made at the expense of a man who had a book dedicated to him in these terms by a man of genius—Mr. Whitley Stokes, the greatest of living Celtic philologists, whom the common voice of the Continent would declare to be the greatest philologist native of these isles:—"*To George Petrie, LL.D., archæologist, painter, musician, man of letters; as such, and for himself, revered and loved.*" If anybody chooses to look on these words as the language of a mere Dublin clique-friendship, they are welcome to the thought, and we wish them joy of it. In conclusion, we venture just to hint that Irish archæology is a study which is by no means without practical bearings. Anybody who opens Dr. Petrie's published collection of native Irish music and songs will understand, for one thing, what an Irish Nationalist means when he says that Moore is no more the national poet of Ireland than of New Zealand; and he will begin to have some insight into a main constituent element of an undying national sentiment, which has nothing to do with reason, and defies all remedial treatment by reason. It is as well, one would think, to inquire, what does constitute Irish nationalism as to go on bothering about the wrongs of Herzegovinians, and the like, on grounds of national sentiment alone.

POPULARISED **ETHNOLOGY.**

January 17, 1866.

ALL work and no play makes a learned society a very dull body. Such societies as the Asiatic and the Philological are very dull bodies. The Royal Society is so great and powerful, and real distinction is so rigorously exacted, or is meant to be so rigorously exacted, as the condition of its fellowship, that it becomes impertinence to think whether it is dull or not. But all these societies are content to take their stand upon their work. On the other hand, it is certain that all play and no work will wear to rags the most scientific of garments worn by a learned society. Foremost among those bodies which prefer play to work, and which seem to care less for the record and transmission of severe scientific observations through their journal than for the engaging presence of ladies and fashionable reporters at their evening meetings, is the Ethnological Society. Of the great Geographical Society we say nothing; the truly scientific part of its work is transacted in its cabinet, and its practical work is in its very essence popular, and requires and deserves all the popu-

larity it can get. But ethnology is not an exact science,
nor yet an outward and popular topic with practical bearings; it is an inexact and tentative science. It may be
defined as being formed of the complex of physiology,
philology, ethnology, or psychology, together with history
and genealogy; and its only claim to the title of science
at all is the strict observance of scientific method on its
part in exercising its own special function. It has to
establish certain principles by determining the exact corre-
lation of its several factors, with the view of ultimately
arriving by science alone at a solution of the problem of
problems—the primary origin of man. It can only do this,
when in its present initial stage, by means of strict inductive reasoning and the accumulation of authentic facts.
When it stands upon firm ground, it is perfectly right to
popularise its ascertained results and exhibit its method.
When this society contributes new facts, it is right to do
so in public. But when it talks beside the purpose for
talking's sake, or unduly stretches its purpose so as to
catch within its net everything comprehensible, it is no
more a scientific society than Discussion Forum or Codgers'
Hall. Public discussion of minute points of comparative
physiology or comparative philology before a jury of
ladies—long-haired and empty-headed ones, as the Turks
say—for referees, is simply turning scientific research into
a thing like Mr. Spurgeon's lectures on shrew-mice, or Mr.
Bellew's lectures on Milton. In this way they discussed
a point of Celtic philology a year or two ago at a meeting
of the British Association, by inviting two disputants to
speak Gaelic against each other. This was as if the great
geologist who then and there presided had invited two
rival theorists to settle the question of a geological formation by picking up the stones and appealing to the test of
a cockshy. It may have amused the ladies, but it certainly killed the science. Yet the only object of handling
the matter at all on such an occasion should have been
to show the outer public that philology was science, not

guesswork. A rival body, the Anthropological Society, dis-
approve of this way of going on. Possibly they are envious
of it, as their *casus belli* with the Ethnologists appears to
be the possession of their platform, or some of their platform, at the British Association. At all events, they
reprove it openly, and craftily advertise physiological discussion *without* the ladies, much as the knowing White-
chapel baker advertised his bread *with* the gin in it. It is
for the Ethnologists to see that their smart and go-ahead
offset, which parted from them in anger like the United
States from England, does not ultimately increase and
multiply and drive them out of the market.

They had a field-day last week, and it is worth while to
examine what they did and how they did it. The first
paper read before them was an excellent instance of their
work at its best. This was a careful series of physical
measurements made upon the Laplanders, at the instance
of the venerable President of the society. Observations
made with similar precision among all the outlying races
of Europe are rare, and are of great importance ; but they
are uninteresting, except professionally ; and under a
ladies' *régime* are naturally postponed to vague speculations or other more attractive matter. The next paper
was valuable, but not ethnologically valuable, or only so
indirectly. It was purely literary in its interest, being the
notice of a Burmese book. If everything were in its right
place, and every society obtained or kept to its own work,
this would have been contributed to the Asiatic Society.
The third paper was upon the " characteristics " of the
South Slavonian races, and was contributed by Miss Irby.
This young lady is already, or ought to be, famous as
having travelled long and extensively in Servia and the
adjacent countries, and as being animated by a strong
enthusiasm in regard to their politics and their religion,
which is fed and sustained by a *bonâ fide* knowledge of
their language such as is not only remarkable, but unique,
among Englishwomen, or Englishmen either. The ethno-

logy of the Slavonians is unknown ground in England, and a contribution on such a subject by one whose knowledge is derived at first hand, whose head is clear, and whose literary abilities are of a high order—as Miss Irby's certainly are—could not fail of being very interesting, if not striking. Yet her paper, to our estimate of which we are guided by the report of an evening contemporary, however meritorious in itself, or excellent as a magazine article, seems to be of no value as a contribution to ethnological science; and what is of no value to this is of injury to it, for it takes up time and perpetuates unsettlement in method. Ethnologically, observations upon the bravery and moral truthfulness and various excellences of the Servians, if authentic, are good as the groundwork of ethnological conclusions alone, and not of political or any other conclusions. Whether the latter occurred in the paper or not we cannot say. But with Mr. Denton, of all men in the world, who was afterwards called upon to speak, discussion drifted off wide as the poles away from ethnology. This gentleman held forth upon the "resources" of the country and its aspirations after civilisation, and the like, in a fashion which simply amounted to politics in disguise, or trembled on the verge of politics. In common fairness the society now cannot possibly refuse the use of its boards to Mr. Layard, let us say, if ever it should occur to that gentleman to hold forth about the "resources" of Turkey, under the veil of a Nineveh lecture, or to a city stockjobber wanting to raise the wind for the next new Ottoman loan. This, however, is a small matter. We have to animadvert upon a more serious one—nothing in itself, yet becoming a breach both of justice and good taste when sanctioned, and in some measure made its own, by the society in its adoption of the present paper. Miss Irby may have travelled in Greek countries, but we apprehend that she knows nothing of the Greek language, the Greek inner life, or the Greek ideals. These things she probably knows well in the case of the Servians. But with this inequality and inadequacy of knowledge, she has no right to institute an *ethnological* comparison between these two races, to the laudation of the noble Slavonian, and to the disparagement of the vapouring and pretentious Greek. Perhaps these hard sayings may be true, but they are *impressions de voyage*, and should not have been treated as first-hand scientific truth. Many people have said worse things of the Greeks than this. But Greeks mind these things the less when they see that they come from people who know and understand them. Mr. Finlay double-thongs them with clean and straight 'cuts down their backs, and his tenderest mercies to them are cruel; yet this they do not resent—for they know that he understands them thoroughly. The highest praise, indeed, from the mouth of a Greek is that which he applies to such men as Finlay and Charles Alison, and very few besides. He does not say, Μᾶς ἀγαπάει, " He loves us," but Μᾶς καταλαμβάνει, " He understands us;" for he knows that such thorough understanding cannot fail of bringing some sympathy in its train. He may relish or despise ignorant praise, but he naturally resents ignorant depreciation. And the Greeks may most justly do so when it comes to them incorporated in the transactions of a learned society, and invested with all the dignity of scientific observation.

Our Ethnological friends will, we hope, take our remarks in good part, for they cannot fail to see that we are actuated by the desire of consolidating their science, and not of impairing its efficiency. Nor should they fail to see that if they go on popularising the merely unfixed and speculative portions of their researches, instead of the fixed and solid results, they are not planting the tree of science, but merely sowing a crop of thorns and thistles, which some day may be used for their incremation by their rivals the Anthropologists.

IRISH PROPER NAMES.

March 2, 1866.

SUPPOSING the Turks, not content with conquest and forcible seizure of the soil in Thessaly and Epirus, had even
waged war against patronymics with the view of crushing
out Greek nationality and Ottomanising the country, had
proscribed all names ending in *ides* and *opulos*, and had
issued firmans and hatti sherifs enjoining everybody, on
pain of the bastinado, to call themselves by Turkish names
or after Turkish towns, rivers, and the like, what would be
said by the historians and the great Elchees and the thirty-
five consuls of each of the sixteen Frank Powers who
make diplomatic capital out of Turkish misdeeds? Let
us imagine it to have been only the other day that the
liberal Grand Vizier took occasion to repeal an offensive
old statute directed against the Klepht, the last and most
noxious of the three noxious beasts—the Greek priest, the
wolf, and the To—the Klepht, whom the old Turks thought
it a religious duty to extirpate where they could. But
stay. Are we not all the while repeating the history of a
country somewhat nearer to us than Turkey, and not so
very ancient a history either? We recommend Lord
Lifford to study this history before he again argues, from
the modern Irish tendency to recast their English proper
names in as Celtic a form as they can, that this process
indicates any sort of antecedent English descent, and that
there is no difference of race between Englishmen and
Irishmen perceptible in detail. The Irishman began to
take his English name—his Saxon name, as the cant
phrase goes—at a time when Mac and O' might legally
cost him his land at least, if not his life; and he continued to do so in even an accelerated ratio in later times,
when the obnoxious prefixes only degraded him socially
or kept him down in his worldly career. The old Gaelic

nationality of Ireland is dead, and the race is transmuting its type; but whatever the modern English-speaking Irishman may be, there is one thing which he is not, and will not be for some time to come, and that is an Englishman without a difference, or with the difference of religion alone. But the new body is haunted by the old spirit, and from time to time is torn and convulsed by it as with a demoniac frenzy. We have before this alluded to the extra-rational or sentimental element of nationalism, existing in spirit when the form and reality is gone, as being perhaps the taproot and ultimate cause of the dull smouldering Irish discontent so incomprehensible to the practical understanding and strenuous sense of justice of our modern and liberal English generation. Of course we are talking of fuel, not of the application of fire by conspiracies from abroad. The tendency to revert to the old Celtic names is not "ludicrous" at all; it is a sign at once of English liberality and of the Anglo-Irish revivalism so conspicuous in poetry and in the antiquarian turn of the modern Irish; it is part of the same sentiment which has hurried a modern practical Irish grammar through a sale of three editions in as many years—too late, indeed, to do more than barely galvanise the dying language, but showing beyond a doubt the passionate ardour and longing regret with which the modern reading generation has been striving to imbue itself with the spirit of the old wild Ireland. The whole statement of the case, as regards the names, will be found in an essay by the late Dr. John O'Donovan, prefixed to his edition of the "Topographical Poems of O'Duvegan and O'Huidhrin," an old Irish metrical survey of Ireland arranged according to the clans, written in the fourteenth century. O'Donovan's essay is most masterly and fascinating; nobody over here, to our knowledge, has made use of it except, to some extent, Miss Yonge, in her history of Christian names; but the English reader will get more fresh information from it upon an important collateral branch of historical inquiry than from any other

work of the kind. More than anything it will broaden
his views and enlarge the scope of his survey while
brought by it to look at Irish history as a whole—the
strange and sad history of a conquered country half
digested, which its conquerors would not abandon when
alive and struggling, and which their posterity cannot
assimilate now that it is dead and swallowed. The comic
aspect of the Irish revivalism is undoubtedly shown to
perfection in the splendid brag of the inimitable Pagan
O'Leary about the spelling of his own name—a treasonous
felon who has our warm heart. No Irishman whose dis-
affection was of the old national or of the more modern
and priest-moulded type could possibly have flourished
and flaunted a sham paganism in our faces after this
defiant fashion; and it certainly shows the influence of
ideas from that great country which, among other portents
and monsters, has produced Walt Whitman. But Heaven
knows there is nothing else ludicrous, as Lord Lifford says
there is, in an Irishman reverting to his O'. As for pre-
fixing it to "Saxon" names, we are not aware of his doing
anything of the kind. Boyle, alleged to be "Saxon," is a
pure old Donegal name, and if any Mr. Boyle likes to call
himself O'Boyle, we do not see why he should not. If he
reads O'Donovan's essay, he will at any rate see that the
O' does not in the least degree imply nobility, such being
a purely popular error; and he might therefore have let it
alone.

ROMANS, ROUMANS, AND ROUMAINS.

March 10, 1866.

OUR worthy friends on the Lower Danube, who have just
risen into new prominence in Western Europe through
quarrelling with the stopgap of their own selection, whom
they found so useful in 1858, seem to require a fixed
English name as well as a steady-going Hospodar. As

yet we are likely to hear about these people through news-papers alone. We should, therefore, like to see them called therein by some uniformly recognised name, rather than Roumans one day and Roumains the next, and Moldo-Wallachians the third, and Daco-Romans—their own term used for brag and self-laudation, corresponding to our "Anglo-Saxon"—the fourth.

As a general rule, we are anything but sticklers for uniformity and system in these matters, so far as current writing is concerned; holding that anybody in a news-paper may spell Gortchakoff just as he likes, within certain limits; nor have we the least wish to reprimand a jour-nalist who, for instance, takes his news about the ruler of Japan from a French source and calls him Taïkoun in one column, and then takes more news about him from an English source and calls him Tycoon in the next column. So long as we see what is meant we are quite satisfied, and, indeed, think that to cavil at it as an inconsistency betokens a certain pedantry of nature which values husks rather than kernels. And we are thankful for so effective an instrument of criticism all the while. But the line must be drawn somewhere, and for one thing we would fain draw it so as to exclude so utterly barbarous and un-English a word as "Roumain." Its termination is purely French, and has no business in English as it stands. "Rouman," though somewhat un-English in appearance as to its first syllable, is perhaps the best word to be had for the people, and Roumania for the country. Both seem to be now settling down into established use. Wallack, a good English word, is the best ethnical name for the whole race, or for the individuals ethnically treated. This, of course, includes not only the natives of the Principalities, but their brethren in Transylvania and Bessarabia, the nomad shepherds far away in Northern Greece, and the strange unnoticed and unaccountable fragment now at the point of breathing out its national life at the very gates of Trieste. It cannot, therefore, be used restrictedly for the people of the Principalities alone. The word itself in a Rouman mouth is not " Rouman " at all. The first syllable is an *o* rather than a *u*, and the second is not an *a* at all, or at most only so by etymological courtesy, being an obscure sound fostered under Sclavonic influence, indescribable in English. " Romoun " would best give the idea of it. But the wild nomad of the Pindus, whose dialect, being quite unsophisticated, is much the most valuable to the philologist, calls himself honestly " *un Rĕmanu,*" with as broad a vowel as in a real *bocca Romana* of old Rome—the first syllable, however, being slightly obscured. Mr. Boner seems to have been told in Transylvania that this name is a recent revival, like " Hellene " in Greece. In this he was told quite wrongly, for it is nothing of the kind. It is also quite wrong to say, as many papers—otherwise treating the political part of the subject with marked ability and correctness of appreciation—are saying, that the Principalities are inhabited by a heterogeneous population. These are of mixed origin and mongrel to any extent, no doubt; but as they stand now, they are as entirely homogeneous as Norfolk and Suffolk, Jews and gipsies apart; and the very essence of their position is, that of all the motley political divisions of Eastern Europe, theirs stands alone in this perfect actual unity of race. The case, in fact, is the Italian case over again, with Transylvania for the Rouman Venetia, and Bessarabia for its Corsica—more or less.

MR. ARNOLD ON CELTIC LITERATURE.

March 19, 1866.

WE have been waiting for a week or two in hopes that some adequate notice of Mr. Matthew Arnold's remarkable paper on Celtic Literature might have been taken by an authority competent to deal with the subject as a master. There is doubtless no great novelty in the view that the

English nation is destined to be affected beneficially by some considerable infusion of the artistic and imaginative faculty through a more complete incorporation of the various Celtic fragments existing within its bosom, which it has been absorbing and has yet to absorb. But this has always been put in a merely rhetorical and suggestive way, or in a bare dry ethnological way, and without the remotest reference to the actual nature and extent of that faculty as possessed and manifested in detail by the Celts. It has been reserved for Mr. Arnold to deduce this conclusion legitimately from a true knowledge of the Celtic ideals obtained by a direct study of the highest and most standard works on Celtic literature. And there is the greatest novelty in boldly challenging public attention and admiration on behalf of these ideals from an independent point of view. Mr. Arnold's style needs no laudation at our hands, nor do his special opinions require any exposition. It is not difficult to construct his argument out of his previous writings, nor to imagine the contrast between the Celtic children of light and the Saxon Philistines which may be assumed to pervade the present essay, without even taking the trouble of cutting the leaves. We presume everybody has read it; otherwise we might say that anybody might thus write its main argument for himself. We may further say that, even if he did that alone, he would be very much the better for so doing; so entirely do we concur in the conclusions to which Mr. Arnold is led, in some measure no doubt by the spirit of antipathy, but in a far greater measure by the keen instinct of a just and long-withheld sympathy. But Mr. Arnold, so far from meeting with the criticism of appreciation or depreciation, has hardly met with any notice at all. His subject is new and just now appropriate, and it is represented in a way both original and striking. We consider that it requires some notice, and that any notice is better than no notice. We are but as proselytes of the gate ourselves in Celtic matters, with no authoritative knowledge of Celtic details, yet we feel moved to hazard a brief remark or two in the present case, more with the intention of assisting Mr. Arnold than of criticising him. Celtic literature, indeed, and the study of the Celtic past—we may as well say all Celtic questions, past, present, and to come—bear much resemblance to the face of nature in a Celtic landscape. There is fair display of cultivated ground, in which it is the fertility of the soil which strikes the eye rather than the art of the cultivator or the bounty of the crop; there is the wild alternation of mountain and lake and sea, and there are the dreariest stretches of bog and moor and swamp, impracticable and interminable. It is given to very few to traverse with impunity, or even to set foot upon, the quaking bogs of Celtic archæology. We own that we gazed with no small trembling as we found Mr. Arnold, who knows no literary fear any more than his French friends know physical fear, venturing boldly upon this dangerous surface; and we cannot but admire the great skill with which he has as yet managed to plant his foot upon firm ground, or extricate himself from the quagmire before sinking more than knee-deep at most. We would fain lend him such assistance as lies in our power, by placarding the unsafe portions of his course, and writing "dangerous" in very large letters over Gomer and the Cimmerians, over the attribution of antiquity to any Celtic language as we have it, and over everything connected with the Scotch Highlanders, whom he has fortunately left alone for the present.

If Mr. Arnold means seriously to insist upon his classification of writers upon Celtic literature and antiquities, wherein he divides them into Celt-lovers and Celt-haters, and to uphold it as an exact or exhaustive one, or as one which is at all justifiable in the present day, we must beg him to change his mind forthwith, and shall do our best to convert him as fast as we can. It is·not a just one now, and it was not a just one in the days of Edward Lhuyd at the beginning of the last century. It is only just when applied to the intervening period when chaotic nonsense reigned supreme, when the Celtomaniacs had it all their own way in Wales and Ireland, their absurdities being incorporated into the national self-love, and when these extravagant pretensions called into existence the reactionary extravagances of Pinkerton and his school. This state of things is all past and gone now, or, if it lingers at all, it abides with the body of the people as a matter of vulgar prejudice, not with their leaders as a matter of enlightened belief. It is only found among Welsh and Irish Philistines on one hand, among Gothic Philistines on the other hand, and we would fain warn Mr. Arnold of the danger of falling among these. The dawn of the neutral and scientific spirit, first manifested in Dr. Prichard's excellent little book, became as the meridian light of full noon after the publication of Zeuss's immortal "Grammatica Celtica." The great German, dying, founded a school of Celtic philology which is one of the most conspicuous and flourishing branches of the new and irreversible science for which the world is indebted to Professor Francis Bopp. This school works upon language alone as its subject-matter; but it has been able thus to construct a firm basis of general scientific investigation upon all other points. Celtic archæology is now only trustworthy when in harmony with the teaching of the Zeussian school. If their doctrines are not accepted in England, it is not for want of any inculcation of them, for they have been presented over and over again to the public, notably so in certain articles which are to be found in the earlier numbers of the "Saturday Review." Upon the anonymous authorship of these we care not to intrude, further than to advert to the fact of our having recently cited their writer under his own name, as being emphatically a man of genius, and the ablest philologist of the new school who is native to these isles. The real name of "*Mac dá Cherda*," the gifted "Son of two Arts," is better known in Germany than in England, and we take shame

for this. These topics in England are left to grow wild
and to run adrift; nor do we admit them into the canon
of science until they have undergone what is called public
discussion, or have been sanctioned by those who have got
the right of affirming and denying things, and who act as
our bell-wethers. On the Continent it is the common
consent of an authoritative and competent body which
admits truth at sight in such points, and which then proceeds to work on further by means of the principles thus
obtained. Here, when such a theory is started for the
first time, all persons, *docti indoctique*, have a voice in
discussing it, without any ascertained principles of discussion; it has to be read a second time, and the Ethnological Society has to go into committee about it, and it
has to be read a third time, and then it is sent to our
recognised hereditary legislators in philology, such as Mr.
Crawfurd and Mr. Farrar, and the new cuneiform man
who made an exhibition of himself in the "Fraser" of last
November; and then it has to be sent up to the Sir Cornewall Lewis of the period to receive his royal assent, before
it can pass among us as law. This is well in politics and
Reform Bills, but it is anything but well for questions
such as that whether Welsh is in the category of Basque
or in the category of modern French to pass through the
hands of unqualified vestrymen and jurymen, with nothing
but common sense and the coarser Minerva to help them.
Yet thus it comes to pass that in England there are real
living men who doubt the mutual affinity of the Indo-
European languages, who know nothing of the details of
their comparative grammar, and who listen to Mr. Crawfurd quite as seriously as to that Professor Bopp whom
the universal academic world of the Continent at this
moment is uniting to honour. But the Irish Academi-
cians have identified themselves actively with the new
learning; and the leading Welsh scholars, such men as
Mr. Basil Jones, or Mr. Longueville Jones, or Mr. Williams
of Rhydycroesau, fully adopt its principles, and would be

ashamed to repeat any of the weary and **ridiculous outbursts**
of national self-love in **which** their forefathers gloried. **Mr.**
Nash, an Englishman, who has honestly studied the sub-
ject from the beginning, and who has received unqualified
praise from the Celtic Saturday Reviewer alluded **to** above,
has, we think, been most unfairly classified by Mr. Arnold
among Celt-haters. **Mr.** Nash undertook to expose, and
succeeded in exposing, the " dishonesty and blundering,"
the " scandalous suppressions, mistranslations, and forgeries," **with which the old** school of writings on Welsh
literature **teemed, which** alienated Englishmen from the
study of **that literature, and which** misled even such men
as Sir F. Palgrave **and Bunsen.** This is **not hatred of**
Celts; it is destroying **the** tares planted by Celts in the
field of science, and Mr. **Arnold is** hardly right or just in
attributing to Mr. Nash, a **conscientious** and valuable
workman of the new school, a preconceived anti-Celtic
animosity. The words in inverted commas **are** not **ours,**
they are the words of the Celt who is **the first authority**
on the subject. The classification should stand, **not as**
Celt-lovers and **Celt-haters,** but as science-lovers and
party-lovers—those **who are** urged by the partisan's **Phil-**
istine spirit, **and those whose path** is lighted up by the
scientific spirit. **We must do Mr.** Arnold the justice to
say that he hesitates **before committing** himself. Mr.
Nash does not hate the **Welsh;** he chastises them. His
position towards them is, in fact, precisely Mr. Finlay's
position **towards** the modern Greeks.

One **word more.** There is a touch here and there in
Mr. Arnold's delightful picture of the chattering French
maid, moving among her Celtic cousins, who speak her
own ancestral language about her unconscious ears, which
affects us with a pang of dreadful misgiving. How comes
the French maid **to be a** daughter of Gomer, and how
come the Welshmen or Cymry to **be** his sons? What was
" the common dwelling-place in the heart of Asia "? Who
were the Cimmerians of the Euxine who " came in on their

Western kinsmen"? and by **what kinship are they kinsmen?**
When the Welshman calls **white and red and** rock and
field and church and lord, *gwyn* **and** *goch* (lege *coch*) and
craig and *maes* and *llan* and *arglwydd*, in the genuine
tongue of **his** ancestors, **how** old does Mr. Arnold suppose
that tongue to **be?** This last point had better be settled
at once. Till thirty years ago it was usual to attribute a
mysterious and unfathomable antiquity to the **two** Celtic
main languages. Their history was uninvestigated; **nobody knew** or thought of asking whether or not **they had
any recorded stages** of development; on their surface **they
were utterly** unlike anything else in the world; and **this
halo of age and** mystery pleased their speakers and com-
pensated them for the loss of political power. But the
result of recent **inquiry,** which has admitted them into **the**
fullest and most equal right of brotherhood in the great
Aryan confraternity of speech, **has, in so doing,** broken
down the charmed circle **and dissipated the o**bscuring and
magnifying **halo.** **These languages are no granitic or pro-**
tozoic formation of the **elder** world; they are, **broadly
speaking,** the mere detritus of an older speech, **just as**
French **or** English is a detritus. It redounds to **the credit**
of the leading Welsh and Irish scholars that they can look
at this honestly in the face without blinking, accept it as a
definite principle, and embody it in their teaching. These
words, old **as they** may be for a modern language, as these
go, **are not in** their old **form;** they are phonetically cor-
rupt; they have lost their case-endings; **and two of them
are** simply Latin of the later Empire. *Llan* is *plana,* **an**
enclosed level ground; *coch* is *coccinus,* red, in modern
Greek κόκκινος. **Strangely enough,** the later Latin words
for yellow **and red,** *melinus* **and** *coccinus,* **survive nowhere**
—the Greek excepted—but in **Welsh, and in that queer**
little **tongue,** the Rumonsch **of the Grisons, w**here they
appear as *mellen* and *cotschen.* **The first work of** the
Zeussian school was to **restore** conjecturally, by means **of**
comparison of **all existing or** recorded forms found **in the**

Celtic languages, the older speech from which they were held to have been derived. Now it cannot be too often repeated that these conjectural forms, restored with such wonderful acuteness, have since been literally verified by their actual discovery in inscriptions written in the old Gaulish language which have recently come to light. These are inadequate as regards the verb, but are simply identical as regards the noun. Next to the resurrection of the ancient language of Persia, this is surely the greatest triumph of comparative philology yet achieved. The old Proto-Celtic language may be defined, in a word, as having Welsh or Irish roots—the primitive difference being but small—inflected with terminations after the Latin fashion, all but identical with the Latin ones themselves. The word Cymry has nothing whatever to do with Cimmerians, nor with Cimbri. It is later than the Romans; it was once written with two *m*'s, and its oldest form was demonstrably Combroges, meaning a united or confederate people, as opposed to Allobroges, or alien people. All this, since Zeuss's proof, has been accepted without a dissentient word, except where dissent signifies nothing. As for Gomer, he belongs to Dr. Cumming by vested right, and Mr. Arnold had better leave him to the patentee. We conclude by hoping that Mr. Arnold will not be long in perceiving that the one man who has done more irretrievable harm to the proper appreciation of the imaginative literature of the Gael than ten thousand Pinkertons is James Macpherson, the fabricator of one of the greatest delusions upon earth, and the incarnation of literary injustice to Ireland.

OLD AND NEW IRISH NATIONALITY.

March 27, 1866.

ABOUT a hundred and thirty years ago there flourished in Dublin a schoolmaster of some repute in his day, by name Teige O'Nechtan, translated into English as Thaddeus

Norton, according to that queer fashion, the conventional
"translation" of Irish names into English, which was to
some extent compulsory in the early days of conquest and
oppression, and ended by becoming voluntary during the
subsequent period of degradation.   Norton was a man of
learning in the old lore of his country, the study of which as
a living pursuit had not even then fully died out.   We may
fairly contrast his Hibernology with that of the Hibernolo-
gists of the present generation, the Reeveses and Todds, in
the same way that we can contrast the Arabic or Sanskrit
lore of natives, the leading Cairene Sheikhs or Benares
Pundits, with that of the De Sacys and Lanes, the Wil-
sons and Müllers, of Europe.   He it is who was mainly
responsible for raising the absurd Phœnician ghost which
has since haunted the purlieus of Irish archæological inquiry.   He was first in the field with the Irish version of
the immortal Punic passage in Plautus.   He never published this himself, however; but his manuscripts which
contained it fell into the hands of General Vallancey, who
brought it before the public as his own discovery without
the slightest acknowledgment, apparently under the impression that he was appropriating something of value.
Many Irish scholars made a grievance of this plagiarism
when detected, and perhaps they were right, looking to
the General's motive, and not to the worth of the stolen
article.   But Norton is chiefly memorable for an extem-
pore Irish stanza which he was provoked to utter upon
the sight of an Englishman hanging from a tree.   "*Rath
do thorad hort, a chroinn,*" said he: "Increase to thy fruit,
O tree,—and may every tree in Ireland bear a goodly
crop of it ere long." Hardiman gives the words with a
slight difference, but we quote from O'Reilly.   Now we
are well accustomed to sentiments of this kind in the disaffected Anglo-Irish poetry of the present day.   But in the
latter case they are traditional rhetoric, and nothing more,
for no man can say now what makes an original Irishman,
and what makes an Englishman in Ireland; while in the

mouth of Norton they represent a living and bitter sense of national hatred, founded on the fact of a real national difference, then as yet unextinguished, though on its way to extinction. We refer to the schoolmaster's stanza as a good example for the purpose of illustrating in detail that traditional hostility to England assigned as a main cause of Irish difficulties by Lord Dufferin in his masterly speech of last week. That hostility is now but a tradition; yet only four generations ago three-fourths of the country at least were divided from the other fourth by a difference greater than that between Pole and Russian, and in some respects not less than that between Turk and Greek. Few Englishmen realise to themselves how recently the Irish nation kept some sort of distinctive corporate existence alive. The assimilative operations of English influence began early, but these were both gradual and partial, and did not affect the country at large until a late period, in spite of over-statements made by Elizabethan writers, arguing for a set purpose, who contradict themselves in the next breath.

In the face of the surviving consciousness of a real national existence within so few generations, it is both idle and unfair to reproach the Irish with want of appreciation of our brief thirty years of equitable and conscientious policy. It is equally idle to talk of past "misgovernment." What did Norton and his Catholic contemporaries care about English misgovernment? It was the presence of the English which they loathed, not their misgovernment. There is something almost shocking in the easy and reckless levity in which our present generation—drunk, as it were, with the strong drink of conscientiousness and virtuous intention—is turning its back upon its ancestors and reviling them for their misgovernment in Ireland. They conquered the country, and could only hold it down when alive and struggling by dint of such acts as constitute misgovernment. When nationally dead, we can now afford to govern it well; had we been in the place of the

Elizabethan or the Cromwellian or the Williamite conquerors, we should have done as they did and no better.
When did thirty years ever suffice to obliterate the abiding
sense of ancient wrong, more especially if there exists an
influential body whose professional business it is not to
let the memory of that wrong die out, but to foster it for
their own purposes ? The forces which are to determine
the future fate of Ireland stand arrayed on either side
ready for the muster. On our side we count Time the
healer, and the admirable system of national education,
which has done more than anything else to reclaim the
Irish middle classes, to give them a British soul, and in-
corporate them in the body of the empire. · On the side of
the anti-English powers of darkness is the new disturbing element of a paradise realised in life, a future state
beyond the Atlantic, which any man may reach by the
outlay of a five-pound note, where the landlord ceases
from troubling, and the weary tenant may rest—yet no
passive paradise, but a belligerent and vengeful heaven,
that is ever coming clothed in terror to redeem the op-
pressed and chosen people in their old island home. Of
what avail is petty redress of absenteeism and Protestantism and the like in presence of this mighty and absorbing
hope of a Yankee advent?

While mentioning Protestantism, we take occasion to
close with one word about the Established Church in
Ireland. Doubtless it is a great inconsistency, and perhaps it may be a great evil. The mass of the Catholic
people may not feel it as a grievance in practice, but we
know that there are certain parties who do feel it as a
grievance. To be sure, if we trace these people upwards,
from inferior to superior, it will probably be found that
the centre of operations whence their feelings are attuned
into accord and discord with England is at Rome rather
than at Dublin, and is therefore un-English in nature, and
may be anti-English, too, when it seems good. But that
may be let pass; if justice must be done, we must of course

take our chance of pulling heaven down in the process. The theory of the Irish Church is not what it should be, that is certain; and if it is not a popular grievance, it ought to be one. Lord Grey is aware that it is not one, and conceives that the conclusion therefrom deduced, to the effect that we should leave the Church alone for the present, or hesitate before at once easing it off, is a very shallow observation. What we want to say is, that it *is* an observation, and as such is more valuable than a speculation. An ounce of the one is worth a pound of the other. This charge of shallowness was no doubt brought by the German philosopher against the Englishman who went to Arabia to study his camel. Lord Dufferin has lived all his life with his camel, and has studied it under every possible light; and thus we consider that his view of Irish questions—especially this one of the Church— must be held to supersede that of Lord Grey, who has only elaborated one out of his moral consciousness. A residence in Corfu, or an hour's interview in person or in print with impartial Ionians or uncorrupted Ionians, would have made Lord Grey hold his hand before committing himself to the sweeping measure which ran its unavoidable course, and which has ended in the retardation, if not the destruction, of material prosperity and moral progress in the islands for half a century at least. Anybody who ever talked with Ionian peasants in their own language knows that their wish for union with Greece belonged to the extra- rational part of their nature, and had nothing to do with Otho's kingdom. Their souls aspired for union with an ideal Greece, not with the real Greece. In like manner it is well for us to be on our guard against pushing doc- trine to extremes in estimating the condition of Ireland, by overvaluing the immediate present, and overdoing reme- dial work, when things are either beyond remedy or not ripe for remedy. In the Irish nature the ideal elements go for much, but they must not be mistaken for the reason- ing element, any more than they should be ignored.

We have the highest and warmest respect for Lord
Grey, but we think he is too much of a *doctrinaire*, and
too "thoughtful," if we may use without offence a word
rapidly passing into slang. Excess in doctrinarity and
excess in " earnestness " are threatening to set their mark
on the new political generation, and we are glad to have
an opportunity of entering our protest against these when
out of all moderation, unchecked by any misgivings, and
unsweetened by a drop of the sense of humour or of omni-
lateral sympathy.

OLD AND NEW FENIANS.

April 1866.

" A VAGRANT " has just written another of his long, ram-
bling, discursive letters to the " Times " about the' ancient
Fenians. This, like the former one of last October, is full
of information which, if not very new, nor very recondite,
nor very practical, is very little known to the present
metropolitan reading generation, although bearing directly
upon a chapter of literary history which was at one time
thought of sufficient importance to send the great patriarch of literature himself from Fleet Street to the
Hebrides, when these were more difficult of access to
Londoners than Montenegro or the Atlas are to ourselves
at the present day. This letter is the best of the two; not
that there is any method in either, nor does any object
seem to have been aimed at by the writer beyond that
of scattering his information in a desultory way, and of
pointing a plain moral or two by dint of running an occasional parallel between the ancient Fenians of tradition
and the modern revivalist Fenians. The main point seems
to be that the ancient Fenians were volunteers and fine
fellows, and that their real legitimate descendants are not
rebels but loyal volunteers and fine fellows too, especially
the London Scottish, with Lord Elcho for their Finn

M'Coul. These letters are open to criticism in many places, albeit such treatment would hardly be fair, as they were evidently not written with the prospect of encountering criticism. Yet we would fain take occasion to recommend the writer to beware of over-estimating the scientific value of nursery tales, popular legends, and the like, as a branch of comparative mythology; and to be on his guard against his own tendencies and proclivities in this direction, such as the reader feels to be latent below the surface of the present letters. Comparative mythology, if a science at all, is as yet but an unfixed and embryonic science, with no certain basis save that of comparative philology, and only to be treated by those who are masters of this last. It is clear that our author has yet to serve his apprenticeship in both the principles and details of comparative philology, even from his brief remarks about the local names on the Brighton Downs, which he conceives to afford evidence that speakers of Gaelic as well as speakers of Welsh once existed there.

Now we say, as we have once said and shall say again whenever we have an opportunity, that nobody has any right to speculate in print upon Celtic philology, much less to lay down the law about it, unless he has previously sat in all docility at the feet of Zeuss and Norris and Whitley Stokes. We shall hammer this nail on the head till we have driven it well home into the public mind; and when we are tired, Mr. Matthew Arnold will come and relieve us. However, our own object in the present notice is not so much to censure such points as the author's refusal of the word " bourne" to the forefathers of the South Saxons until they came and found it in Britain—a refusal which would have mightily astonished Bishop Ulfilas — as to appeal to his letter, so full of citations from genuine and beautiful Ossianic poetry, taken from Irish records of the twelfth century, as an excellent means of illustrating and enforcing what we said the other day when reviewing Mr. Arnold. We said that the one man who did more irre-

parable mischief to the correct English appreciation of
genuine Gaelic poetry, and who committed more injustice
to Ireland, in a literary point of view, than any or all
other men and circumstances, was James Macpherson, the
arch-fabricator and father of distortion. Nobody can read
the true Ossianic fragments, such as those cited in this
letter, without at once feeling how their discovery would
have entirely altered their position in our literature had it
taken place naturally, primarily, and on a large scale, instead of their having been brought forward by piecemeal
as incidents of attack or defence in the controversy about
the false Ossian.

SLAVONIC PROFESSORSHIP.

April, 1866.

WE have an impression that about a year ago there was a
small paragraph in one or two papers which announced
that the late Lord Carlisle had left some money to one of
the Universities, probably Oxford, for the purpose of founding a professorship of the Slavonic languages; or at any
rate, for we are not sure of our details, and only speak
from uncertain recollection, of promoting the cultivation
of these languages by some process of academical encouragement. Whether good or not, this idea, if truly re-
ported, was at least an original one; but it fell by the
wayside for aught we see to the contrary, and was trampled
under foot in the crush of our bustling public life, or was
cast on the stony soil of indifference, and withered up in
a day.

Such seeds as this never can come to maturity in this
country unless they are fostered by the warm sun of popular favour, or by the official patronage of a great man, such
as in this case would probably have been afforded if Lord
Carlisle, a wide-minded and scholar-like man, with genuine
and many-sided, even if occasionally feckless sympathies,

had lived. This idea is now brought very forcibly to our
recollection by the sight of the Russian "Galignani," if we
may so call it, appearing once a week or oftener at Brus-
sels. There is no savoury hash of gossip here, like that
so bountifully served up by our own purveyor for English
tastes; there is nothing but leading articles and strong
political writing, into which we can only obtain a glimpse
through the very brief French summaries or dockets of
each separate article which precede the whole on the first
side of the paper. One is almost appalled at having it
brought before us in this striking way how far the whole
bulk of our educated and cultivated community is shut
out from the study, at first hand, of the real thoughts and
words of seventy millions of men, of one of the most
powerful nations in the world, rising to unwonted political life, and exulting in their new and almost uncon-
trolled freedom of the press. The Russian press abounds
with most important and valuable scientific and literary
periodicals, corresponding to our monthlies and quarterlies;
and, as regards geography at least, the cream of these is
now generally made public under the auspices of Sir
Roderick Murchison and the Messrs. Michell. Yet these
gentlemen, like the late Emperor Alexander, are but fortunate accidents. But it is dreadful and tantalising to
see political articles about Turkestan and Germany and
Moldo-Wallachia wrapped up in the impenetrable veil of
a language to which there is here neither royal nor any
other road, clothed in an alphabet which looks to the common English eye like the Greek Lexicon in a dream after
a supper of pork chops, as Mr. Sala says, with his usual
reckless, happy buffoonery. It is really a pressing need,
that of easy access to the free play of Russian opinion on
those public matters which must be influenced by that
opinion sooner or later; and we consider that for this
reason alone the vernacular acquisition of Russian by
system, and not by haphazard, is deserving of great and
immediate encouragement. The method of its acquisition

and the enormous importance of the Slavonic dialects in the scheme of Aryan comparative philology, so strangely ignored or slightly dwelt upon in the usual English expositions of that scheme, are questions separate from the above, which we may have occasion to treat some day.

"GREEK SLAVS."

May 11, 1866.

WE have been wondering for the last ten days what can possibly have induced our respected contemporary the " Spectator " to call the Wallachians or Roumans " Greek Slavs." What purpose is served, or what point is illustrated, by so doing? In calling them " Roumans," as other people do, there is perhaps a lack of surface cleverness, but there is certainly safety. What is a Greek Slav, as such? What are the characteristics whereby he is denoted? Has any human being, now or at any time, ever beheld such a thing as a Greek Slav people? In the greater towns of European Turkey there are certain families reputed to be of mixed Greek and Armenian descent, and thence called in the Greek tongue by the queer-looking name of Khaikhorúmides, or Armeno-Greeks. These, if the assertion be true regarding them, represent an extreme case in the way of hybridity between incompatibles. So do the natives of Scio, according to the jocose ethnology of the non-Sciote Greeks, who are fond of imagining them to be lineal descendants of the Ten Lost Tribes, as well as of Homer's fellow-citizens of Chios ; founding their imputation on a certain turn for shrewd and sharp practice now well known over the whole commercial world. But a community of Greek Slavs north of the Danube must be a strange mixture, and is worth looking for. It is not enough to say simply that the Wallachians are not Greeks and are not Slavs, nor yet the product of the two together. So far as they have any national antipathy at all, or have ever asserted themselves with anything remotely approaching to a national feeling in their past history, it has been notoriously anti-Greek on one side and anti-Slavonic on the other. When they took up arms in 1821 under Theodore Vladimiresco, their hands were against the Turkish absentee landlord, but their hearts were against the Fanariote middleman. When they joined Maghero's abortive attempt at an organised resistance in 1848, it was against a Russian invasion of their territory, perpetrated for invasion's sake on a sham diplomatic pretext, such as is but too likely to recur at any time. What the exact genealogical factors of the modern Wallachian may be it is very hard to say, nor does it matter for any practical purpose. It is enough for us that he chooses to think of himself as a descendant of the Romans, to lay stress on his Romanic elements, and to put himself into as close a connection as he can, both socially and politically, with the leading Romanic Powers of the West. He has as much right to do this as the Greek—much purer in language, but hardly less impure in blood, except locally—has to work the leverage of his ancestral connection, and call himself a Hellene. The Rouman has some Slavonic blood in his veins doubtless; and so, for the matter of that, have the Turk and the Greek, and everybody else in these parts. But it has no more bearing on his character or his present politics than the Slavonic blood alleged by Schaffarik to exist in Wiltshire has upon the elections at Calne and Devizes. The whole history of modern literary movement and literary cultivation among the Roumans is simply the detail of their efforts to purify their language by elimination of its intrusive Slavonic elements. They have not done this satisfactorily nor according to any consistent rule of analogy, for they are without the groundwork of a solid Latin education, owing to their connection with the Eastern Church. But the spirit of their modern culture is anti-Slavonic in the most thoroughgoing sense. A consideration of these Slavonic elements is well worth

the while of philologists. They have, of course, received
due attention in Germany, and not one single syllable of
notice in England. The best account of them is contained
in a recent monograph by Francis Miklosich of Vienna,
who holds within the domain of Slavonic comparative
grammar the same master's position as that held by Zeuss
in the Celtic, Jacob Grimm in the Teutonic, Diez in the
Romanic, and Bopp in the Pan-Aryan domains respectively. They are larger than the Teutonic elements in
French, the most Teutonized of the Neo-Latin languages,
but far less than the Romanic elements in English. They
are not only lexical, but have distinctly affected the phonology, the idiom, and, in a small degree, the forms of Wallachian. The number of words of Slavonic origin found in
the latter as given by Miklosich—many of them root-
words, fathers of families—is little short of a thousand.
We have naturally no space here to enter into their most
interesting details. But, while referring to the Wallachian
language, we must find room for adverting to one fact.
This important language may, in some measure, be called
the keystone of the Romanic arch. It has been completely separated and finally disconnected from the
Romanic languages of the West, from the time of Aurelian
downwards. But it is in an almost identical stage of development with Italian, and, its Slavonic accretions apart,
may be taken for a rude mismanaged Italian dialect. The
importance of the conclusions deducible from this would
not fail to strike our philologists, if we had any school of
philology—we do not count people who, knowing no languages, speculate on the origin of Language, as philologists.
Yet the one book which we possess on the subject of the
Romanic languages and their origin, that by Sir Cornewall
Lewis—an inadequate, inexact, and most overrated work
—absolutely makes no mention from beginning to end of
the one derivative of Latin which is the co-ordinate, not
of any single one among its Western congeners, but of the
entire group collectively, and illustrates them at every step.

Q

SLAVONIC AT OXFORD.

May 24, 1866.

LORD ILCHESTER'S bequest of a thousand pounds for the promotion of the study of " Polish and other Slavonic languages" has at length been accepted by the University of Oxford without opposition, but in a thin house. The subject certainly is one not likely to create enthusiasm among M.A.'s of the ordinary type; and as for opposition, surely no one would have the heart to oppose the bequest on principle, or the knowledge wherewith to oppose it in detail. We have some curiosity, not to say anxiety, to know how its provisions will be put into practice, now that it has been fairly adopted, and whether it is in contemplation to adhere strictly and literally to the arrangement whereby Lord Ilchester assigns priority to the Polish in preference to any other Slavonic language. Now these languages, like all other languages, are capable of being taught in two ways and for two distinct objects. They may be taught with the apparatus and for the purposes of the modern science of comparative philology, with the view of illustrating each step of their own special history and each point of their interdependence among themselves, as well as their general position and bearings in that vast domain of Aryan speech of which they form so important, well-defined, and thoroughly surveyed a section. Or they may be taught not as ends, but as means, for the purely practical purposes of life, in the same way that we teach French or Hindustani. The Polish language does not possess any such inherent right of priority over the other Slavonic languages as would entitle it to be selected as the medium of instruction upon either of the above grounds. It does not stand towards them in the same position as Ulphilas's Gothic towards the other Teutonic languages, or Sanskrit towards the other Aryan languages. It is on precisely the same footing as its sister tongues, with no special advantage, except in the archaic retention of certain final nasals—an advantage which can only be made of avail or appreciated at all by treating the languages as a whole, and not singly. If they are to be thus treated, and if decision be given in favour of teaching them philologically, it is obvious that the basis of instruction should be the old Church Slavonic, which does occupy a position like that of the Gothic among German forms of speech, though in a far less marked degree, and which can be made to act as a solvent or key of the peculiarities and deviations of each special dialect. Broadly speaking, and apart from the merits of individuals, which have to be considered in detail, instruction in this old tongue is not to be expected from a Polish quarter, for it has never been studied as a book language or a Church language by the Poles, a Catholic people, who have always been careful to keep up their Latin cultivation.

If, on the other hand, any Slavonic language is to be taught simply for the purpose of linguistic acquisition, it becomes still more reasonable and necessary to inquire why Polish should be the one chosen. It is difficult of acquisition, not only grammatically, but organically; for it is full of minute shades of pronunciation, of birdlike trills and twitterings such as it is almost impossible for our adult or adolescent organs to reproduce; and it leads to nothing except, at best, to the study of a few striking works of poetical genius. All Poles with whom an Englishman is likely to hold intercourse speak French, English, or German. As for the Polish peasantry, the Polish Jews, or others who speak Polish alone, he is no more likely to have dealings with them, or to need their language—much less likely, in fact—than with Bosnians or Bulgarians. And— we write it with pain, but it must be written, whatever may be the sacrifice of sentimental regret—there is only too much reason to forbode a position of subordination and inferiority for the Polish language henceforth. A moment's

reflection will show that it must be so. On the other
hand, the position of Russia will be that of predominance,
and of an extension to which, in two directions at least, it
is difficult to assign limits. Our direct personal intercourse with the Russians of all classes is increasing in the
same ratio that the development of public life, an unfettered
press, and a self-confident spontaneous nationalism, replacing servile imitation of the West, are increasing among the
Russians themselves. It is full time that the language of
seventy growing millions of people should be rendered
accessible to us by systematic cultivation, instead of being
left to be picked up at haphazard and by rule of thumb.
Lord Ilchester's bequest gives us the opportunity of saying
this now, but we should have said it sooner or later, irrespectively of any bequest. And we shall have to repeat it
and harp upon it too, for it has been observed by people of
experience that one tap of a hammer has never yet been
enough to drive a nail into the "Anglo-Saxon" head. As
for the University, our recommendation would be for it to
resign itself implicitly into the hands of Mr. Watts, of the
British Museum, and procure a report from him as to the
most advisable plan of action, for he alone, to our knowledge, is master of the subject in all its bearings, and of
Slavonic bibliography into the bargain.

DAM ALTAFHOO.

May 30, 1866.

THE exalted Order of the Star of India has just been
divided into classes, into Knights Commanders and ordinary Companions ; and it has all been duly registered and
decreed by Hatti-Sherif, or royal rescript. In this way
Dam Altafhoo, who was but plain Dam before, has now
come to be Sir Dam Altafhoo, for they have made him a
Knight Commander. Let us hope that he will rise in
good time to be Knight Grand Cross, and will some day

sit in the highest seats among the chosen ones of the age,
next to our old friend Sir Furzund Dilbund Rajegan. Of
course, it is open to himself or anybody to call him Sir
Shreemun Altafhoo, should it so seem good, for the choice
of names is as great and as picturesque as in the case of
Sir Furzund. His full style, in fact, is the Rajah Shreemun Maharajah Chuttroputte Shahabe Dam Altafhoo;
and a pretty style it looks too. There is one comfort,
that nobody can go wrŏng about the Rajah, not even in
the "London Gazette" office. It certainly seems odd that
the higher title of Maharajah should form part of the
name, being as though King Victor Emmanuel, or King
Pepple, or King Theodorus were to bear the name "Emperor" as part and parcel of those given them in their
baptism. But then we have never been to India, and
have, doubtless, no business to go about cavilling at what
we do not understand. Yet we own that we wished to
verify the Dam when we first saw it. It is not a proper
name for anybody belonging to a Christian order of knight-
hood. Thomas Hood would have resented it, and made
his printers treat it as he made them print Amsterd—m
and Rotterd—m. Having begun by disliking it, we went
on to doubt it. We consulted dictionaries and grammars
of the Guzerati, the Marathi, the High Tamul, the Low
Tamul, the Canarese, the Malayalam, the Brij Bhakha, the
Pushtu, Puk'hto or Afghan, the Parthian, the Mede, the
Elamite, the Cretan, and the Arabian. We tried to consult Colonel Sykes—getting at him in the disguise of a
Taeping, with samples of rebel-grown silk. We knocked
up Sir Henry Rawlinson at an unearthly hour, rousing
him out of his beauty-sleep. We went the rounds of all
the club porters, and the great butlers, and the chaperones,
in order to try and find out who were the real London
"authorities" in Eastern matters—the people who are
most sought after, and get most invitations to dinner as
Oriental lions, and are most thought of by the best men.
We got plenty of edifying information, but not about the

Dam. Neither grammars, nor lexicons, nor Colonel Sykes, nor the leading servants, nor the servant-minded ones, could relieve our doubts, or unriddle us the Dam, except to make us aware that no such a name existed anywhere. There are places where it is said to mean a copper coin quite below marketable value ; also places where it means a trap wherein unwary creatures are caught. Either of these will do for its meaning in the " London Gazette " office— the second for choice. Not but what the first well represents the current value of our modern official Orientalism —just what it is worth.

Some eighteen months ago a contemporary review—if we may use that form of words in speaking of articles written before our own birth—indulged both in facetiousness and indignation at the absurd and discreditable—not to say shameful—way in which, at the time of Sir Furzund of Kuppoorthulla's investiture, that potentate's names and titles were insanely jumbled up with the headings of his letters in Persian, and suchlike purely Oriental honorific adjuncts. These, at first written in dog-Persian, were transcribed into the Roman character promiscuously, just as the letters might happen to come uppermost into the compositor's hand, and without a word to show our English public that the ridiculous amalgam was no name at all, and had no more to do with an Asiatic proper name than " I am, sir, your obedient servant," has to do with an English proper name. So it is in the present case, to be serious with it at last. Dam Altafhoo, with its absurd capitals, is no part of the honest man's name, but simply the Arabic formula, *dáma altáfuhu,* " may his favours continue." It, or its like, is used in the direction and the opening preamble of all letters among Mahometans ; places where, in Oriental correspondence, honorific epithets and vows for welfare are always accumulated, and complimentary titles set forth at length. But what may here call for special remark, over and above the original crowning absurdity, is this, that both socially or morally and grammatically, it is irredeemably wrong, alike bad grammar and bad etiquette. *Altáf*, "favours," the plural of *lutf*, requires its verb to be in the feminine singular, by a rule analogous to that whereby Greek neuters plural take a singular verb. Semitic verbs, it should be said, as Hebrew scholars know, distinguish the genders of their persons. To be good Arabic, it should be *Dámat altáfuhu.* But that is nothing compared with the joke of making the Empress of India appeal with gratuitous humility to a little Mahratta princeling for the continuance of his favours and kindness towards herself. The words used, just as "favours" in English, distinctly imply and acknowledge the superiority of the person whose favours are in question. All Mahometans, from the Moors at Gibraltar to the Tumongong of Johore, can understand each point, and all will be in convulsions of laughter if ever they come to hear of them. If Oriental words are worth using at all, they are worth using rightly. But here, whatever may be the process by which this sort of stuff contrives to filter through layers of copying clerks and stratum after stratum of officials into the "London Gazette," it is clear that the persons who manage the titles at the Oriental Heralds' College, be they "nigger" moonshees or albino aides-de-camp, have no more idea of Eastern verbal etiquette than of Arabic grammar.

After all this, it would be merely trifling to inquire why, when you have got Oriental names by the gross, forming a compact body, you spell them either quite chaotically, or at best with a separate system for each name. This is quite a different thing from the principle we advocate, of spelling them in current newspaper writing just as we find them, flagrant errors apart. There was a capital opportunity, not to say a necessity, for system in the present list, and it has been thrown away.

LATIN PRONUNCIATION.

September 4, 1866.

AUTUMNAL newspaper controversies are like the Indian banyan-tree. The main stem sends off its branches towards all quarters of the heavens; and these stretch down and take root in the earth, and forthwith become themselves as new trees. The great grammar controversy in the " Times "—not that it is a controversy as yet, for the correspondence has all been on one side till yesterday— has just shot forth a promising young sapling indeed, which may end by waxing much mightier than the parent stem, if its growth be properly looked after. " J. R. A.," who has taken part in the discussion with some sensible and practical remarks upon the original question of me-chanical *versus* ultra-philosophical teaching in the case of very young boys, ends his letter by himself raising a separate issue of the highest importance. This is no less than the substitution of a reasonable for an utterly bar-barous pronunciation of Latin in English teaching. Now as regards theory, it is merely flogging a dead horse to estify against the Eton pronunciation. No one defends it in theory, or has anything better to say in its favour than that it is the custom of the country. But no one seems to conceive that it is within the limits of possibility to give it up and replace it by the one pronunciation which prevails over all the rest of the world, with a certain minimum of local variation in each country. The ques-tion is one of practicability and of goodwill, not one of theoretical accuracy; and is literally nothing more than whether or not it is within our power to teach the Latin vowels with their Continental instead of their English sounds. Now there is not the remotest difficulty in so doing, because there is no organic obstacle in the way. Such an organic obstacle we may exemplify by the instance

of a Greek θ, which no Frenchman or Italian could pronounce unless he learnt it in childhood from an Englishman, an Icelander, or a modern Greek. The most he could
do would be to bear the theory in his mind, and do the
best he could in practice, with a sense of its being a
makeshift. But we have all the Latin vowel sounds as a
natural part of our own utterance, only we express them
by different letters or combinations. Is there any conceivable reason why these should not be introduced into
English schools, if not from abroad, at least from Scotland? As for the consonants, they may take care of
themselves. The main point of difference would merely be
whether *g* and *c* should have their hard or their soft sound
before *e* and *i*, whether *que* and *qui* should be simple or
compound sounds, and maybe one or two more points,
which may be left to take their chance, and are quite
subordinate to the chief question.

THE GIFT OF TONGUES.

September 6, 1866.

THE Vienna correspondent of the " Times" has just drawn
up a list of the various languages which an Austrian
official may be called upon to learn in the course of his
duties—an appalling list indeed. There are no less than
ten of them. It is almost impossible for an Englishman,
who knows absolutely nothing of language-questions, or
of race-questions determined by language—for the Irish
language is virtually extinct—to realise such a state of
things as one in which not only have ten languages got
to be learnt and mastered by the aggregate central government, but they actually serve to denote ten separate political questions, each of which is more or less menacing to
the very existence of the empire. These languages, indeed,
are not merely symbols of the political questions; they

are of their very essence, the pivot on which they actually turn. But it will perhaps be more to the purpose if, instead of going into general reflections about these matters, we were to make a correction here and there in the list before us; for it requires correction, and is, otherwise, sufficiently accurate to make it worth while to correct. To begin with, there is a curious misprint; Vaids instead of Vinds or Winds, as the writer no doubt had himself written it—meaning the Slovenians, or Carniolan Slavonians. This word must be carefully distinguished in current use from the Wends of the north-west, though the two words are originally the same, being in fact our true native name by which Teutons have in all times called their Slavonic frontagers. Our own old English form of it was *Weonodas. Selovenisch* should not be translated *Sclave,* which is rendering a specific term by a generic one, and thus, by meaning everything means nothing. It should be translated Windish or Slovenian. *Russinisch* (Russian) seems safe enough at first sight, but there is enough latent fire smouldering under the ashes here utterly to burn up the unwary foot that may be set upon it. What turns on the rendering here is neither more nor less than the ultimate fate of Galicia. We are not going to handle the question ourselves here, warned off as we are therefrom by the sound of much uproar and gnashing of teeth. It is enough to say that, whatever the Ruthenian or Russine language may be, it is most certainly not the Great Russian of St. Petersburg and Moscow, nor a dialect of it, but as much a co-ordinate of it as Polish or Bohemian. It is, in fact, Little Russian, the language of the Ukraine. The Austrians love to coquet with it and encourage it as against Polish. They try to make a literary language of it, and have invested it with all the dignity of the most ancient form of Cyrillic black-letter type, which looks very imposing on a bank-note or official document. It must be borne in mind, however, that five out of these ten languages are closely akin to one another;

varying from a dim, imperfect, mutual comprehension to
a difference which is barely even one of dialect. What is
the amount of difference between Croatian and Servian?
Miklosich, in his Comparative **Grammar of the Slavonic
Languages,** treats the two as one, and **they** hardly **seem** to
vary more—idiom and single words apart—than in tone,
accent, and **one** or two phonetic peculiarities, **such as the**
retention **of the** final *l* in active participles **in Croatian,**
where the Servian vocalises it into *o.* The book-language
seems absolutely the same in Agram that it is in Belgrade
or Ragusa. As regards **popular** language, the details **on**
this point, in English **at least,** are certainly insufficient.
Miss Irby, who has the philological faculty, might do an
essential service in this direction **if** she could be **kept**
clear of politics. We think **it is fair to say** that any **man**
who is thoroughly master of **one** Slavonian language is
practically master of all, in so far as regards the power of
comprehension. Unless endowed with the special linguis-
tic gift, he may not be able to shift his speech from one
form to **the other form so as to talk in each; in doing so**
he **would** always **run the risk of missing his grammatical**
tip, to borrow **Mr.** Sala's inimitably happy **phrase; but a**
few days' **practice** would be all that was necessary to
enable him to understand the sense of his interlocutor's
words. Mr. Wratislaw, in his **preface to** his ancestor's
delightful journal of his Turkish captivity, says he **tried**
this at Prague in the extreme case of a Bulgarian. **He**
did not succeed in understanding **him** by means **of Bohe-**
mian, **as** was hardly to be expected, seeing **that Bulgarian**
has passed from synthesis to analysis, **and has adopted**
Turkish **and** Greek vocables **to a** large **amount; but** he
could have **felt** his way **to comprehension with** a fortnight's
intercourse before him, **and it is probable that** he might
have understood what **he heard, had he seen** it written
down on paper.

GREEK PRONUNCIATION.

September 14, 1866.

SIR,—Your correspondent the "Turk" is but a violent and
arbitrary Ottoman if he really attributes to your previous
correspondent, " C. B. C.," any tendency to advocate the
modern Greek system of pronouncing ancient Greek
merely because he objects to our pronunciation and re-
proves our total neglect of accents and our untruth to
ourselves in the matter of adhering to the rhythm which
we profess to respect. It by no means follows that, because a man says we are wrong, he necessarily implies
that the moderns are right, or *vice versâ*. There is not a
word from beginning to end in " C. B. C.'s " letter which
commits him to any advocacy of the moderns, nor any
necessary indication of his holding such an opinion in
reserve. Our diphthongs are bad, he says, but it does not
follow that he may not think the modern ones are worse
—being, in fact, no diphthongs at all. No doubt the
" Turk " may be right in availing himself of " C. B. C.'s "
letter as a favourable opportunity to lift up his voice and
testify against modern Greek heresies, but such testimony
is volunteered testimony, and does not in the least follow
from the terms of " C. B. C.'s " letter. I venture to think,
sir, that it is just as well for an outsider to set this
straight, because it is out of imputations volunteered and
suggested in this way that aimless, resultless interminable
newspaper controversies arise, whereof no man may see
the advantage or the end. In your columns at least there
is no elbow-room for them, and at best they would be like
a prize-fight in an ocean steamer's state-rooms. I cordi-
ally concur in your own opinion that the current topic of
discussion, the rectification of Latin pronunciation, should
not be allowed to drift into the utterly distinct question of
the theoretical accuracy of the various systems of Greek

pronunciation; and that, when treated at all, it should be restricted to those who are able to approach the question from the three sides combined of comparative philology, recorded evidence, and vital knowledge of the true modern theory and practice. The subject is far too extensive for a newspaper topic, the simple reason of this being that nobody except benighted Dons and bigoted Greeks any longer continue to uphold any system as an aggregate, wholly right or wholly wrong, but treats each phonological detail by itself, to stand or fall by its own merits. As for the accents, the question *solvitur ambulando.* Professor Blackie, an enthusiastic and perfervid man, with a will of his own, does actually teach tone-accent consistently with unimpaired prosodial quantity, precisely as an old Greek pronounced, and as a modern Lithuanian pronounces. How he does it himself it is not difficult to conceive ; how he enforces his teaching I own puzzles me ; how to ensure a succession of Professor Blackies is an impossible problem. Still, he does it, and he has thus achieved a triumph of principle which both Don and Greek will do well to bear in mind.—I am, &c.,   VEXATUS TOTIES.

THE LANGUAGE QUESTIONS IN THE TYROL AND ISTRIA.

September 15, 1866.

WHATEVER may be said by physiologists in objection to the employment of language as an absolute test of race in questions of ethnological descent—and we do not pretend to deny that it has been overvalued, and can only be used thus absolutely in default of other evidence—it is certain that, in all questions of practical ethnographic delimitation in Europe, language does happen to be the one recognised test for determining the race of any given people as it now stands, and for asserting its political rights consequent upon the principle of nationalities. Apart from force and the strong hand, the ultimate decision on such a test must, no doubt, rest on the will of the people under consideration, guided by the view which it may choose to adopt as regards its own national affinity. The Bulgarians, for instance, a uniform race, who constitute the great mass of the Christian population of the Eastern Peninsula—to use Mr. Grant Duff's excellent new formula—subject to the direct rule of the Porte, are as yet in that fluid or half-consolidated state which admits of their moulding themselves into the shape of more than one kindred race. Fifty years ago, as a matter of fact, they were content to think of themselves as Greeks like other Greeks; that being a period when religion, and not language, was the test of race. It is open to them now to think of themselves as Servians, or to think of themselves as Russians, or as something standing by itself, independent of both, and of the same ordinal value as either; and they do actually think of themselves in each of these three directions. But the final issue, as regards practical result, will clearly rest, not on the actual ethnological fact, but on their own interpretation of the fact, subject, of course, to the final and superhuman authority of the lords of the world, the Emperors of the East and the West, and of the Centre, if there is to be one. As regards abstract ethnological truth, however, the issue rests with the scientific inquirer alone, and if he would attain it, he had need keep his science clear from his own or other people's political conclusions. In registering and criticising linguistic facts, therefore, as we are about to do, in the case of any particular nationality inclined to base practical conclusions on those facts, it is necessary to premise, as we have done, that the political part of the argument, however properly it may be conducted, is secondary to its scientific part, and under undisturbed circumstances turns on the will and opinion of the people in question. As a corollary to this it may be added that, in current questions of this kind, temptations are great, and few scruples are shown in recklessly distorting and misrepresenting facts in order to create such an opinion on the spot itself and elsewhere. The ethnological politician handles his facts his own way, according to scheme or predilection. But the non-political ethnologist must keep aloof from political questions, and must deal with his facts in as strictly abstract and scientific a spirit as he can, so long as he remains on scientific ground. In examining the state of the case, therefore, in the Southern Tyrol and Istria, we think it quite legitimate for us to admit, as politicians, that neither may be wholly Italian, and still to recognise their claim to become Italian, if they are mainly and increasingly Italian, and have set their heart on becoming Italian. Our only quarrel would lie, as ethnologists, with those who chose to distort the facts for the sake of the politics, and averred that Istria was already Italian if it were nothing of the kind. That is the unpardonable sin to all concerned in the integrity of scientific truth.

The case of the Southern Tyrol, indeed, is clear enough, and has no difficulty about it. Trent is as thoroughly and absolutely an Italian city as Rome itself. The frontier line of the Italian language coincides with fair accuracy, subject, however, to some marked exceptions, with the main ridge of the Central Alps. On one point alone it has crossed the Alps, and is established on Swiss territory in the Val Livigno, a wild primitive pastoral upland of the Eastern Grisons, only now coming into notice among our Alpine travellers. The case is reversed in the upper valleys of the Pennine Alps, and notably in the valley of the Adige. The chain here trends northwards, and is crossed by the lowest, or nearly the lowest, of all its passes. The German invaders have thronged into Italy by this way for a thousand years, and they have completely occupied or Germanized all the upper valleys of the Adige. These are certain always to remain as thoroughly German as they are now. If Trent is as Italian as Rome, Meran is as

German as Innspruck. Yet the tables are being slowly turned on the Germans in the main valley, and the tide of ethnic occupation is setting northwards. Italian is gradually encroaching upon and displacing German within the Cisalpine Tyrol—if we may use a Roman's term in the Roman's sense. The two adjoining villages of Mezzo-Lombardo and Mezzo-Tedesco, in German *Deutsch* and **Welsch** *Metz*, once formed the frontier, but German has now receded far north of this. The town population is bilingual, as all towns are on ethnological frontiers within the frontiers of political States. Italian can hardly be called as yet the predominant language of Botzen, the chief town of the doubtful district, but it bids fair to become so in fifty years' time, to whatever State the town may be assigned. Rural populations, as a rule, are everywhere unilingual, except when a language is undergoing the process of actual displacement, as in the remote districts of Ireland; and such process hardly lasts more than three generations in one spot. Where the line of demarcation is to be drawn in the valley of the Adige for the present generation it is hard to say, for our own travellers do not observe these phenomena, and we cannot lay our hands on such German or other records of them as we have had the luck to fall in with from time to time. But one thing is certain, that the Germans of the main valley of the Adige are what is called a retiring population; in other words, are either bodily retreating, or else changing their language;—wherever the temporary line of demarcation may happen to be drawn. The encroaching Italian, it need hardly be observed, is not book-Tuscan, but the natural speech of the country, assigned by Biondelli to the Venetian family, and thus clearly marked off from its Lombard neighbours to the west, the frontier here coinciding with a political frontier, or what once was such. Where Italian has surrounded and insulated a fragmentary German population it has killed it outright. That strange relic of a Bavarian settlement of the twelfth century, the Sette Communi of the Vicentine territory, whose uncouth old speech was only taken down *in articulo mortis*, has only been extinguished thus within the present generation, if indeed it be yet fully extinct. Probably some Dolly Pentreath still survives, however, as a curiosity.

How far is the case in Istria the same with that of the Tyrol? The language used by the Italians in urging their claims gives us no reason to believe that any difference exists between the two cases. Both are alike called Italian, and both ought equally to belong to Italy—both being Italian to the same extent and in the same way, for ought we are told to the contrary. Now the real fact is, that Italian in Istria is in precisely the same category as Italian in Corfu and Zante; if not in the Corfu of this generation, assuredly so in that of fifty years ago. The country, as a whole, may be called a bilingual country; but its rural population speak one language, and one language alone, and that is not Italian, but Slavonian of the Croatian type. The urban population, whose blood may be mainly Italian, dwelling in the numerous and very interesting little towns which fringe its long line of coast, speak two languages—the enchorial Slavonian, and, side by side with it, the foreign Italian, implanted, or at least fostered, there by Venetian intercourse and dominion. It would perhaps be nearer the truth if we were to arrange the languages horizontally rather than vertically, for the Italian is uppermost. It is in reality the language of culture, of business, of trade, of the sea and all that concerns it, here and throughout the Adriatic. Every man as he rises in life must learn it, as a Welshman, to rise, must learn English. But it is not the one language of the country. Throughout the Eastern Adriatic, and wherever the direct rule of the Venetian Republic extended, the linguistic phenomena are precisely the same. An enchorial language, easily coexisting in the towns with Italian as the language of culture, has gone on from generation to

R

generation without the slightest friction, or mutual displacement or encroachment. This was the case in Dalmatia, on the North Albanian coast, and in the Ionian Islands, precisely as much as in Istria. The rural population, uncivilised or half civilised, spoke, and continues to speak, its own language, and that alone, in all these countries. The Austrians who have ceded Venice are only too glad to inherit a language of culture common to all South-Eastern Europe more or less, and have themselves been a means of keeping up Italian on these coasts. Bilingualism is here more marked, and rests more strongly upon each of its limbs, than, perhaps, anywhere else in Europe. Anybody who has overheard the crews of the Austrian Lloyd's—nay, even Corfiote ladies and gentlemen of the old school—keep up a sustained conversation, knows that it is impossible to say, if a speaker begins to talk in one language, whether or not he will end his sentence in the same. Each comes equally well and natural to the tongue, somehow; though it is odd to the outside listener to find the light blown out, as it were, and himself suddenly plunged into the utter darkness of Slavonic or Greek without a warning. The speakers, however, seem as wholly unconscious of all incongruity as the polyglot little Russian or Levantine children who skip about from speech to speech as a matter of course, without a thought or the power of thought on the subject.

The best test wherewith to measure the accuracy of a parallel between these two cases would be the detailed history of the displacements in each case, if we could but get at it. Is there a third language, if not actually aboriginal, at all events quasi-aboriginal, and as old as we can find, either in Istria or the Tyrol; and if so, is it German or Italian which has overpowered it in the Tyrol, Slavonian or Italian which has overpowered it in Istria? Now it is a very curious circumstance that in each country there does happen to be a language, one, indeed, no older than Roman rule, which can be made to do duty as an aboriginal tongue, and by means of which we can bring the issue fairly to the test. Each is a rude wild form of Romanic, broken off, or otherwise far removed, from its immediate congeners—themselves but rustic half-cultivated dialects at best—and each at this moment actually expiring under our eyes. The eastern branch of the Upper Adige above Botzen is joined at points far apart by two tributaries, respectively named in German the Enneberger, or Gader Thal, and the Grödner Thal. Each of these, communicating with one another by their heads, is inhabited by a population quite distinct from its neighbours, speaking an ill-kept dialect of the same language which is spoken in the Grisons far to the west in the valleys of the Upper Rhine and the Inn. They are, in fact, true Quere-Welsh, and the curious evidence of the very peculiar local names covering the whole of this country, evidence into which we have no space to go ourselves, distinctly proves the former continuity of this one race over a very extensive area of Central Europe. The Gader Thal is a wild rugged valley thinly occupied by woodcutters. This population is being Germanized under the congenial influence, as it would seem, of the mountain Tyrolese of the north. The Val Gördeina, on the other hand, as it is called in its native Quere-Welsh (we are not going to use so unsightly a word as Rumonsch, nor so clumsy a one as Rhæto-Romanic, to please anybody), comes under lowland influence, for it is a rich valley, well cultivated and well peopled. It prays in Italian, it writes in Italian, and it has learnt to talk in Italian. Of its twelve priests, eight preach in Italian, three in Quere-Welsh, and one in German. But still nearly every man understands and speaks German. Here it is clear that the strongest, the advancing, and the civilising influence is the Italian.

When, some months ago, we were suggesting the propriety of getting rid of the French word *Roumain* as an English name for the Wallachs, and otherwise discussing their various national names, we adverted to the existence of an outlying fragment of that race, under the surface, at the very gates of Trieste. With the exception of a brief incorrect notice cited by Dr. Latham from Biondelli, who at that time had no means of knowing anything about them, no account has ever been given of this population in English, nor, indeed, does anybody seem of late years to have been anywhere more than barely aware of their existence until the publication of Miklosich's very valuable monograph on the Slavonic elements in Wallachian two or three years ago. In an appendix to this work the Vienna professor gives a detailed account of these interesting people, chiefly on the authority of local parish priests and of some special contributions to a Trieste newspaper of 1846. This handful of men, by some stated as amounting to six thousand, by others as three thousand only, now occupy a few villages in a district stretching from the roots of the great Istrian mountain, best known by its Italian name of Monte Maggiore, down the Val d'Arsa. Their former occupancy, however, was demonstrably far more extensive. They are genuine and unmistakable Wallachians. But their native language, the only available test for determining their race, has so far died out, that it only survives as a family language, disused out of doors, and kept up by the women alone,—a *lingua di confidenza*, to use the reporter's words. As for their history, and how they came to be where they are, it is wholly unknown. We are so accustomed to associate the word Wallachian with the inhabitants of the Danubian Principalities—the only portion of that race who, having obtained political standing, speak their own language exclusively, and have made a written speech out of it, such as it is—that we are apt to lose sight of the fact that the great mass of the special evidence points to the countries south of the Danube—to Thrace and Macedonia—as the original seat of the development of the Rouman language out of colloquial Latin, and growth of the new **race out** of a **Romanized native** population, with a maximum of other foreign **elements.** Now, the language of the Istrian Roumans is **not of the North** Danubian **or** Daco-Roman type. **It is of the South** Danubian or Macedo-Roman type; the language **of Métzovo** and Kalarítes,—nay, of Thebes and Athens,—rather **than** of Bucharest **and Jassy; the** mother tongue **of Coletti, not** that of Couza. **The** test-words—we use **this term with** repugnance, **so much abused** by half-learned **critics of local** nomenclature—are **sufficient** to establish the fact **clearly.** On the Danube the word for " beautiful " **is** *" frumós,"* from *formosus.* **In** Istria **and the Pindus** both the **word is "** *mashátu,"* **the final** *u* being sounded in the latter, con- trary to the North Rouman practice. Miklosich calls **it an obscure** word, **but it is** probably **neither** more nor less **than from** a low Latin *formosatus.* " Where " is *" unde "* at Bucharest; **in Istria and Thessaly, "** *iù."* **These** cases might be multiplied, even **out of Miklosich's** necessarily scanty speech-samples. **But the** gist **of** the **matter is that** the outdoor language that **is** replacing the dying Walla- chian is not Italian, which, from its strong special affinity with Wallachian, would have **nine** points in its favour, but the alien Croatian. Such a sentence as the proverb, *Shi* **vaca neagra** *ab lapte* **are,** " Even a black cow has white **milk,"** is pure Rouman everywhere, with the one exception **of** *ab* for *alb.* **Any** one who knows Latin can see the **meaning for himself.** But **no** Latin will help in a sen- tence like *Odprosté nam a nostru pekat,* " Forgive **us our** sin," **except** by taking a **shot.** The first words **are pure** Slavonian as they stand, **verb,** pronoun, construction, **and all.** For all **this,** Italian has left some mark on the lan- guage. *Maltraté, divertit,* **donche** *(dunque;* in Wal. *atunci)* are Romanic, **but** not Rouman, and **are of course** Italian. So is *e* for *and,* side by side **with** the original *shi,* old French *si,* from *sic.* But, in the language of Dr. Miklosich's main authority, these little - known people *slavizzarono tutti.* They have merged their national life into a Croatian, not

an Italian, existence; and not even Cæsar's decree nor
Dantesque writ can avail to make their country a *bona fide*
and integral portion of Italy in the eyes of the ethnologist. We think that these two cases show sufficiently
that the Southern Tyrol is, and that Istria is not, an essentially Italian country, to be ranged in the same category
with any part of Italy proper.

CELTIC AT OXFORD.

September 22, 1866.

MOST of our contemporaries who have been prevented by
want of space or inclination from giving an account of the
late Eisteddfod at Chester with any fulness of detail have
concurred in selecting Mr. Matthew Arnold's letter, recom-
mending the institution of a Celtic Professorship at Oxford,
as the most important or prominent feature of the proceedings. This concurrence of opinion, fixing upon the
one circumstance which served to connect the Welsh
festival in a practical way with a project of supposed
general interest beyond the limits of the Principality, is
certainly a noteworthy fact. The Eisteddfod council
appear to have adopted Mr. Arnold's recommendation
warmly and promptly, and embodied it at once in a formal
resolution. Under these circumstances it may not be
superfluous to inquire what it is that Mr. Arnold really
wants, how far his object be definite or attainable, and
how far, supposing the University to decide upon the
establishment of such a professorship, it can find in any
part of the world a source of supply equal to a demand for
a single individual likely to meet Mr. Arnold's idea. Let
us firstly premise that the word "Celtic" itself is entirely
a bookman's word. No Celtic or other population now
calls itself, or its neighbours, or anybody else, Celtic. The
word is entirely a conventional word, transferred from the

historical **Celtæ** of Julius **Cæsar's time to** a group of modern fragmentary peoples **who are** their kindred **no** doubt, but are so by presumption **alone.** The word in its modern acceptation is bookwork, **not** vernacular record. Its constant use as a convenient ethnological generalisation is apt to lead modern writers into laying **undue** stress upon the continuance of their common character **of** identity unimpaired, **and** far into the historical period, **without a** shadow of **evidence** being adduced in justification **of such a** course. **It is in** the domain of philology, and **of phi-lology alone,** that their modern divergent species **can be raised into the** common term **of a** single ancient one. **By philological** investigation **we are able** successfully to **get rid of all the old** ideas of primæval separation between **the two** main branches of the Celtic race, **of Gaelic waves and** Cymric waves and the like,—ideas which **seem** still as rife as ever outside the **Zeussian school.** But **there** is no other way of reducing **these two languages under a** common term than by philological **treatment.** The recorded litera-ture of each branch **developed** itself altogether **separately** from the other; those who formerly cultivated **and who** still cultivate **the** literature of each country, **whether for** antiquarian purposes, as in Ireland, or for both vernacular and antiquarian **purposes,** as in Wales, **are wholly and** altogether out of mutual communion and intercourse with **their respective** congeners. No Gael knows anything whatever **about** Welsh literature. No Welshman knows anything whatever about Irish literature. Such an excep-tion **as that** of the venerable Mr. W. Skene only proves **the rule. Mr.** Arnold sees **in** the translated literature **of each branch, in so** far **as it has** come before him in an appreciable form, the **common** property **of a** delicacy and spirituality which he would contrast with certain qualities alleged to denote both the **English and the** strictly Teu-**tonic** literature. But who **is to illustrate** this view and work it out in detail by **means of** a common exposition of, **say,** the Black Book of Carmarthen and the Yellow Book of

Lecan? It is Mr. Arnold who generalises and combines, not the Celtic scholar himself; and the impracticability of finding a suitable professor would be at once perceived the moment an attempt were made to look into details. Even within the Britannic branch we are told by the high authority of one of the ablest writers in the "Archæologia Cambrensis," a most excellent periodical, that not half-a-dozen Welshmen have ever bestowed a thought upon the Cornish remains, or know anything about them. Within the Gaelic branch the Scotch Highlanders are doing all they possibly can to set themselves up as co-ordinates of their Irish progenitors, and in so doing are only cutting themselves adrift from the safe moorings of modern philology, as well as from the best records of their own antiquities. The convergent tendency of archæological and literary treatment is only now setting in among the Celts, and until a generation be past, and a special class of men be formed, who may be termed by the old Scotian phrase of *Fir dâ leithe,* "men of two halves"—*i.e.,* of Ireland and its colony in North Britain—men capable of doing equal justice both to Welsh and Irish literature, we think that the only alternative lies between appointing a professor whose work would be solely philological, with Zeuss for his text-book, or having two professors, one for each language. If this last plan were adopted, we may foretell that, according to the best diagnosis of the rules of patronage and promotion in England, the selection would probably fall on the eldest, most influential, or most pushing Jones on the books of Jesus or on John Brown the gillie. ·

ZMUDZO-LETHONIANS.

January 28, 1867.

CAN it be possible that there still exist any survivors of the Old-Prussians, as appears to be indicated by the Russian statistics of the recruitment of 1866, giving the

proportion furnished by each different race of the empire ?
These state that there were 852 recruits contributed by the
" Zmudzo-Lethonians," who are described as being " Old-
Prussians, a nearly extinct race of Lithuanian descent,
formerly inhabiting the now German province of East
Russia." East Russia is obviously a misprint for East
Prussia in this passage. Who are these people ? The
description seems to point to a migration of the old race
at some period when they were in retention of their old
speech, or otherwise had means of keeping up a distinctive
character of race-descent. But there is no account of any
such migration in any ethnological work accessible to
English readers, nor is any mention made of them or their
dialect in any of the important German works recently
written on the Lithuanic languages. The true Old-
Prussians of Prussia are known to have lost their language since the end of the seventeenth century—a few
old people alone having spoken it in 1689—and they are
now perfectly undistinguishable from any other German-
speaking Prussian, unless possibly by physical tests, of
which, however, we have no record. Zmudz is the Polish
form of the word, which we are more accustomed to see
in the Latin form of Samogitia. It is a strong corruption
of the full-mouthed native Lithuanian term Zemaitis,
plural Zemaitei (the z by rights bearing a mark to show
that it is sounded like a French j), meaning a Lowlander,
as opposed to the Upper Lithuanians of Prussia. The word
is the correspondent, in fact, both in sense and etymology,
of a Greek χαμαίτιος, if one may venture to create such a
form for illustration's sake. But these Samogitians are
not Prussians, but true Lithuanians, and, in so far as the
authorities have hitherto informed us, certainly do not
speak the extinct Prussian, which differed from Lithuanian
as a substantive language, not as a dialect. They speak
true Lithuanian, only differing dialectically from that of
the Prussian kingdom. The difference is important
enough, for the one dialect, under Polish influence, accents

its words uniformly, as in Polish, while the other has actually retained in all but perfect integrity an independent tonic accent coexistent with prosodial quantity. It is thus the exact living counterpart of Hellenic Greek during the Homeric and classical period; and a reference to it, or a comprehension of its method, may be called indispensable to an understanding of the ancient Greek sound-system, to say nothing of its beautiful completeness of archaic diphthongation. This alone would make it of sufficient importance to justify our seizing a passing opportunity of allusion to its existence. But the real fact is that the Lithuanian language is, for reasons into which we would gladly enter had we space, as much the most important of living European tongues in the eyes of the comparative philologist as French is the most important to the practical linguist. In the Prussian kingdom it has gone down by the run; it is dying out rapidly, and is only to be heard in the peasant's hut; yet Schleicher speaks naturally when he compares his exultation at coming across its "herrliche Formen" in living speech, after going through hardship and trouble to obtain them, with that of the botanist who has at last come on a rare plant, after searching through brakes and swamps. Nor does Diefenbach unpardonably exaggerate when he says that what may be called its discovery excited hardly less sensation among the learned of Europe than even that of Sanskrit itself. Surely an Eton master, and even an Eton boy, might be moved at hearing that there are Europeans alive who not only called their sons *sunus,* their beer *alus,* and their bulls *bullus,* but who actually decline them like *gradus* into the bargain, with the *us* short in the singular and long in the plural.

"*IRANIAN*" *AND* "*ARYAN.*"

March 30, 1868.

Sir,—Pray allow me the liberty of making one or two observations upon your recent able reviews of Professor Max Müller's—" remarkable," the Professor calls them— late reprint of his minor pieces. I should like, and it is full time, to call attention to a very curious neologism, or rather solecism, which you have therein employed in the general terms used by you for the purpose of classifying the various languages of the world. I need hardly say that the first impulse after reading those articles is one of thankfulness that somebody has at length come forward who can criticise the brilliant Professor as well as repeat him; who, to take one point for instance, is not in the least inclined to accept his purely negative group of Turanian languages in the positive and all-comprising sense which he would fain confer upon it. But there already exists in these matters so much confusion of thought and so much misconception, through cross purposes created by the ambiguous or twofold use of general terms for classification in ethnological and philological science—the same word being now used generically, now specifically, now in a comprehensive, now in a restricted sense—that I venture to think that no time should be lost in making an appeal to an able writer to forego the use in a generic sense of a term as yet universally recognised and employed by all other writers in a specific sense only, when such neological use is altogether peculiar to the able writer himself, and tends but to make confusion worse confounded. Here, at the outset of your second article, you say, " Mr. Max Müller is, as always, bounded by the myths of the Iranian or Aryan world." Now a genuine student at first hand of Bopp and Pott, not to speak of the aggregate of English readers who get their Indo-European comparative philology

through Dr. Müller alone, being accustomed to meet the
terms of that science as used in their ordinary acceptation,
will at once wonder at this, and will be set speculating as
to which of the two worlds can be meant, the larger or the
smaller.   He will be still more surprised farther on when
told of the Professor's " brilliant exposition of the comparative mythology of the Iranians," for, as he has always understood that word, used as it is by his school *semper, ubique,
et ab omnibus* in one sense, and one only, there can be in
his eyes no possibility of instituting any such comparison,
through sheer want of the necessary records and materials.
All his knowledge tells him that the ancient Persian mythology as related to us in the Avesta and by the classic
historians, or as dimly echoed down to modern times in
Firdausi's great romance, is absolutely the sole recorded
mythology of any Iranian people; being indeed, as perhaps
it is not unnecessary to say parenthetically, in presence of
the great fuss which is now making by theologians and
amateurs about the Zend writings, little more than an offshoot or a distortion of the more archaic Indian mythology set forth in the Vedas.   Persian mythology cannot
well be compared with itself, and there is none other within
the Iranian domain.   There is no Armenian mythology,
nor is there any Kurdish or Lurish or Beluchi mythology,
nor any Afghan mythology, not the faintest trace so far as
the ground has been explored; while of the Irôn or Os-
setes of the Caucasus, the only remaining Iranian people
according to the established usage of the word, there is
nothing to show but a handful of nursery tales. But on
reading farther your true meaning becomes clear.   It is
at length seen that the word Iranian with you really means
the same thing as the word Aryan with Professor Müller,
the French, the Italians, and, under his influence, most of
ourselves.   That word Aryan is not popular with the Germans generally, and it is in reality very inconvenient,
being so for the same reason, only less in degree, that the
word Iranian is inconvenient; that is to say, it is wanted

for a special conventional use, which of right intrinsically belongs to it, as comprising the Eastern branch of the whole family, the Indians together with the Iranians, specially connected for many ages after separation from the Western branches who settled in Europe, and needing distinction therefrom by a proper term. The Germans prefer to use the word *arisch* in this last sense, and not as denoting the whole family, which they now mostly call *arisch-europäisch*, too long a word for us, but very accurate, if not very convenient. It is too late for us to stop the word Aryan for the general family, but we should at least do well to supplement it by the word *Aric* for the special family of the Indians *plus* the Iranians; of course retaining the latter word in its usual sense, for which it is wholly indispensable, and from which, I venture to submit, it should never henceforth be moved. To use such an expression as "the Greek and other Iranian myths" is to unsettle the fixed terminology of a definite branch of science upon a point where all its teachers are fully agreed.

TATHÂGATA.

March 30, 1868.

SIR,—May I ask your leave to make a personal explanation? Mr. Max Müller did me the honour to call me a Shemite; my courteous critic in your number of to-day identifies me with the lamented Bunsen. He asks me "to forego the use in a generic sense of a term [Iranian] as yet universally recognised and employed by all other writers in a specific sense only, when such neological use is peculiar" to me, &c. My critic must be aware that in the "Philosophy of Universal History" (vol. ii. pp. 6, 7) one of the three great groups of language is called the "Iranian," among the subdivisions of which is the "Arian," divided again into the Arian proper, and the Arian of India.

I frankly admit that the generic term Iranian is a bad

one, and that it is a shade worse than the now usual Aryan or Arian. But if the modern Irán be etymologically identical with the Airyana (Airyanem vaêgo) of the first Fargard of the Vêndidâd, the difference between Iranian and Aryan, when employed in modern science, actually disappears.

My critic says, " It is too late to stop the word Aryan for the general family." One who combines a scientific hatred of vicious terminology with a Turanian hatred of all that is Iranian can surely do something better than accept Aryan for the group, and suggest Aric for the Indo-Persian division. Would he not render a great service to comparative philology, by opening a discussion on its terminology at the next meeting of the British Association ?

THE REVIEWER OF MR. MAX MÜLLER'S " CHIPS."

SIR,—I am afraid that I was not the least aware of Baron Bunsen's use of the word Iranian in a sense identical with that assigned to it by your reviewer of Professor Max Müller's " Chips." I wish your reviewer all the benefit of a precedent carrying such weight in this country. But meanwhile I beg to repeat my assertion, that no comparative philologist of the school of Bopp or Pott, either now or ever, will be found to use the word otherwise than in one sense and one only. This seems contradictory ; but catch me reconciling it out loud in England. Elsewhere explanation is not needed. Bopp and Pott and their school may be wrong not to acknowledge the Baron's authority as we do, but as a matter of fact they do not. Nobody else but your reviewer uses the word, and I may further take leave to add, now that he no longer speaks with the editorial voice, that it is by such solecism that his individuality becomes known when he writes, as he always does with perfect mastery of his own subject, in your and other columns. My letter, which I am glad he found courteous, was an appeal to him, a high Semitic authority, to forego the use of such solecism henceforward, and to refer him to the strictly defined usage assigned to the word by the universal consent of working comparative philologists. Let your reviewer go to the original German workshop and see the practice for himself. He is far too valuable to be allowed to rest under any misconception as to who is and who is not in authority there.

I do not see how I can "do better" with regard to the next particular point than recommend, as I have done, the term *Aric* for the German *Arisch*, which is quite in harmony with the genius of our language, keeping that of *Aryan* for the whole family; not quite liking this last term, but perfectly ready to make the best of it, and subordinate myself to the current usage as fixed by the great authority of Professor Müller. The only improvement I see would be to use the word *Pan-Aryan* in the latter sense. What your reviewer means, I think, is rather that I could do more, raise further issues, and subject the whole of our current terminology in these matters to criticism, so as to remedy its vagueness and looseness. Well, I should like to try and do so. But one voice does little, as the opera says. I, in turn, would strongly recommend your reviewer to do much better than to read Bunsen's book for Aryan comparative philology, unless it be such parts as are directly contributed by Aufrecht and Müller. He surely would not himself admit of an Aryan student's reference to, say, Dean Stanley as a *primary* authority upon the technical usage of general terms within the domain of Semitic ethnology and philology. The accepted generalisations of Bopp and Pott are, I think, to be found in the *Vergleichende Grammatik* and the *Etymologische Forschungen* and their teeming progeny, rather than to be looked for in Bunsen, in which books also will be found the correct method of transcribing the Zend language. I hope it is your printer, and not your reviewer, who is responsible

for the vaêgo and the Vêndidâd. I strongly suspect that
the vaêgo should really be laid at the door of Professor
Müller and his unsatisfactory way of writing our *j* and *ch*
as italic *k* and *g*, which is enough to perplex any printer.
It is usual, moreover, in transcribing Zend, to mark the
quantity of short ĕ as in th-ĕm of neuters and masculine
accusatives equal to the Sanskrit ăm—that is to say,
Burnouf, Bopp, Spiegel, Haug, and everybody do so.

If Bunsen does not, 'tis pity for Bunsen.

May I say a personal word in conclusion? Being so
mighty sensitive under Professor Max Müller's epithet of
Shemite, your reviewer might surely have thought twice
before calling me a Turanian, in so far as he calls me one
by talking of my "Turanian hatred of all that is Iranian."
A man is a wise child who knows his ethnological father,
but I believe I am as safe in saying that I am not a Turanian, as you in replying editorially on his behalf to Professor Müller that your writer was not a Shemite.   That is
to say, each epithet is correct enough in an illusive or subjective sense, and each intended it in that sense—not but
what the Professor, who is a bad hand at literary detection,
meant it in a literal sense as well. What should make
your reviewer say I hate all things Iranian I do not know ;
between you and me they are the pet hobby-horse in my
little stable.   I am, in fact, so put out by being called a
hater of things Iranian, that I am just on my way to
the new Iranian *chargé d'affaires* to get a certificate of
friendly feeling towards things Iranian. This I shall be
happy to submit to you in original, together with a translation for your benefit and that of——   But I will keep courteous to the end of the chapter, and not pour cold water
upon hot broth, as the Turanians say in Turkey.

TATHÂGATA.

"*CUI BONO*" AND "*VIDI TANTUM.*"

April 20, 1868.

A VERY pretty little question is suggested for the behoof
of philological casuists by our current and strictly British
use of the Latin words *Cui bono*, in the sense of the
French *à quoi bon*, "what's the good of it?" Innumerable schoolboys of this generation must know, and a
great many adults cannot have altogether forgotten, that
the Latin words mean nothing of the kind, at least in
Latin. They know that they are simply a quotation from
a forensic speech by Cicero, wherein that orator, usually
considered a very good authority upon the use of Latin
words, advises that when it is wanted to ascertain who is
a guilty party, inquiry should be made whose is the profit
by the guilty deed. *Cui bono* in Cicero is Latin for
"whose is the profit." But, for all that, it has come to
be modern newspaper English for "what's the use." It is
not unknown in the House of Commons : perhaps it might
even mount up to the Lords but for the beneficent despotism wielded by a great scholar in that august chamber.
It has worked its way to this elevated position by dint of
sheer iteration, and by, we hope we may say without
offence, an abnormal development of our imitative
faculty, or hypertrophy of the pithecoid organs of our
brain. "The children of men," said the Emperor Akbar
in the immortal letter which he wrote to the King of the
Franks for an authentic copy of the Christian Scriptures,
"are slaves of the rope of imitativeness"—*asvî î ribkah i
taklîd*—and hard enough it is in our part of the world to
find a child of man who is not, let alone Akbar's world.

This absurd new idiom seems to be tickling our fancy
in the same way that a nice new ball of pretty coloured
worsted attracts the kitten's fancy; at least we have no
other way of accounting for it, for we could never be so

S

rude as to hint that it arose from those who adopt it not knowing how to construe Cicero. Let us be thankful that there are people left who neither do nor would adopt it. You will not find it so used in the writings of Mr. Goldwin Smith, who is said to be a master of the English language, neither of Mr. Goldwin Smith above, nor of the working classes beneath, who manage to express what they have to say quite well in English composed of English words. But the surface of our English mid-earth, between Mr. Smith and the workmen, is overrun with this queer sprout of damaged Latin as with a rank weed growth. It is now English, not Latin; as English it has to take its chance of living or dying, and the scholars have no more power over its life, to banish it from the English language, than "Punch" had to kill crinoline. There is no more use in crying out against it than in crying out against *cottage ornée* and *thé dansante* for being such atrocious French. But it is both a deed of justice and of necessity to wash poor Cicero's hands of this unpleasant Britannic idiom in public; and high time to do it, moreover. Just think what Cicero would think of our *cui bono*—with *cui* pronounced *kye*, too.

What sets us writing about *cui bono* is the rapid growth of a younger brother or companion in misery, who in these latter days is visibly waxing strong under much the same circumstances and conditions. This is poor little *Vidi tantum*. These are quite good Latin words taken apart; taken together, and as used by the author quoted, they mean, "I saw him and no more," "I was not able to do more than just to see him." The quotation is turned to account with entire aptness and accuracy by Mr. Thackeray in a passage where one of his characters—we do not immediately remember who or where, but that is matter of easy reference—in describing some noteworthy person of a previous generation, conveys a regret that he was too young to have done more than just see him; that he was unable to hear him or hold intercourse with him.

Thackeray here, as always, was perfectly felicitous in his Latin application. But Thackeray is now fallen among a generation of imitators, who openly seek to array themselves in his garments; who freely help themselves to his ornaments of Latin citation, without having the remotest idea where and how they should be worn so as to make the literary raiment look all right and as though it were the wearer's own. It is from Thackeray, not from the classics, that *Vidi tantum* is now quoted, and it is not with its proper meaning, but with the meaning of " I saw that much," " I saw what I am telling you I saw," that it is being encountered; we run against it here, there, and everywhere, in a certain class of writing. It is a nuisance, and it must be stopped before it gets, as it assuredly will if not stopped, to those lady novelists who are the shadows of Thackeray's and other substantial authors' shades. Now we have a great relish for this desipient literature, which is a sweet thing in its right place, as the Pagan poet observes, nor is it always less wise than the writings of the sapient; but its votaries and chief professors, who are mainly answerable for these small depravities, are apt to spoil all our relish for their very pleasantest fooling by little tricks of the kind. As for the chief master of the school, he is incorrigible. It is no use reviling and punishing him, and it is no use appealing to him to give his versatility, his kindliness, and his genuine native humour, something like fair play in a more decorous literary garb, and a more staid and seemly behaviour, if only for the sake of the generations to come. We must take him as we find him. Still we cannot possibly harden our hearts against him and his whimsies. But to his followers, and to the comic school in general, we recommend total abstinence from stock classical quotations, coupled with a wholesome mistrust of one another as authorities for the conveyance and interpretation thereof.

CHANGE IN ENGLISH PRONUNCIATION.

July 23, 1868.

SIR,—Pray let me say that I do not think Lord Winchilsea's criticisms are worth so much powder and shot as he is getting on all sides. At all events, I am sure they are not worth any second volley. But there is one prime fallacy upon which his remarks upon the hypothetical Milton's rhymes rest which is worth some notice, for it is of constant recurrence in untrained English criticism of the versification of past times. By this I mean the fallacy of assuming that the English of Shakspeare or Milton was, as a matter of course, pronounced in identically the same manner as the English of Lord Winchilsea. In a general way and loosely, perhaps, we are most of us aware of this in principle ; but when we come to details, I suspect that none of us fully realise it, save our handful of thorough working phonologists of the type of Mr. Alexander Ellis ; for the fallacy, which is that of the modern Greeks, is a perfectly natural one after all. To base minute criticism at all upon such an assumption is mistaken enough ; but to base sweeping negative propositions upon it, and to propound them, if not with downright arrogance of manner and flippancy of tone, at least with that curious dogmatism and absence of all misgiving which is the unmistakable mark of the tyro as distinguished from the master, is rather too bad, and in the present case gives very natural offence to Lord Winchilsea's readers, as may be seen anywhere in the press. For all purposes bearing on the current controversy—into which Heaven keep me from embarking while the whole host of æstheticians are hard at it—it is quite enough to say that, by the universal consent and practice of all our chief poets, English rhyme tolerates a certain occasional looseness, and does not require an absolute, but is now and then content with an

approximate, identity of sound. If, consequently, rhymes
of this sort be found in the true Milton, that is quite
enough justification of the hypothetical Milton, in so far
as rhyme goes. Into this æsthetic part of the controversy
I have neither the will nor the power to enter. But I
hope, notwithstanding, that you will allow me the use of
your columns to warn intending controversialists who may
seek to lay down the law about this matter of rhyme in past
stages of English of the risk they incur in so doing, without
some previous mental reservation as to the probability of
the rhyming words having been pronounced differently
from what they now are, and, therefore, of what to our
ear is a dissonance having really been a true rhyme to the
author's. Here, for instance, are the long polysyllables of
Romanic origin in *y*, which are constantly made to rhyme
together, and to which objection is taken on that account.
Milton's rhymes of that kind are enough to justify the
epitaph, as far as that is concerned; but, then, how did
Milton himself come by such rhymes, for the probability
is, on the whole, in favour of these words having been
accented in his day as they now are, rather than otherwise? The answer to that is, by poetical tradition, and
carried down in an unbroken catena of conscious observance from a period typically represented in Chaucer's
verse, when these words were vernacularly pronounced
with the accent on the last syllable, and when, therefore,
such a combination as " felicity " and " misery " would
have been genuine rhyme. But I venture to doubt
whether anybody, perhaps not even Mr. Ellis, is in a position to say *exactly* when the accent in these words shifted
to its present place in common speech. Again, Milton, as
quoted in Mr. Caldwell's letter in the "Times," rhymes
pair and *are*. Was this only meant for a mere approximation, as it now seems, or was it a real consonance to his
ear, and if so, which sound was it? So also which was it
in his rhyme of *where* and *sphere?* Many may laugh at
such a question, but it is a question nevertheless; cer-

tainly it is one in the latter couple. *Par* for *pair* may be dismissed as improbable, yet not without reservation either. That, if anything, would be a Southern and Western vulgar Americanism, on the analogy of *har* and *bar* for *hair* and *bear*, on the age of which I do not like to pronounce. But it is by no means so absolutely certain that Milton may not have said *air* for *are*, like a genuine down-Easter, though I do not think he did. The form *arrn* in the Ormulum certainly indicates our present pro-nunciation of the vowel for the thirteenth century, and though it may possibly have changed and re-changed since then—for such is the way of language—I am pretty sure that we are more likely in this case to have kept the right tradition than the Yankees are to have retained an inter-mediate one in their *air*. This last is likely to be modern, and to have got in through orthographic influence on speech among a generally cultivated and widely lettered people; but, *à priori*, their tradition of spoken English is quite as good as our British tradition, and indeed, from the absence of dialects, is even less liable to disturbing influences; that is to say, in its headquarters in rural New England at least. But I hold that no man can settle the point off-hand and peremptorily; for any amount of rhymes such as with *war* or with *far*, for instance, are altogether short of settling the point, however much they may help to determine probability when in assured majority.

PAR.

INDEX.

THE END.

PRINTED BY BALLANTYNE, HANSON AND CO.
EDINBURGH AND LONDON

PHILOLOGICAL WORKS

PUBLISHED BY

TRÜBNER & CO.

Arnold.—A SIMPLE TRANSLITERAL GRAMMAR OF THE TURKISH LANGUAGE. Compiled from various sources. With Dialogues and Vocabulary. By EDWIN ARNOLD, M.A., C.S.I., F.R.G.S. Pott 8vo, pp. 80, cloth. 2s. 6d.

Asher.—ON THE STUDY OF MODERN LANGUAGES IN GENERAL, and of the English Language in particular. An Essay. By DAVID ASHER, Ph.D. 12mo, pp. viii. and 80, cloth. 2s.

Beames.—A COMPARATIVE GRAMMAR OF THE MODERN ARYAN LANGUAGES OF INDIA (to wit), Hindi, Panjabi, Sindhi, Gujarati, Marathi, Uriya, and Bengali. By JOHN BEAMES, Bengal C.S., M.R.A.S., &c.

Vol. I. On Sounds. 8vo, pp. xvi. and 360, cloth. 16s.
Vol. II. The Noun and the Pronoun. 8vo, pp. xii. and 348, cloth. 16s.

Bleek.—A COMPARATIVE GRAMMAR OF SOUTH AFRICAN LANGUAGES. By W. H. I. BLEEK, Ph.D. Vol. I.—I. Phonology. II. The Concord. Section 1. The Noun. 8vo, pp. xxxvi. and 322, cloth. £1, 16s.

Caldwell.—A COMPARATIVE GRAMMAR OF THE DRAVIDIAN OR SOUTH INDIAN FAMILY OF LANGUAGES. By the Rev. R. CALDWELL, LL.D. A Second, Corrected, and Enlarged Edition. Demy 8vo, pp. 805, cloth. 28s.

Childers.—A PALI-ENGLISH DICTIONARY, with Sanskrit Equivalents, and with numerous Quotations, Extracts, and References. Compiled by ROBERT CÆSAR CHILDERS, late of the Ceylon Civil Service. Imperial 8vo. Double Columns. Complete in 1 Vol., pp. xxii. and 622, cloth. £3, 3s.

The first Pali Dictionary ever published.

Cleasby.—AN ICELANDIC-ENGLISH DICTIONARY. Based on the MS. Collections of the late Richard Cleasby. Enlarged and completed by G. VIGFÚSSON. With an Introduction, and Life of Richard Cleasby, by G. WEBBE DASENT, D.C.L. 4to. £3, 7s.

Contopoulos.—A LEXICON OF MODERN GREEK-ENGLISH AND ENGLISH-MODERN GREEK. By N. CONTOPOULOS. In 2 Vols. 8vo, cloth. Part I. Modern Greek-English, pp. 460. Part II. English-Modern Greek, pp. 582. £1, 7s.

Douse.—Grimm's Law; A Study: or, Hints towards an Explanation of the so-called "Lautverschiebung." To which are added some Remarks on the Primitive Indo-European *K*, and several Appendices. By T. Le Marchant Douse. 8vo, pp. xvi. and 230, cloth. 10s. 6d.

Haldeman.—Pennsylvania Dutch: A Dialect of South Germany, with an Infusion of English. By S. S. Haldeman, A.M., Professor of Comparative Philology in the University of Pennsylvania, Philadelphia. 8vo, pp. viii. and 70, cloth. 3s. 6d.

Hopkins.—Elementary Grammar of the Turkish Language. With a few Easy Exercises. By F. L. Hopkins, M.A., Fellow and Tutor of Trinity Hall, Cambridge. Crown 8vo, pp. 48, cloth. 3s. 6d.

Hunter.—A Comparative Dictionary of the Languages of India and High Asia, with a Dissertation, based on The Hodgson Lists, Official Records, and Manuscripts. By W. W. Hunter, B.A., M.R.A.S., Honorary Fellow, Ethnological Society, of Her Majesty's Bengal Civil Service. Folio, pp. vi. and 224, cloth. £2, 2s.

Kellogg.—A Grammar of the Hindi Language, in which are treated the Standard Hindí, Braj, and the Eastern Hindí of the Ramayan of Tulsi Das; also the Colloquial Dialects of Marwar, Kumaon, Avadh, Baghelkhand, Bhojpur, &c., with Copious Philological Notes. By the Rev. S. H. Kellogg, M.A. Royal 8vo, pp. 400, cloth. £1, 1s.

Newman.—A Dictionary of Modern Arabic.—1. Anglo-Arabic Dictionary. 2. Anglo-Arabic Vocabulary. 3. Arabo-English Dictionary. By F. W. Newman, Emeritus Professor of University College, London. In 2 Vols. crown 8vo, pp. xvi. and 376–464, cloth. £1, 1s.

Newman.—A Handbook of Modern Arabic, consisting of a Practical Grammar, with Numerous Examples, Dialogues, and Newspaper Extracts, in a European Type. By F. W. Newman, Emeritus Professor of University College, London; formerly Fellow of Balliol College, Oxford. Post 8vo, pp. xx. and 192, cloth. 6s.

Oriental Congress.—Report of the Proceedings of the Second International Congress of Orientalists, held in London, 1874. Royal 8vo, pp. 76, paper. 5s.

Oriental Congress.—Transactions of the Second Session of the International Congress of Orientalists, held in London, in September 1874. Edited by Robert K. Douglas, Honorary Secretary. Demy 8vo, pp. viii. and 456, cloth. £1, 1s.

Palmer.—Leaves from a Word Hunter's Note-Book. Being some Contributions to English Etymology. By the Rev. A. Smythe Palmer, B.A., sometime Scholar in the University of Dublin. Crown 8vo, pp. xii. and 316, cloth. 7s. 6d.

Redhouse.—The Turkish Campaigner's Vade-Mecum of Ottoman Colloquial Language. Containing a Concise Ottoman Grammar; a carefully-selected Vocabulary, Alphabetically Arranged, in Two Parts, English and Turkish, and Turkish and English; also a few Familiar Dialogues; the whole in English characters. By J. W. Redhouse, F.R.A.S. Oblong 32mo, pp. iv. and 332, limp cloth. 5s.

3

Rhys.—LECTURES ON WELSH PHILOLOGY. By JOHN RHYS. Crown 8vo, pp. xii. and 458, cloth. 12s.

Sayce.—AN ASSYRIAN GRAMMAR FOR COMPARATIVE PURPOSES. By A. H. SAYCE, M.A. 12mo, pp. xvi. and 188, cloth. 7s. 6d.

Sayce.—THE PRINCIPLES OF COMPARATIVE PHILOLOGY. By A. H. SAYCE, Fellow and Tutor of Queen's College, Oxford. Second Edition. Crown 8vo, pp. xxxii. and 416, cloth. 10s. 6d.

Schele de Vere.—STUDIES IN ENGLISH; or, Glimpses of the Inner Life of our Language. By M. SCHELE DE VERE, LL.D., Professor of Modern Languages in the University of Virginia. 8vo, pp. vi. and 365, cloth. 10s. 6d.

Schele de Vere.—AMERICANISMS: THE ENGLISH OF THE NEW WORLD. By M. SCHELE DE VERE, LL.D., Professor of Modern Languages in the University of Virginia. 8vo, pp. 685, cloth. 12s.

Schleicher.—COMPENDIUM OF THE COMPARATIVE GRAMMAR OF THE INDO-EUROPEAN, SANSKRIT, GREEK, AND LATIN LANGUAGES. By AUGUST SCHLEICHER. Translated from the Third German Edition by HERBERT BENDALL, B.A., Chr. Coll. Camb. Part I. 8vo, pp. 184, cloth. 7s. 6d.
Part II. Morphology. 8vo, pp. viii. and 104, cloth. 6s.

Sophocles.—GREEK LEXICON OF THE ROMAN AND BYZANTINE PERIODS (from B.C. 146 to A.D. 1100). By E. A. SOPHOCLES. Imp. 8vo, pp. xvi. and 1188, cloth. £2, 10s.

Sophocles.—A GLOSSARY OF LATER AND BYZANTINE GREEK. By E. A. SOPHOCLES. 4to, pp. iv. and 624, cloth. £2, 2s.

Stokes.—BEUNANS MERIASEK. The Life of Saint Meriasek, Bishop and Confessor. A Cornish Drama. Edited, with a Translation and Notes, by WHITLEY STOKES. Medium 8vo, pp. xvi., 280, and Facsimile, cloth. 15s.

Stokes.—GOIDELICA—Old and Early-Middle Irish Glosses: Prose and Verse. Edited by WHITLEY STOKES. Second Edition. Medium 8vo, pp. 192, cloth. 18s.

Stratmann.—A DICTIONARY OF THE OLD ENGLISH LANGUAGE. Compiled from the Writings of the XIIIth, XIVth, and XVth centuries. By FRANCIS HENRY STRATMANN. Second Edition. 4to, pp. xii. and 594. In Wrapper, £1, 11s. 6d.; cloth, £1, 14s.

Whitney.—ORIENTAL AND LINGUISTIC STUDIES. First Series. The Veda; the Avesta; the Science of Language. By WILLIAM DWIGHT WHITNEY, Professor of Sanskrit and Comparative Philology in Yale College. Crown 8vo, pp. x. and 418, cloth. 12s.
CONTENTS:—The Vedas.—The Vedic Doctrine of a Future Life.—Müller's History of Vedic Literature.—The Translation of the Veda.—Müller's Rig-Veda Translation.—The Avesta.—Indo-European Philology and Ethnology.—Müller's Lectures on Language.—Present State of the Question as to the Origin of Language.—Bleek and the Simious Theory of Language.—Schleicher and the Physical Theory of Language.—Steinthal and the Psychological Theory of Language.—Language and Education.—Index.

Whitney.—ORIENTAL AND LINGUISTIC STUDIES. By W. D. WHITNEY, Professor of Sanskrit. Second Series. CONTENTS:—The East and West—Religion and Mythology—Orthography and Phonology.—Hindú Astronomy. Crown 8vo, pp. 446, cloth. 12s.

Whitney.—LANGUAGE AND THE STUDY OF LANGUAGE: Twelve Lectures on the Principles of Linguistic Science. By W. D. WHITNEY. Third Edition, augmented by an Analysis. Crown 8vo, pp. xii. and 504, cloth. 10s. 6d.

Whitney.—LANGUAGE AND ITS STUDY, with especial reference to the Indo-European Family of Languages. Seven Lectures by W. D. WHITNEY, Professor of Sanskrit, and Instructor in Modern Languages in Yale College. Edited with Introduction, Notes, Tables of Declension and Conjugation, Grimm's Law with Illustration, and an Index, by the Rev. R. MORRIS, M.A., LL.D. Crown 8vo, pp. xxii. and 318, cloth. 5s.

Williams.—A DICTIONARY, ENGLISH AND SANSKRIT. By MONIER WILLIAMS, M.A. Published under the Patronage of the Honourable East India Company. 4to, pp. xii. and 862, cloth. £3, 3s.

Williams.—A SANSKRIT-ENGLISH DICTIONARY, Etymologically and Philologically arranged, with special reference to Greek, Latin, German, Anglo-Saxon, English, and other cognate Indo-European Languages. By MONIER WILLIAMS, M.A., Boden Professor of Sanskrit. 4to, cloth. £4, 14s. 6d.

Wright.—THE HOMES OF OTHER DAYS: A History of Domestic Manners and Sentiments during the Middle Ages. By THOMAS WRIGHT, Esq., M.A., F.S.A. With Illustrations from the Illuminations in Contemporary Manuscripts and other Sources, drawn and engraved by F. W. FAIRHOLT, Esq., F.S.A. 1 Vol. medium 8vo, pp. xv. and 512, handsomely bound in cloth. 350 Woodcuts. £1, 1s.

Wright.—THE CELT, THE ROMAN, AND THE SAXON: A History of the Early Inhabitants of Britain down to the Conversion of the Anglo-Saxons to Christianity. Illustrated by the Ancient Remains brought to Light by Recent Research. By THOMAS WRIGHT, Esq., M.A., F.S.A., &c., &c. Third Corrected and Enlarged Edition. Numerous Illustrations. Crown 8vo, pp. xiv. and 562, cloth. 14s.

Wright.—FEUDAL MANUALS OF ENGLISH HISTORY. A Series of Popular Sketches of our National History, compiled at different periods, from the Thirteenth Century to the Fifteenth, for the Use of the Feudal Gentry and Nobility. Now first Edited from the Original Manuscripts. By THOMAS WRIGHT, Esq., M.A. Small 4to, pp. xxiv. and 184, cloth. 15s.

LONDON:
TRÜBNER & CO., LUDGATE HILL.

www.ingramcontent.com/pod-product-compliance
Lightning Source LLC
Chambersburg PA
CBHW020923120726
47905CB00008B/2357